OLIVE ODYSSEY

JULIE ANGUS

OLIVE ODYSSEY

Searching FOR THE SECRETS OF THE **FRUIT** THAT SEDUCED THE WORLD

GREYSTONE BOOKS
Vancouver/Berkeley

For Leif

14 15 16 17 18 5 4 3 2 1

Greystone Books Ltd.
www.greystonebooks.com

Cataloguing data available from Library and Archives Canada
ISBN 978-1-55365-514-5 (cloth)
ISBN 978-1-77100-006-2 (epub)

Editing by Nancy Flight
Copy editing by Shirarose Wilensky
Jacket and text design by Jessica Sullivan
Jacket photograph by iStockphoto.com
Photographs by Julie Angus and Colin Angus
Printed and bound in Canada by Friesens
Distributed in the U.S. by Publishers Group West

We gratefully acknowledge the financial support of the Canada Council for the Arts, the British Columbia Arts Council, the Province of British Columbia through the Book Publishing Tax Credit, and the Government of Canada through the Canada Book Fund for our publishing activities.

Greystone Books is committed to reducing the consumption of old-growth forests in the books it publishes. This book is one step toward that goal.

CONTENTS

Introduction 1

1 | A Modern Boat for an Ancient Voyage *11*

2 | Ancient Olive Groves *45*

3 | Searching for Wild Olives *63*

4 | An Ancient Food for Modern Foodies *77*

5 | Coveting Virginity *103*

6 | Illumination and Inspiration on the French Riviera *125*

7 | Ancient Civilizations, Ancient Oil *151*

8 | The Science of Olives *177*

9 | How to Live Like a Centenarian *193*

10 | The Olive Solution *217*

11 | Something Old and Something New *237*

12 | The Birthplace of the Olive *255*

Epilogue 273

Acknowledgements 277

Notes 279

References 286

APPENDIX A: *Tips on Hosting an Olive Oil Tasting Party* 298

APPENDIX B: *Top Questions about Olive Oil* 304

APPENDIX C: *Olive Oil and Olive Recipes* 313

INTRODUCTION

I INHALED DEEPLY, savoring the smell of roasted garlic, browned lamb, and exotic spices that perfumed my aunt Noura and uncle Nabi's apartment in Aleppo. Their faux-wood coffee table with its skinny aluminum legs struggled under the weight of pomegranate-infused lamb stew; chicken baked in a creamy yogurt sauce; salad topped with fried triangles of pita bread; bowls of steaming lentil soup; and platters of cigarlike rolls of meat and rice tightly wrapped in vine leaves, stuffed baby eggplant, and torpedo-shaped patties of fried bulgur and ground beef known as kibbeh. This feast was to celebrate our arrival, my first trip to Syria in twenty-five years, and my husband Colin's introduction to my extended Arab family. Pushing aside feelings of guilt about the extravagance of our meal, I heaped food onto my plate and ate unabashedly. All of it was delicious, but one item stood above the rest, not for its complexity or the effort required to prepare it but for its simplicity and purity. It was a food that I had eaten all my life but that had never evoked such a response. It was fresh and clean, like summer grass, and made my mouth tingle. It was olive oil.

I dipped a pita wedge into a faded blue bowl brimming with olive oil, or *zeit*, as my Arab family called it, and coated it in *za'atar*, a finely ground mix of roasted sesame seeds, sumac, thyme, oregano, and marjoram. The taste and smell took me back to childhood breakfasts, when my father made heaping bowls of *foul*—fava beans, tomatoes, and parsley in lemon juice and olive oil—while I nibbled on *zeit o za'atar.*

"Mmmm. This is delicious," I said, pointing to the oil.

My aunt's plump face spread into a wide smile, deepening the creases around her brown eyes. "It is our oil. We pressed it this year"—as they did every autumn. Between forkfuls of tomato and parsley salad gleaming with olive oil, Noura told me that they had grown olives for generations on their farm on the outskirts of Aleppo, near the Turkish border, where their hundreds of trees grew among endless olive groves that stretched all the way south to the border with Jordan. Most of Syria's 100 million olive trees grow here, producing a tenth of the world's olive oil and making Syria the fifth-largest olive oil-producing country in the world.

I drizzled oil onto my lentil soup, lamb stew, and baked chicken. Everything contained olive oil already, but my family also used it as a condiment, and I followed suit. It seemed to make everything taste better, bring out new and more intense flavors, add richness, and enhance the texture. How could such a simple ingredient that I'd eaten my whole life impart such a complex flavor? Why was the oil here so different from what I was used to? I was hooked. Like a whiskey aficionado who had just discovered single malt Scotch or a chocolate addict sampling his or her first truffle, I had tasted something divine and unforgettable.

I had visited Syria once before, when I was eleven. Then, my main interests were eating my aunt's honey-drenched baklavas and playing hide-and-seek with my cousins. This time, however, I wanted to learn about my family's lives and piece together my history. A first-generation Canadian with a Syrian father, I had no extended family in Canada, and my only window into Middle Eastern culture came through the media, often a one-dimensional portrayal, particularly after September 11.

I had come to Syria to understand the cultural undercurrents of my childhood and their influence on me, and as I listened to my family's stories, I realized that the olive was a fundamental part of that history. My relatives had been growing olive trees for hundreds of years, and the fruit's rhythms and cycles guided their lives—what they ate, whom they married, and how much money they made. The olive tree was at the core of who they were. It wasn't just a commodity, as corn in Iowa might be, but was regarded in an almost spiritual way, like a talisman passed through a family for generations. The bounty of these trees was something to be cherished and shared, and the trees were nurtured so that they would continue to provide for their descendants.

The pride my family felt toward the olive was palpable. According to Kurdish lore, Afrin, the region where my family cultivated olives, was the birthplace of the domesticated olive, planted some 20,000 years ago, after one Zoroastrian clan presented olive trees and branches to another as a peace offering for taking and marrying a woman from their clan, an act banned during an era that allowed only intra-clan marriages. In the nearby archaeological site of Ebla, scientists discovered 4,400-year-old clay tablets describing olive oil, the oldest written evidence of olive oil. Other archaeological evidence suggests that the first olive trees were grown here, some 6,000 years ago, when communities were just beginning to form in the cradle of civilization. The olive is as much a part of the landscape as the minds and spirits of the people living in the regions in which it flourishes. My family considers the olive tree sacred, as do many Muslims, who are well aware of the olive's revered role in the Koran. The three great monotheistic religions are united by their respect for the olive tree, and the Bible and the Torah also praise it as a symbol of peace and a tool for healing. I was beginning to understand that an olive is so much more than a green orb at the bottom of a martini glass.

My family's excitement about the olive ignited my curiosity. I wanted to understand the origins and history of the fruit that meant so much to them and, in many respects, had subtly helped shape my character. And so, like an olive pit cast on dry, rocky earth, an idea was sown that, against all odds, would thrive, and three years later I would return to try to understand the mystery and meaning surrounding the fruit that had shaped humankind and continued to do so—the world's most influential and seductive fruit.

BACK HOME, my interest in the olive tree continued to grow. I'd always enjoyed olives and olive oil, but I had never given them much thought. Olives were something I had on pizza or in salads, and olive oil was just another oil in the cupboard. Sure, I knew olive oil was supposed to be good for you, but I didn't know that it should enhance and complement food like a fine wine. Now I began to understand that my indiscriminate approach was robbing me not only of olive oil's taste but also of its healthful properties.

I learned that corruption is rampant within the industry and that as much as half the extra virgin olive oil on supermarket shelves doesn't meet international standards or is outright fraudulent. Although studies have found that olive oil improves cardiovascular health, prevents certain types of cancer, and helps slow Alzheimer's disease, we aren't getting these benefits if our "extra virgin" olive oil has been diluted with hazelnut oil or worse. Not only is this oil not good for us, but in some cases it can make us sick. Perhaps the worst example of this occurred in the early 1980s, when adulterated olive oil sold in Spain killed almost a thousand people and sickened twenty-five thousand.

As I researched the olive tree, I learned that in many ways olive oil was the original oil, highly valued, fought over, and prized for a myriad of uses. It was once worth its weight in silver, and cutting down an olive tree was punishable by death. To the great civilizations of the Mediterranean—the Egyptians, Phoenicians, Greeks, and Romans—olive oil was one of the most important commodities. Olive oil lubricated machinery, made soaps, tanned hides, and provided a base for perfumes. It fueled lamps, oiled athletes, and anointed the pious, the newly born, and the deceased. During war, it was thrown from castle walls to deep-fry attackers and brought along to nourish armies and seafarers. The Punic Wars were fought over olive oil trading routes, and Greece's capital is named Athens because the Greek goddess Athena gave Greece the olive tree. For thousands of years, when people said oil, they meant olive oil.

Olive oil and olives have been worshipped and have played a significant cultural role for millennia. Homer called olive oil liquid gold, and Oedipus was told to offer olive branches to purify his sins. A dove brought Noah an olive leaf to signify the end of the flood, and Prophet Mohammed said olive oil cured seventy diseases. King Tutankhamen was buried with olive branches in his tomb. The original Olympic athletes were slathered with olive oil before exercising, and afterward the remaining oil, along with sweat and dirt, was scraped off their bodies and sold to aspiring athletes. Olive branch wreaths crowned the winners, and they took home thousands of liters of oil in prizes.

North Americans consume more olive oil than ever, twice as much as a decade ago, and Europeans use even more, with Greeks topping the list at some twenty-six liters a year per person. That's like drinking a wine glass of olive oil every other day. Yet despite the olive's popularity, or perhaps because of it, myths, untruths, and mysteries surround it. Where did people first grow olive trees? Was it the olive or its oil that was first eaten? Does olive oil really prevent cancer, Parkinson's, and stroke? What do "virgin," "extra virgin," and "pure" mean, and how can we be sure we're getting what we pay for?

To find the answers to these questions, I needed to taste olive oils, touch olive trees, and meet the people whose lives are intertwined with this tree. My home on Vancouver Island wasn't exactly a hotbed of olive oil production; our rainy springs, overcast days, and frosty temperatures are a little too unappealing to the heat-loving *Olea*. I needed to travel somewhere warmer and drier, to the places where the olive tree was born and most of the trees now grow: the Mediterranean. There I could meet olive farmers, tasters, government regulators, agronomists, archaeologists, plant scientists, and retailers, and see endless varieties of olive trees, all shapes and sizes.

As I began to plan for the journey, I realized that we still didn't know the answer to the most basic question about the olive—how did it originate? Was the olive tree originally domesticated in the Middle East? And if so, how did it spread to the rest of the Mediterranean? It was one of the olive's greatest mysteries, albeit one many were struggling to unravel. Some believe that the olive tree was simultaneously domesticated in many areas throughout the Mediterranean; others insist that it was first domesticated in the Middle East and that those trees were spread through the Mediterranean by trade and human migration.

Because domestication occurred many millennia ago, there is little archaeological evidence to guide us. But scientists have other tools at their disposal, and a new approach that offered promising insight was genetic testing. As a molecular biologist, I knew that examining DNA can allow us to understand events that happened thousands, even millions, of years ago, and I wondered what we could learn by studying the DNA of ancient olive trees. I brought this idea to my publisher, *National Geographic*, several granting agencies, and one of the leading olive tree scientists. The response was enthusiastic, and slowly I began to put together the funding and expertise to make this project a reality.

My project was based on the question that if the olive tree was taken from the Middle East and planted on distant shores, who did this and how could we prove they did it? Given that domesticated olive trees have been growing on the opposite side of the Mediterranean, in Spain, for more than two millennia, someone must have bridged that formidable gap, and only maritime traders could travel those distances in 500 BC. Few groups had the ability to voyage great distances, and the most far-ranging early sea merchants were the Phoenicians, who made their living trading over long distances and who lived in what is now Syria, Lebanon, and Israel, the region that most likely gave rise to the domesticated olive. They set up trading posts and colonies throughout the Mediterranean, in Spain, Portugal, France, Italy, and Africa, trading in olive oil, wine, ostrich eggs, and silver. Could they have also carried olive pits or even seedlings in their boats and planted them on foreign shores?

To find out, I wanted to retrace their trading routes, stopping in the places where they traded and at the colonies they founded and searching for olive trees that bore their mark—a genetic signature linking them to ancient Phoenicia. Because of the olive tree's long life span, often reaching a thousand years or even three times that, only one or two generations would separate the trees we'd find from those that grew during the Bronze Age.

There was even the possibility that we'd find an olive tree planted by Phoenicians.

As I expected, it was not hard to persuade my husband, Colin, to go on another adventure.

"We can sail, just like the Phoenicians," Colin said. "That will be the best way to follow their trading routes. It'll allow us to anchor in the same harbors they sheltered in and stop in places that might only be accessible by water."

It was true that sailing would allow us to better understand Phoenician voyages and the challenges the mariners faced, as well as enable us to explore the places where they might have planted olive trees. But I wasn't convinced it was the best way to travel.

Colin sensed my hesitation. "Plus, it'll be a fantastic way to travel with Leif," he added.

I looked down at my bulging belly. Leif would be ten months old when we planned to leave, and although I didn't have any experience with infants, I had read enough books to know that parenthood was challenging. We had our worries, but in the end we decided that living on a boat might even be better for a baby than being on solid ground. After all, how different was the gentle swaying of a boat to a cradle? And didn't traditional societies throughout the world successfully raise their children in far more nomadic circumstances?

Over the next year, we planned and plotted and convinced ourselves it was the perfect idea. I had never sailed before, and we knew very little about conditions on the Mediterranean, but I reasoned that this could all be learned. We would start near the western perimeter of Old World olive groves and voyage east toward the origins of the olive tree. We would buy a sailboat at the start of our journey and sell it wherever we finished. I liked the idea of ending the journey in Syria, returning to my family's olive farm, the place that seeded the idea for this journey, but we would have to wait and see where the olive and its secrets took us.

The rest of the logistics and planning were also falling into place. I was able to finance most of the project through a book advance from my publisher, Greystone Books, and various granting agencies. *National Geographic* awarded me an expedition grant, and three other organizations awarded me literary and research grants. Even the genetic analysis would be possible, and an Italian university agreed to collaborate with me and conduct DNA analysis on ancient olive trees I sampled. Finally, we were ready to begin our journey, more than two years after a meal changed my life, propelling me and my young family on an adventure that would take us to some of the most ancient and fascinating parts of the world.

1

A MODERN BOAT FOR AN ANCIENT VOYAGE

"The whole Mediterranean ... all of it seems to rise in the sour, pungent taste of these black olives between the teeth. A taste older than meat, older than wine. A taste as old as cold water."

LAWRENCE DURRELL, *Prospero's Cell*[1]

"I CAN'T DO THIS," I screamed, my voice stolen by the wind before it reached Colin. Our sailboat raced across the water, heeling over like a drunk at an open bar. My stomach churned, and I was hyperventilating. Below, our ten-month-old baby shrieked. He was only 4.5 meters away, but I couldn't do anything. I couldn't leave the tiller until Colin returned from adjusting the boom vang for the mainsail, and even if I could have, going inside that dark, rocking cabin would have made me vomit.

How could Colin be so calm? He was staring at a block and tackle system that wasn't working properly with a perplexed look on his face. He seemed completely oblivious to the ridiculous angle of our boat or the steep waves casting spray over the entire vessel. He probably couldn't even hear Leif's shrieking.

My panic attack seemed to trigger a secondary wave of anxiety. What was wrong with me? The winds were only twenty to twenty-five kilometers per hour. I recalled from my reading just two hours earlier that this was force 4 on the Beaufort scale, an empirical measuring system for wind and sea conditions. Force 4, I struggled to remind myself, is defined as a moderate breeze. *A moderate breeze?* It felt like a gale. I wanted more than anything to be back on solid ground. I wanted to hold Leif in my arms, to stroke his flaxen hair and soothe him. I wanted to be anywhere but on this boat.

Having solved the boom vang fandangle, Colin returned to the cockpit with a couple of well-placed steps. He glanced at my face and immediately looked alarmed.

"What's the matter?"

"Leif! Can't you hear him?" I could barely speak, and my words came out in great gasping gushes.

"Yeah, why don't you go down and calm him? No big deal. I'll turn the boat around and we can head back to the marina. The boat sails beautifully, eh?"

"I can't," I murmured, flooded with shame. "I'll throw up if I go inside."

"No problem. Just keep steering, and I'll check in on him."

I nodded gratefully, looking away so that he wouldn't see the tears slipping down my face. But he noticed something was amiss.

"Are you all right?" he asked, his voice gentle with concern.

"No," I sobbed. "I can't do this."

"Can't do what? If you're having trouble steering, I can..."

"I can't do the sailing trip," I shouted.

Colin didn't say anything, but he looked surprised. I felt like such a failure. We'd spent an entire year planning this voyage, and just three days ago we'd handed over $11,000 cash to buy this boat. Now I was backing out.

Colin loosened the mainsheet, the line holding in the mainsail, and the boat slowed slightly.

"Don't worry," he said. "Let's head back to the marina and we can talk things over there."

TWO WEEKS earlier, we had left Vancouver Island, our home rented out and our cat in the care of neighbors. We arrived jet-lagged in Madrid with a screaming baby and shoehorned our camera gear, boat equipment, clothes, diapers, stroller, books, computer, and life jackets into the diminutive trunk of a rented Fiat Uno. A tangle of freeways marked the start of our life on the road as we drove four hundred kilometers to Valencia, the coastal city where we hoped to buy our sailboat.

It wasn't long before we saw our first olive trees. Silver leaves shimmered in the valleys along the motorway, standing alone or in small groves. They were planted in perfectly straight lines with dry, cracked earth between them. Their solid trunks and thick foliage hinted of life and permanence in an arid land that could support little else.

Spain has more olive trees than any other country and produces three times as much olive oil as its nearest competitor, Italy. In the 2011–12 season, Spanish growers pressed 1,571 million liters of olive oil, nearly half of the global supply and Spain's most fertile year in almost a decade. Spain produces more than twice as much oil as Spaniards use, making it the only European country that makes enough oil for its own consumption. The country also grows nearly a fifth of the world's table olives, and even though the 2011–12 harvest was down 14 percent from the previous year, it still produced a staggering 471 million kilograms of olives, enough for every Spaniard to eat 10 kilograms of olives.

Olives are crucial to the Spanish economy. As one of the country's most important export commodities, olives bring in significant revenues, and the olive industry employs hundreds of thousands of people. There are 413,000 olive farms and almost a thousand olive cooperatives in Spain, as well as olive mills, packing plants, and refineries for inferior olive oil that is unpalatable. Lampante oil, which needs to be refined, makes up about a third of Spain's olive oil, and the remainder is split relatively equally between virgin and extra virgin, a ratio that shifts from year to year, depending on growing conditions. Some of the world's largest olive oil companies are here, including Hojiblanca, which expects to produce 300 million liters of olive oil in 2013, and the Acesur Group, which exports to eighty countries and had revenues of $537 million in 2010. There is also a litany of smaller producers and more than a hundred brands. More than half of Spanish oil is exported; 80 percent of that goes to other EU countries, with Italy purchasing the bulk of it, and the rest goes to Japan, Australia, the United States, China, and other, smaller olive oil–consuming nations.

Spain's ascent to olive superpower can be partially attributed to the past policies of some of the greatest civilizations of the Mediterranean—the Phoenicians, Romans, Greeks, and Arabs. The Spanish term for olive oil, *aceite de oliva,* reflects this broad influence. *Aceite* comes from the Arab term for olive juice, *al-zat*, and *oliva* is Latin. The Romans adapted *oliva* from the Greek word "*elaíwā*," which comes from prehistoric Greece and the Mycenaeans, who chiseled "*elava*" on clay tablets in Linear B script.

I was excited to be here, finally embarking on an adventure we'd planned for so long. My feeling of well-being was further buoyed by the sight of Leif sleeping peacefully in his car seat, and I felt a glimmer of hope that sailing with Leif would be the pleasurable experience we had dreamed of.

Valencia sits on the coast, tucked into the Costa del Azahar (Orange Blossom Coast). This vibrant university city is Spain's third-largest city and is home to a Formula One Grand Prix circuit. It is also a foodie's dream, producing not only excellent olive oil and wine but oranges so sweet that an American cultivar was named after the region. Our hotel was next to the City of Arts and Sciences, an architectural marvel of physics-defying curves, twists, and arches that housed art galleries, museums, and an opera house.

The city hummed with countless attractions, but we were here for only one reason—to find a sailboat. Our hunt for the ideal boat had been going on for nearly a year; we had scoured newspapers, magazines, online boat classifieds, and yacht brokerages. There was no shortage of boats for sale, but very few met all of our requirements. Not only did it have to be seaworthy and fit a family of three, but it had to be affordable. We would use the boat for our journey and try to sell it afterward. If we couldn't, we would take a large or complete loss.

After a wearying night consoling our jet-lagged son, we began our search for a boat in nearby Port Saplaya, a recently constructed seaside community of pleasant mid-rise apartments curving around a man-made harbor filled with pleasure craft. Topless sunbathers and young families dotted the honey-colored beach and splashed in the shallows, cooling off from the fierce August sun, and a string of cafés faced the sea, empty except for a pair of aged men, talking animatedly over empty espresso cups. We strolled along the marina, searching for the twenty-eight-foot sloop that matched the dog-eared printout Colin carried. This was the boat that had brought us to Valencia, the sailboat we hoped to buy.

"Maybe he's out sailing," I mused after we'd completed a circuit of the marina.

Three other mid-sized sailboats were advertised as *en venta,* and in a nearby mall, Colin made the phone calls using Skype and our newly purchased Internet stick while I played with Leif.

"*Hola,*" Colin said into the headset. "I'm sorry, but I don't speak Spanish. Do you speak English?"

There was a long pause.

"Umm . . . uh . . . boat . . . sale?"

More silence.

"*Parlez-vous français? Non?*"

"Uhhhhhhh . . ."

Leif, mesmerized by the tortured expression on his daddy's face, paused in his efforts to untie my shoelaces—Colin's eyes narrowed with concentration. Suddenly, he smiled, remembering a Spanish word from past travels.

"*Barco?*"

The single word meaning "boat" was enough to convey the gist of his inquiry. A look of disappointment came over Colin's face, and he finished the call.

"*Vendido,*" Colin said, taking off his headset. "It's been sold. I guess that's why it's not in the marina."

After several more awkward conversations, we learned that the other boats were much too expensive. Our quest to find the perfect boat wasn't going as we'd hoped. We'd exhausted all leads in this region, and the next boat on our list was four hundred kilometers away.

BEFORE BECOMING a mother, I read stacks of books and solicited advice from other parents. I thought I was prepared, but it was as though I had crammed for an exam only to discover I'd studied the wrong subject. My first time holding a baby was when the nurse placed our screaming newborn in my arms, and when we left the hospital two days later, I felt anything but prepared.

Leif was smaller and more helpless than I had expected. He did not spend most of his days eating and sleeping, as I'd mistakenly believed he would. Nor did he lie at my bosom like a cherub, gently nursing. He slept as though we had fed him Red Bull, not breast milk, and between those mercilessly short and shallow naps, he screamed. Even nursing couldn't provide an escape. He'd writhe and struggle, pushing away and shrieking as though he were being tortured. Colic was often suggested, but whether I went dairy free or gluten free—sometimes recommended as a treatment for colic—didn't seem to matter. We spent the first ten months as new parents in a sleep-deprived haze, desperately trying every soothing trick we heard of, from swaddle wraps and white noise to nightlong pacing sessions.

Given the challenges of parenting at home, we were almost happy with how things were going so far. Although Leif had screamed throughout the flight and wasn't sleeping at night, he was almost angelic during the day. The vibrations of the car would lull him to sleep, and he would catch up on his night's rest while we scanned the passing countryside through heavy, bloodshot eyes. Today was no different, and as we drove to Cartagena, Leif slumbered peacefully in the back.

The highway took us inland, through groves of olive trees and away from the endless seaside communities, resorts, and apartment blocks. Olive trees, ubiquitous in this region, are to the Mediterranean what the Great Barrier Reef is to Australia or the great boreal forests to Canada. They are an emblem of the Mediterranean, and it is unimaginable to think of this place without olive trees, not only as fixtures in the landscape but also as pillars in the culture and livelihoods of the people who live here and who keep them close to their hearts. In both wild and domestic form, olive trees have coexisted with humans throughout the rise of civilization, each shaped by the other's rhythms, needs, and cycles. The gnarled old trees seem to symbolize humans' ability to harness the world around them.

The olive tree is rarely taller than a two-story house and often much shorter, even shrublike. Its evergreen leaves are elongated and come to a rounded point at both ends, like tiny canoes. They are two-toned, forest green on top and silver green on the bottom, giving the tree its characteristic shimmer. The trunk is braided and contorted, a dense wood that grows slowly and reaches widths that can rival its height. In the spring, tiny white blossoms with four feathery petals erupt on the previous year's wood, clustered like bunches of grapes. Most, but not all, trees can self-pollinate, but cross-pollination results in higher and earlier rates of fertilization. When the olives form, they are green, and as they ripen, they turn black. There are no green or black olive varieties, just olives at different stages of maturity. Some olives are picked in October, whereas others aren't ready until February; it depends on the variety, location, and desired ripeness. A single tree can produce from five to five hundred kilograms of olives, depending on size, cultivar, conditions, and year. Olive trees are biennial, producing a bumper crop one year and half or less the following year, as though the tree needs time to recuperate.

If conditions are right, the olive tree grows with little effort. It thrives in calcareous soils, which contain more rock than earth and would make other plants shrivel and die. But sudden frosts kill it, and olive groves on the edge of their climatic zone are periodically annihilated by precipitous temperature changes. The olive tree can endure extreme drought and grows in near-desert climates, but many orchards are irrigated to improve production, a practice others claim compromises the flavor of the olives and oil. The olive tree can even survive fire and axe, growing back from its roots. It is one of the longest-lived trees, easily growing for hundreds of years, and some specimens are believed to be two thousand or three thousand years old. Because new olive trees can grow from ancient roots, a tree could be even older, leading some to call it "the tree of eternity."

The olive tree belongs to the family Oleaceae—which also includes jasmine and forsythia—and the genus *Olea*. There are forty species within *Olea*, including *Olea europaea*, which is further divided into six subspecies, including *europaea*, the olive tree we know. *Olea europaea* subsp. *europaea* is further divided into two varieties, the domesticated olive (var. *europaea*) and the wild olive (var. *sylvestris*). Wild olive trees are commonly called oleasters, as are feral ones, which result when domestic olives crossbreed with wild forms or revert to a wild shape through uncontrolled breeding and which are often indistinguishable from truly wild olive trees. There are thousands of names to describe the vast array of domesticated olive cultivars.

According to pollen traces, *O. europaea* has grown in the Mediterranean for 3.2 million years. But the subspecies *europaea*, at some 500,000 years old, is much younger. *Olea europaea* subsp. *europaea* is believed to have arisen from the crossbreeding of two other *O. europaea* subspecies, the African *cuspidata*, often called ironwood tree for its hardy wood, and *laperrinei*, from the Saharan mountains, a tree now verging on extinction. The wild olive tree then spread from eastern Africa throughout the Mediterranean. In Israel's Negev desert, 43,000-year-old fossilized wild olive wood has been found, and on the Greek island of Santorini, there are 39,000-year-old fossilized imprints of wild olive leaves. The last glacial period devastated wild olive trees throughout the Mediterranean, but pockets survived, and from these the population rebounded.

When and where the olive tree was domesticated is the most controversial issue in the olive's history. Everyone agrees it was domesticated about six thousand years ago and is one of the earliest cultivated trees. But where and how that happened is still a mystery. Before people domesticated the olive, they used it in its wild form. Wild olive pits and charcoal from nineteen thousand years ago were found in Israel at the Ohalo II site, a hunter-gatherer village on the shores of the Sea of Galilee. The earliest signs of the domesticated olives are found just north of the Dead Sea, in Teleilat Ghassul. Here archaeologists discovered olive pits that are too large to be wild and dated them from 3700 to 3500 BC. These are the oldest evidence of domesticated olives, supporting the theory the olive tree was domesticated in the Middle East and migrated westward throughout the Mediterranean.

Neolithic people in Spain and France also used wild olive trees, and some researchers suggest that olive trees were simultaneously cultivated here. In 3800 BC, people in southern Spain ate wild olives, leaving behind the characteristically small pits (five to nine millimeters) in the Caves of Nerja and charcoal from olive wood they used to fuel their fires. Spain's Cova de les Cendres, Cave of Ashes, contained olive wood charcoal dated between 5500 BC and 3300 BC. Similarly, in coastal France, just north of the Spanish border, 6,590-year-old olive wood charcoal was found in the Cova de l'Espérit.

According to Dr. Jean-Frédéric Terral, an archaeologist at Université Montpellier 2 in France, some of the ancient charcoal found in Spain may be from domesticated trees, but despite his detailed analysis of growth rings and cellular structure, it is difficult to differentiate between wild and cultivated olive trees. Even if people weren't growing domesticated olives, he argues that by 1600 BC, they were pruning olive trees to improve yield, a deduction supported by the type of olive wood charcoal found. Around this time, the olive wood burned changed from large mature trunks to smaller branches and twigs, a sign that the olive tree was no longer felled for wood but pruned for productivity.

But turning wild olive trees into domestic ones is not an easy task, and therein lies another challenge to the theory of multiple domestication events. From ancient Greek literature, we know that the Greeks pruned wild olive trees to improve yields and tried to better the quality of the olives through selective breeding. But try as they might, they were never able to turn wild olive trees into cultivated ones. The founder of botany, Aristotle's student Theophrastus, wrote extensively about olive trees in the fourth century BC. In his book *Enquiry into Plants*, he wrote that *Olea europaea*, the domesticated olive, could not be made out of *Olea oleaster* by cultivation.[2] Not only could the ancient Greeks not turn wild olives into domestic forms, but domesticated trees easily reverted to the wild. "The seed produces wild form," Theophrastus wrote of *Olea europaea*, and sometimes "changes to *[Olea oleaster]* spontaneously."[3] Instead of trying to convert wild olives, ancient Greeks relied on pruning and transplanting to improve their yield. Theophrastus explained that the wild olive "produces more fruit than *[Olea europaea]* but ripens less,"[4] a comment that reflects the wild olive's lower oil content and increased bitterness.

As our Uno sped along the coastal highway and we looked across a sea of olive groves, I could see how important the olive tree was today and could imagine the crucial role it played in the past, in both its wild and cultivated form. The olive had witnessed humankind's transformation from hunter-gatherer society to civilized nation, and now we were part of the team trying to understand its transformation from small, bitter fruit to fat, oily orb.

Beyond the olive groves lay the Mediterranean, its subtle silver and brown hues giving way to a vast expanse of white-flecked blue, the two distinctly different yet indelibly intertwined. Ancient Greek philosophers believed olive trees could not grow more than sixty kilometers from the sea, and the French author George Duhamel wrote that "where the olive tree disappears, the Mediterranean ends."[5] That may be true, but I was struck and a little unsettled by their incongruity, the chaotic and unpredictable deep blue waters of the Mediterranean contrasted against the orderly patterns that ruled the olive farms. Perhaps it's because I'm half German, but I took comfort in this symmetry, whereas the randomness of the Mediterranean made me nervous.

The Romans called the Mediterranean Mare Nostrum, Latin for Our Sea. In the Bible it is the Great Sea. In Hebrew, Arabic, and German it is the Middle Sea or White Middle Sea. The Portuguese, Spanish, French, and Italians all use variations of the name Mediterranean, which when you understand its meaning makes perfect sense. In Latin, *medius* means middle and *terra* is earth; thus, "Mediterranean" may be translated as "in the middle of the earth." When it was named thousands of years ago, people thought that this continent was the center of the earth and that the Mediterranean dominated it, entirely surrounded by land except for the narrow Strait of Gibraltar connecting it to the Atlantic.

As a result of this confinement, the water in the Mediterranean is saltier than that of the nearby Atlantic. Evaporation increases the salinity of the Mediterranean, and there is not enough circulation through the strait to compensate for that increase. The strait is essential to maintaining the sea's levels, however, since the rain that falls on the Mediterranean and its catchment basins amounts to only one-third of the water lost through evaporation. If the Strait of Gibraltar were to completely close, the entire Mediterranean Sea would dry out in 1,000 to 2,000 years. This happened 5.5 million years ago, when a shift in the earth's crust pinched off the entrance to the Mediterranean and closed it for 700,000 years. Throughout this period, the Mediterranean seabed was the lowest place on earth, 3,000 meters below sea level and 2,600 meters lower than the Dead Sea, which now occupies the lowest point on earth. Oxygen levels would have been more than two and a half times those found at sea level, and only half the UV radiation would have penetrated the thick atmosphere, creating a very different environment.

Despite the astonishing rapidity with which the Mediterranean could evaporate, it is not a small or inconsequential body of water. Plunging to depths of 1.5 kilometers on average and more than 5 kilometers in places, it stretches over 2.5 million square kilometers, about ten times the size of Great Britain, and borders three continents. Its shores gave rise to three of our greatest religions, and it nurtured the most influential civilizations of antiquity, including the Greeks, Egyptians, Phoenicians, and Israelites. Today, twenty-one countries border the Mediterranean, and millions of livelihoods depend on it through fishing, tourism, salt farms, and trade. It is one of the busiest shipping regions in the world, floating one-third of the world's merchant ships, and in the past it played an even more important role in trade and commerce.

The first seagoing merchant boats were most likely built by the Phoenicians and used for fishing. The Phoenicians, who were descended from the Canaanites, lived along the coast of the area now known as Syria, Lebanon, and Israel and were defined by their affinity for the sea. By felling Mount Lebanon's huge cedars, they built ships and created an empire based on maritime exploits. Their boats probably started as dugout canoes, which were later enlarged by adding wooden planks to the sides. Eventually, the Phoenicians progressed to carvel-constructed ships thirty meters long and seven meters wide, as big as those Christopher Columbus sailed 3,500 years later. They were propelled by a square rig sail and twenty or so muscled rowers and could travel some forty to eighty kilometers a day, leapfrogging along the coast before coming ashore each night to rest.

These seaworthy vessels and skilled boatmen began trading goods with neighboring villages and gradually voyaged farther afield. Eventually, the Phoenicians reached Egypt, four hundred kilometers away, and encountered a wealthy kingdom hungry for foreign treasures and capable of rewarding seafaring merchants with staggering sums of gold and other precious materials. Although the Egyptians had a flourishing internal maritime trade system—they proficiently navigated the Nile to connect the various fiefdoms of their country—their flat-bottomed reed boats were unstable and treacherous in the turbulent open sea. They also had planked boats, but they were small, limited by the spindly nature of Egypt's trees, and it wasn't until they had access to the Phoenicians' great cedars that they built larger ships.

Trade between Egypt and Phoenicia began at least 5,200 years ago, making them the first long-distance maritime trading partners. Lebanese cedars were discovered in a temple from 3200 BC in the ancient Egyptian city of Hierakonpolis, and Egyptian art depicting foreign ships and their Phoenician mariners, identified by their distinctive beards and embroidered gowns, suggests that Phoenician ships carried or towed this cargo to Egypt and not the other way around. In 2600 BC, an Egyptian scribe wrote that forty Phoenician ships had arrived with a cargo of Lebanese cedar. Phoenician ships became so ubiquitous that all seafaring ships were nicknamed Byblos ships, even if the boat did not come from Byblos, the Phoenician capital. Throughout the third millennium BC, sea trade in the Middle East blossomed, and the Phoenician merchant vessels were soon joined by Minoans from Crete and, in the second millennium BC, by the Greek Mycenaeans.

Olive oil was one of the most important trade commodities. It was carried in amphorae, large ceramic bottles with a spouted top and handles, and sealed with a plug of wood. For thousands of years, amphorae were the main vessels for transporting olive oil, and amphorae dating back 5,500 years have been found off the coast of Phoenicia. Olive oil quickly became a vital product for all nations the Phoenicians traded with, not only for food but also to light lamps, make soap, and tan hides, as well as for spiritual ceremonies and more. It was a revolutionary product, and every country it was introduced to became as addicted to it as we are to petroleum today. As Phoenician trade moved westward, so did the demand for olive oil, and by 500 BC the consumption and use of olive oil had permeated the entire Mediterranean, from Portugal and Spain in the west to France and Germany in the north and along the northern coast of Africa.

Colin and I decided that if we wanted to understand the Phoenician mariners, we should start with their boats. One of the only and the best-preserved Phoenician shipwrecks was in Spain, in Cartagena's Museum of Underwater Archaeology. Serendipitously, one of the sailboats on our list was also in Cartagena.

After a four-hour drive, we arrived in the ancient city, tucked between the mountains and sea, a location cherished for its security in the past and its beauty today. Originally named Qart Hadašt (Carthage) by the Phoenicians in the first millennium BC, after their identically named city in north Africa, it was later called Carthago Nova, Latin for New Carthage, by the Romans, to avoid confusion. The Phoenicians used the city as the starting point for their expansion into Spain and as a base for mining operations. Plying the waters with their boats, they ferried goods along the coast and to destinations farther abroad. Now home to some 200,000 people, the city showcases the remains of the various waves of ruling civilizations, and in our short drive to the marina, we saw an enormous Roman theater and a Byzantine rampart.

The waterfront is scenic, lined with palm trees and wide boulevards, and offers a perfect natural harbor, protected by land on all sides except for a bottleneck opening. Leif woke up just as we arrived, well rested from his lengthy nap but hungry and annoyed at the confinement. We parked and I nursed Leif, while Colin rushed ahead to meet the owner of the sailboat we hoped to buy.

The marina is at the back of the port, past a row of eateries, the museum, and the yacht club. It is a modest place filled mostly with day sailers and a few motorboats, and as soon as I joined Colin, I knew this wasn't the boat for us. It was scruffy and neglected, a twenty-five-foot Spanish boat called a Coronado that looked older than its thirty-five years.

"It all runs well at low speed," said Fernando, the boat's owner, a middle-aged lawyer in a crisp polo shirt and spotless khakis who spoke fluent English. "But when the boat goes faster than five kilometers an hour, the engine billows black smoke."

As he continued his forthright appraisal, I couldn't help but think it was a good thing Fernando wasn't a salesperson. Finally, after we'd finished inspecting the boat, he concluded, "If you want the boat, I cannot sell it to you now."

I thought we were the ones supposed to be saying no. "Why not?" I asked.

"The navigation permit has expired. You cannot sell a boat that does not have a permit, and I need to have some repairs done before the inspection. It could take weeks, maybe months," Fernando said. "It is hard to find workers at this time of year, and the government officers are on holidays."

Fernando yawned, as though the thought of it all made him tired. I was melting in the heat and felt frustrated at our inability to find a boat. At least now we knew that it was illegal to leave a marina without the proper permits and, given the language barrier and absentee government officials, that these permits would be nearly impossible to get on our own. From now on, we'd be sure to ask about permits before driving anywhere for half a day.

We thanked Fernando for his time and strolled across the broad promenade to the glass and steel Museum of Underwater Archaeology. The entrance of the modern building was marked with six-foot burnished-metal letters spelling *Arqueología Subacuática,* and inside the dimly lit museum, hidden speakers gurgled underwater sounds. It wasn't a big museum, but you'd be hard pressed to find a better display of ancient Mediterranean maritime trade. Phoenician amphorae, elephant tusks chiseled with Phoenician words, 2,500-year-old ostrich eggs, and other treasures crowded glass display cases. Videos, ship replicas, and hands-on displays described the maritime history and the shipbuilding process and explained how archaeologists make these discoveries. But the real treasures were the Phoenician ships.

Only a few Phoenician shipwrecks have been found in the Mediterranean, and generally little of the vessels is left; the wood has decomposed, and the amphorae and other cargo they once carried are the only indication of the ships' existence. This changed in 1988, when the wood remnants of a 2,700-year-old Phoenician wreck were discovered in the Bay of Mazarrón, just twenty-five kilometers from Cartagena. Sections of broken hull, comprising wood planks and framing, were excavated, along with the remains of the ship's cargo. Ten years later, in the same bay, researchers uncovered the hull of another Phoenician boat, and this one was almost perfectly preserved.

"This is the first time we have the actual ships of the Phoenicians,"[6] said Ivan Neguereula, the museum's archaeologist, in a magazine interview. "Their ships are the key to their colonizing, the way they traveled the Mediterranean. We can't understand them without their ships. Now we can see how they actually cut the wood, how they joined it." It was an enormous discovery, finally shedding light on their exquisite craftsmanship.

Despite the tremendous maritime exploits of the Phoenicians, and although they were probably the first to build boats that could categorically be called ships, almost no physical evidence of their vessels remained until now. Before the Cartagena discovery, most of what we knew about Phoenician boats was gleaned from depictions on reliefs, which were usually very stylized and lacked detail. The most concrete evidence of Phoenician vessels lay in the scope of their empire, an achievement that would be impossible without large seaworthy ships. With the discovery of these Phoenician shipwrecks, much of the conjecture finally came to an end.

What was special about these boats that allowed them to survive? As it turns out, we have seaweed to thank. The ships sank in shallow waters, just a couple of meters deep, where the seaweed *Posidonia* thrives. Thick, grasslike layers quickly covered the wooden vessels, and as the seaweed died, it created a hermetic seal that kept out oxygen and saved the wood from decomposition. The vessel in better condition, *Mazarrón II*, was studied by archaeologists and then encased in a steel vault and left in its original location on the sea floor, where it remains. The other, *Mazarrón I*, was excavated and put on display along with a replica of the *Mazarrón II*.

The *Mazarrón II* replica, which dominated the museum's main room, looked like a large open rowboat. At 8.2 meters long, it was nowhere near the size of the large Phoenician galleys and was probably used to carry cargo from the shore to larger boats or for local transportation. When these vessels sank, they were carrying a full load of lead ingots packed into the boats on top of a layer of brush, which acted like bubble wrap, cushioning the boat from the shifting metal. This would have been a common freight, since the Phoenicians' largest mining operations were in Spain, which had a wealth of silver, copper, iron, and tin, and even some gold, as well as a populace that was largely unaware of the value of its precious metals—much like Peru when the Spanish arrived two millennia later. The Iberians traded silver for the Phoenicians' olive oil and wine, but unlike the later relationship between Spain and Peru, their relationship was amicable and nonviolent.

The discovery of *Mazarrón II* provided insight into Phoenician shipbuilding prowess. The boat was made with an assortment of woods, each chosen for a specific attribute. The body was constructed with pine strakes bonded using mortise and tenon joinery (a tongue-and-groove-like system) with dowels of dense olive wood holding the joints together. The frame was made from fig wood, which is soft and pliable, and the keel was made of cypress cedar, a hardy wood with natural antimicrobial properties that would have prevented it from rotting.

The contents of the boat also proved interesting. Besides the lead ingots, the boat contained an anchor, intact Phoenician knots, amphorae, mills to grind wheat, and a wicker basket filled with personal effects. The anchor, shaped like a fisherman's anchor (imagine Popeye's tattoo) but with one hook coming out of its side instead of two, is made of wood and weighted with a lead core. It is the oldest known anchor that uses shape, as opposed to just weight, to stay on the seafloor, and this is the only such anchor ever discovered.

The crew's personal items give us clues to the mariners' lives. The amphorae probably contained olive oil or wine, and the wicker basket would have carried food, probably sheep or goat meat according to the bone remnants, and olive pits. There is very little evidence of olive consumption in Spain during this period, so we have to wonder where those olives came from. Did they bring them with them, or were they grown locally? The very olives these Phoenician seafarers munched on were probably the seed of a revolutionary change in the way the local inhabitants viewed this bitter fruit.

A few meters beyond the replica, a nondescript Plexiglas case sat beside a number of other exhibits. Inside were the remnants of *Mazarrón 1*: thick wooden planks, the color of rusty nails, held together by a quartet of fig branches as wide as my wrist, and a long square keel post spanning the base of the boat; my mind could fill in the missing pieces. These were the remains of one of the oldest shipwrecks in the world, yet the placard beneath simply stated: "Ships were made from Timber" in English and Spanish. There was no hint that the wood was from a Phoenician wreck, never mind that it was the first time so much wood had been recovered from such an ancient shipwreck. If I hadn't done some research earlier, I would have passed by this modest display without realizing that it was one of the greatest maritime archaeological finds of all time.

The pine strakes were cracked and mottled, but I could clearly make out how the planks slotted precisely into each other. The ribs ran across them at a perpendicular angle, positioned every foot and curving slightly with the shape of the boat, adding enough strength to hold the boat together in the rough Mediterranean waters. I closed my eyes and imagined six muscled men driving the boat and its cargo of lead ingots forward, surging through the waves. What caused the boat to sink? Did the men survive? So many unanswered questions, but still, it seemed a miracle to have this remnant of the Phoenicians in front of me, their vast maritime fleets reduced to these few chunks of wood that had survived the eons.

We emerged from the museum into the blast furnace of Spain's summer. Without the distraction of the Phoenician ships, I began to dwell on our lack of a boat. There were no more potential boats in this region. Our next prospects were in Alicante and then Barcelona, which was seven hundred kilometers away. Leif was crying uncontrollably, and we had no idea where we were going to spend the night. This was not the journey I had imagined. Instead of slicing through the water in a sailboat, anchored in a beautiful harbor every night, we spent most of our days in a shoebox on wheels and our nights in grotty roadside hotels, cringing as our baby kept the world awake. I was beginning to wonder if our plan to buy a sailboat and sail the Mediterranean had been a mistake.

VEHICLES CRAWLED bumper to bumper as we drove back north. Our destination, Dénia, was still hours away.

"Let's pull off on the next farm track," Colin said as Leif moaned with impatience and I grumbled about my stiff legs. "I think we need a break, and it would be nice to check out one of these olive groves up close."

It wasn't long before we came across a tractor track leading off the main highway, but a shapely young woman in a bikini was blocking it as she lounged in a lawn chair, shaded by a beach umbrella. A red plastic cooler sat beside her.

"What do you think she's selling? Olive oil?" Colin asked.

"I don't know. Dressed like that I'm sure she'll get a lot of customers."

We came across several more tractor tracks, each blocked by a bikini-clad woman in high heels relaxing beside a cooler.

"Wow, these farmers sure get their daughters to spice it up to sell their olive oil," Colin said, watching one young woman gyrate her hips for the traffic.

"I don't think they are the farmers' daughters, and I don't think they are selling olive oil," I replied.

A Citroën was parked in one of the farm tracks, and we watched a scantily clad "farmer's daughter" lead a middle-aged man into the olive grove. They were clearly not going olive picking, and I had my reservations about pulling into these olive groves. I did not want us to be mistaken for foreigners looking for some excitement. My limited Spanish would not be able to explain our way out of that one.

But our desire to see olive trees overcame our trepidation, and when we came across an empty tractor track, we turned off the road and bumped down the rutted lane. Olive trees sprouted out of arid, fawn-colored earth peppered with desiccated weeds. It was too dry for anything else to grow, but the olive trees flourished as a result of a drip irrigation system that delivered water through a black hose. Only a quarter of Spain's olive trees are irrigated, and even though the trees could probably survive without irrigation, they produce more olives with a little bit of extra water.

We parked our car in the shade of an olive tree and wandered through the orderly rows. The twisted trees were not much higher than a shed, with trunks as wide as a dinner plate, and they sparkled with color—green and purple olives against silver-hued leaves. The olives were small and oval, probably Arbequina, I guessed, one of Spain's most popular cultivars, which is loved for its high oil content and is primarily pressed into oil.

Colin reached up and plucked an olive from the tree. He tentatively placed it in his mouth and bit into it.

"Yeuchh!!" he sputtered, spitting it out and puckering his mouth in disgust. "I don't know how anybody could have started eating these things."

Colin's response was a typical reaction to tasting a freshly plucked olive. It is completely different from the olives you find in the supermarket, which have been processed to make them edible. Unlike most fruit, the olive cannot be eaten fresh from the tree, since it contains an extremely bitter chemical, called oleuropein, that has to be neutralized to remove the astringent flavor.

The fact that olives are not palatable directly from the tree complicates the story of how this fruit was first used by humans. It's easy to envision how early humans discovered the edibility of many foods; they tried them and if they tasted reasonable and didn't cause any stomach upset or other illness, they continued eating them. But it is hard to imagine anyone biting into this fruit and deciding it was edible.

To enjoy olives, it seems our distant ancestors would have had to learn how to cure them or press them into oil. But neither process is straightforward, and we aren't even sure which came first. Some researchers and scholars are adamant it was olive oil, whereas others argue that consumption of the fruit makes more sense.

The processes required to make oil or to make these drupes, a term used to describe fruit containing a stone, palatable are about equal in complexity. To remove the bitterness, olives need to be soaked in fresh water or brine for a number of weeks. The water is changed daily, and slits are cut into the olives to speed up the process. At the end of this procedure, the fruit tastes similar to what we buy in the supermarket today. Meanwhile, the simplest way to make olive oil is to crush the olives and cover them in water. The olive oil will rise to the surface, where it can be skimmed off.

I had read that children have instinctive taste preferences and aversions that resemble the palates of early humans, and later in Greece, we would meet a historian who expanded on this theory. She explained that the most accurate way to assess the taste preferences of early humans is to look at what babies like. She reasoned that because their immature palates have not been influenced by a lifetime of food choices, complex artificial flavors, and exotic spices, their preferences are closer to what we're hard-wired to enjoy. I looked at Leif crawling beneath an olive tree and wondered if he'd mind being a test subject.

He probed the purple bean-sized fruit before opening his mouth and ripping off a chunk of pulpy flesh with his new white teeth. He munched for a few seconds, then scowled and spewed out the remnants.

"Well, if Leif represents early humans, I don't think they enjoyed olives much," Colin said.

"I guess not, but he also doesn't like plums, bananas, or beef. I'm not sure if he really personifies the average caveman," I said.

Although we don't know if cavemen regularly ate olives, archaeologists have found evidence of consumption dating back nineteen thousand years. In the archaeological site of Ohalo II, preserved wild olive pits dating back to 17000 BC have been found in numbers that imply that humans gathered them. Whereas the earliest indisputable evidence of olive oil production isn't until 5500 BC. In a submerged village near Haifa, Israel, sand preserved thousands of crushed olive pits as well as the mortar and pestles used to smash the olives and make oil.

When the olive was domesticated, people in the Fertile Crescent had been farming and living in communities for four thousand years. In the eighth millennium BC, societies began to shift from hunter-gatherer to farming, growing crops such as wheat, barley, and peas. Cereals and legumes grew easily by seed, could be harvested within months of planting, and stored well, making them ideal crops. Societies still relied on gathering wild food and hunting, and if they needed to move, they could bring seeds with them and in a few months grow crops in their new home. Growing trees, however, was more complicated and was the next significant leap forward in agriculture.

Olive trees were one of the first domesticated trees, alongside pomegranates, grapes, figs, and dates. As Jared Diamond reasons in his book *Guns, Germs, and Steel*, growing trees requires a settled community, since it takes three or more years for trees to bear fruit. But for an established village, these are relatively straightforward trees to plant and care for, as they can all be planted from seed or cutting, a process known as vegetative propagation. At some point, someone probably found an olive tree that bore particularly large or oily olives and planted a cutting near their home. Or perhaps that person lived in an area devoid of wild olives and instead of traveling long distances to collect them planted trees nearby.

In fact, the earliest unequivocal evidence of olive domestication comes from such an event. The six-thousand-year-old olive pits found in Teleilat Ghassul are from an area north of the Dead Sea in modern Jordan that is too dry to naturally support olive trees. The large size of the olive pits indicated that they had been domesticated, and the dry environment suggested that the only way these olive trees could have grown is if people had watered them.

It is possible that people had been growing olive trees two thousand years before that. Nearly eight thousand years ago, olive pollen levels in the Ghab valley in northwestern Syria spiked, and the previously uncommon pollen began to outnumber pollen from all other trees. Farming communities proliferated during this time, and people may have planted olive trees alongside their seeds and legumes. Because it is impossible to differentiate between wild and domestic olive pollen, however, the earlier domestication cannot yet be proven.

Until 2006, it was thought that the first fruit trees were domesticated 6,000 years ago, but then a handful of ancient figs turned that theory upside down. As with the olive, differentiating between wild and cultivated figs can be challenging, but these figs had a genetic quirk that simplified that problem. The 11,400-year-old figs discovered near Jericho, in the Jordan Valley, were parthenocarpic, meaning they had no seeds and were produced by trees that didn't require pollination to fruit. This mutation spontaneously occurs on rare occasions in the wild, but the trees die out after a single generation because they cannot seed themselves. The only way a parthenocarpic tree can grow is if someone plants a cutting. From the quantity of figs found, scientists deduced that people must have grown these trees.

This single finding reordered our understanding of ancient agriculture, for it meant that vegetative propagation had occurred five thousand years earlier than previously thought. People were growing fruit trees a thousand years before wheat and peas, and if they grew one type of fruit tree by propagation, it is easy to imagine they might grow another—especially one like the olive, which had been consumed for thousands of years before that and grew easily from a cutting.

IT WAS EVENING when we reached Dénia, a vibrant coastal city with a carnival-like atmosphere. Revelers crowded streets and sidewalks, and packed seaside restaurants and teeming gift shops defied the beleaguered Spanish economy. Parking was impossible, and after a lengthy search, I leapt out of the car in front of the historic portside hotel La Posada del Mar while Colin motored on.

We had agreed to meet the boat owner in front of the hotel, and as I scanned the crowd, a middle-aged man and stunning young woman approached me.

"Hoolie?" the man said, pocketing his cell phone and reaching out a hand.

"Yes, Julie," I replied. "And you must be Emilio."

"*Sí*, very nice meet you. I... daughter... hmmmm... English," he said pointing to the dark-haired woman beside him.

"My father cannot speak English, and I am here to translate," she said in a clipped British accent.

She was visiting from Brussels, where she worked for the European Commission, and, fortunately for us, had volunteered to help her father show his boat. Emilio was well dressed, poised, and elegant, and like the previous boat seller, worked as a lawyer.

The boat was also a Coronado but in better condition than the previous one. Our luck seemed to have changed. The *Olivia* possessed a valid navigation permit, and everything was in good working order. We liked the boat and made an offer of 7,500 euros.

"It is listed for nine thousand euros," Emilio's daughter said, looking confused. The two conferred before Emilio's daughter finally replied, "Nine thousand is the lowest we can go."

That was more than we wanted to pay, and we demurred. It was dawning on us that Spanish secondhand boat prices were as non-negotiable as the price for Heinz beans in the supermarket. Although we did not get the boat, we ended the meeting with a glass of beer on an outdoor patio, and then, under darkening skies, we slipped back onto the freeway. We had exhausted our boat shortlist, but an Internet search had netted two new prospects in Barcelona, a six-hour drive north. I was beginning to wish we had paid the additional money, just to put an end to the driving.

HOT AIR shimmered above the concrete promenade surrounding Port Olímpic in the center of Barcelona. We strolled past busy restaurants and a tiny McDonald's with an endless lineup. I was suffocating in the muggy heat. Colin and Leif were in even worse shape as they struggled with a fever and flu. We were about to view our very last potential boat. If this didn't work out, we'd have to move on to France or go back to Dénia and bite the bullet with the *Olivia*. I was sick at the prospect of continuing our seemingly fruitless quest.

The brokerage office was a modified houseboat advertising six-figure yachts on an outdoor billboard. Not surprisingly, the boat we were interested in was not listed. In the air-conditioned, wood-paneled office, we met Tito, a short man with closely cropped white hair who explained that our boat was out sailing. "But I have another boat you might like," he quickly added. I felt a prickling of unease and wondered if this was a bait-and-switch attempt.

Tito drove us to the far side of the marina, puffing cigarette smoke out the window as his jalopy covered the easily walkable distance.

"There she is," he said, pointing toward a tidy sailboat stern tied to the pier.

"This is it?" Colin said, pointing to the blue boat.

It was larger and in better condition than any of the other boats we had looked at, and I shared his doubt that we could afford it.

"I don't know much about it, but feel free to look around," Tito said. "It's a Spanish-built boat, Sumplast Super Diamo, and is twenty-eight feet long."

We clambered aboard the boat and opened the main companionway to see a clean and stylish interior with new white faux-leather cushions and mahogany trim. The diesel engine sparkled, and Tito said it worked well. The sails were almost brand new, and the roller furling jib and lazy jack system for the mainsail would ensure easy single-handed sailing. It came with almost all the equipment we required, including an autopilot, spinnaker, flares, and other safety gear.

Unlike the other boats we'd looked at, it had full standing headroom and pressurized water, with sinks in both the kitchen (galley) and bathroom (head). There were two double beds and a single, as well as a roomy V-berth that would be ideal for Leif. It also had a new stainless steel and fabric Bimini to shade the cockpit from the relentless sun, and there was a swim ladder.

"How about the navigation permit?" Colin inquired.

"Yes, yes, our brokerage will make sure it has a navigation permit as a condition of the sale," Tito replied.

"It's perfect," I whispered to Colin when we were alone.

Colin was smiling broadly. "This is exactly what we need. It's a capable and fast design. It's comfortable. The forward room is perfect for Leif. It's well ventilated with these three hatches." We agreed it was better than we could have imagined.

"There's just one problem," Colin said. "I think the price may not be what we're hoping for."

I climbed out the companionway. "Tito, how much did you say this boat is?"

"Seven thousand five hundred euros. The economy is so bad the owner is selling it for much less than it is worth."

We spent the afternoon looking through the boat, emptying cupboards, testing lights, running the bilge pump, unfurling sails, and imagining ourselves on it. Colin jumped over the side with a mask and snorkel and inspected the hull. The boat felt like home. It was as though she had been waiting patiently for us since our arrival in Spain. Even the name, *Isis*, was serendipitous.

Isis was an Egyptian goddess, also worshipped by the Phoenicians and Greeks, often portrayed with a crown of olive leaves. Mythology says she introduced olives to humans and was the protectorate of both olive trees and Mediterranean sailors. Equally fitting, she was idolized for being the ideal mother and wife. Isis epitomized the core tenets of our expedition: olives, family, ancient civilizations, and Mediterranean sailing. The boat's name was a delicious coincidence.

We agreed to pay the 7,500 euros for the boat and celebrated at one of the many marina restaurants, sipping gazpacho and baking in the relentless heat, thirty-six degrees Celsius, according to a large billboard at the marina. We clinked glasses of water and toasted our new boat. We'd been in Spain for a week, and our plan was finally coming together. In a few days, we would be sailing on Mediterranean waters.

TITO INFORMED us that it would take about ten days for the paperwork to be completed but that we could move on board immediately. The marina provided hot showers, electricity, security, fresh water, and a secure berth at the discounted rate of ten euros a day through the brokerage.

We checked out of our hotel, transferred our belongings to the boat, and finally unpacked. The boat contained a plethora of cubbyholes, tiny latched cupboards, and huge pantries. Everything had a place, and at last we could rein in the chaos that had consumed our lives since we'd arrived in Spain. Leif rolled around on the V-berth mattress and dive-bombed the pillows, and Colin scrubbed mildew from dark cabinet crevices with a passion he's never before shown for housework.

Port Olímpic was an ideal location to finally relax and explore Barcelona. The sands of Barceloneta Beach, ranked the best urban beach in the world by the Discovery Channel, lay eighty-seven yards from our boat, just over the breakwater wall, and Barcelona's old quarter and the famous La Rambla strip were a twenty-minute walk away. I felt a great weight lifted off my shoulders.

The following day, we returned our rental car at the airport and took a bus to Plaça d'Espanya, one of Barcelona's largest squares, to transfer to a marina-bound bus, which we couldn't find. After thirty minutes of searching, Leif was in a full-blown tantrum, unhappy with the midday heat and our distracted attention. My shoulder ached from carrying the hefty car seat, and I was worried about the $6,000 wrapped around Colin's waist, more than half the payment for our boat. Barcelona had a reputation for petty crime, and nothing made a better pickpocket target than a lost, overburdened couple distracted by a screaming baby.

"I think the lady from the tourist information booth said it was farther down this street," Colin said.

"I don't think it was this far," I grumbled. "She said it was only a hundred meters."

"Well, let's just go another block and see," Colin said.

"I think we must have passed it," I said. I was hot and tired and didn't want to continue in the wrong direction.

"How about you stay here, and Leif and I will run down the street just to make sure."

Colin trotted down the street with Leif, leaving me to examine a map of Barcelona plastered against a bus shelter. I was about to ask directions from the people standing beside me when a shout interrupted.

"The bus stop is just one and a half blocks down the street," Colin panted.

"Great!"

The bus arrived, but when I reached down to open my purse for bus fare, I made an unwelcome discovery. My purse was already unzipped and my wallet was missing.

"I've been pickpocketed," I moaned in disbelief.

I knew immediately that the three youths standing at the map beside me had not been looking for directions but for an opportunity to get close to unsuspecting tourists. They had unzipped my purse and slipped my wallet out without even nudging me. It was amazing—and disastrous. We went looking for them and peered into trash cans, hoping to find at least the empty wallet, but didn't find anything. Losing the two hundred euros I had just withdrawn hurt, but being without credit cards, bank cards, and driver's license was even worse. It would be impossible to replace my ID until we returned home, four months from now. We would only be able to withdraw cash using Colin's cards, I wouldn't be able to drive, and my only piece of identification would be my passport, which, fortunately, was stored in our boat.

"Thank goodness we didn't put the boat money in my purse," I whispered to Colin.

Colin patted the slim money belt under his shirt and nodded. "You know, I think we should consider this a blessing in disguise. Really, it's just the loss of three hundred dollars and a big inconvenience. We've been carting around thousands of dollars of video equipment, and soon we'll have irreplaceable digital files. We've been far too slack with our security, and this is a lesson to guard our stuff more carefully."

I looked at Leif babbling in his arms and nodded, trying to share his optimistic perspective. I felt violated and sick, but he was right. There was a lesson to be learned here, and things could have been much, much worse. What if Leif had been abducted? We'd never let him out of our sight, not even for a second, but now, seeing how easily my wallet was stolen, I realized we had to be even more vigilant. Together we brainstormed possible crime scenarios—pickpocketings, boat burglaries, muggings—and what we could do to reduce their likelihood. Sophisticated petty criminals were as abundant in the Mediterranean as warm weather, and to stay safe, we would need to keep our guard.

OUR TIME in Barcelona quickly slipped by, the days melting into each other like ice cream in the sweltering Spanish summer sun. We spent a few hours each day chasing after required paperwork for the boat, getting supplies, and readying the boat, and the rest of the time we explored beaches, parks, and the city. We made friends with other sailors and had dinner with a Brazilian couple who lived aboard a beautiful yacht with their boisterous two-year-old. I was getting used to life in the marina and entertained fleeting thoughts of returning one day to live aboard a boat. Even Leif was settling into the new climate and time zone and had just fallen asleep for his afternoon nap. Colin was cleaning out the water tank, and I was relaxing with a cup of tea and learning about the Beaufort scale from my sailing reference book, *The Complete Sailor.*

A knock on the hull pulled me away from the book, and I looked up to see Dominique smiling and waving a piece of paper. Dominique worked for the yacht brokerage, and although he wasn't in sales, he spoke English and thus became our de facto translator. Usually when he stopped by it was to tell us that the permits were delayed or that we needed to complete additional paperwork, but not today. Our boat insurance had finally gone through, and for the first time we were allowed to sail our boat outside the marina.

Colin emerged from the forward cabin, beaming. "It's a great day to go sailing," he said.

I looked out to sea. The moderate southwest breeze would be ideal to test our boat's performance, and I nodded in agreement.

2

ANCIENT OLIVE GROVES

"Except the vine, there is no plant which bears a fruit of as great importance as the olive."

PLINY (23–79 AD)[1]

OUR MAIDEN VOYAGE didn't unfold as I'd dreamed. My panic subsided as we chugged back into the calm waters of Port Olímpic, slipping past throngs of beachgoers and tourists on the promenade, but I was no longer certain about our journey.

I was shocked at my reaction to the sea. Four years earlier, I'd rowed across the Atlantic Ocean; I'd spent five months in a tiny boat and survived two hurricanes. Yet now, a moderate breeze nearly caused me to break down. I couldn't understand it. Had motherhood changed me? Was it hormones or some kind of primal reaction ignited by my son's cries of distress?

"You're looking better now," Colin said gently as he maneuvered the boat toward our berth.

"I don't know what came over me. It seems so silly now," I said. In the calm marina waters, with Leif babbling in my arms, my terror seemed so misplaced. Yet it had been real and paralyzing, and if it happened while we were at sea, it could jeopardize our safety.

"Don't worry. Sailing in open waters for the first time frightens many people. Something just doesn't seem right when the boat is heeling over like that," Colin said. "We'll just spend some time in smaller waves and lighter winds, and in no time you'll get used to it."

I hope you're right, I thought as I took the tiller from him. I eased the boat into our narrow slip while Colin clambered onto the bow and leapt onto the dock with the dock rope and secured it onto a cleat.

This was our first time berthing at a Mediterranean marina, and although we'd rehearsed the routine beforehand, we were nervous. Unlike North American marinas, where each boat has a designated dock finger to pull up to, here boats are sandwiched together with just the bow or stern butting onto a central pier or dock. When Colin finished securing the boat, I pulled up a line anchored to the seafloor and tied it to the stern. Now our boat was anchored at the bow and stern and perfectly squeezed into its narrow parking spot. Our docking had come together seamlessly, and my smooth handling of the boat buoyed my spirits. Maybe there was hope for me yet.

The slowness of Spanish bureaucracy meant *Isis* was still a few days from being truly ours, giving us time to take her out for a few more sails before our journey began. Unlike previous delays, this one made me happy. A little more practice in calm waters was just what I needed, and the extra time would give us a chance to visit the ancient Spanish olive grove we'd heard about.

The highest concentration of ancient olive trees in the world—four thousand in an area smaller than London—grows one hundred kilometers southwest of Barcelona, near the Sénia River. These trees are estimated to be upward of a thousand years old, and some might even be old enough to have been planted by Romans. During Roman times, millions of olive trees covered Spain, quenching the empire's insatiable thirst for olive oil, which was primarily Spanish, as indicated by the olive oil amphorae discovered in Rome, 80 to 85 percent of which are Spanish. At peak production, 15 million liters of oil were shipped from Spain just to Rome every year. Spanish olive oil was also sent to other Italian cities and even as far away as Britain and Germany, as indicated by amphorae archaeologists have found there. The remaining olive trees are just a small remnant of the early domestic trees that once covered Spain. It is a miracle that they survived so many centuries, withstanding droughts, fires, and great battles, but they are now slowly disappearing under a new threat.

Ancient olive trees have become the must-have garden ornament for wealthy estate owners and upscale hotels. Angelina Jolie spent $18,500 on a two-hundred-year-old olive tree she bought Brad Pitt for their $60 million Provençal estate. France's Stanislas Machoir auction house sold an olive tree with a diameter of seven meters for $81,000, and that was just one of forty-five ancient Spanish olive trees in their May 2012 auction collection titled "Ancient Olive Trees—Living Sculptures from the Roman Era."

In Taula del Sénia, the region we were about to visit, between 1,000 and 1,500 ancient trees had already been uprooted and sold. The same is happening in other regions of Spain, and a 2008 article by William Snyder in the *Wall Street Journal*, "New Market for Old Trees," reported that several thousand ancient olive trees had been removed from the southern province of Andalusia. The trees are often sold through intermediaries, auction houses, garden stores, or landscape architects. In his book *The Angel Tree: The Enchanting Quest for the World's Oldest Tree,* the landscaper Alex Dingwall-Main wrote about his search for an ancient olive tree for the garden of a wealthy client and his ultimate decision not to unearth any ancient trees.

During our quest to find our boat, we stumbled across a garden center by the highway with olive trees in pots the size of small swimming pools. Sitting among full-sized palms and other oversized trees, the fenced compound looked like a garden shop for giants. Curious to learn more, I approached the salesclerk, a thin blonde woman with fresh dirt under her fingernails. She spoke no English but in fluent German explained that the big ones came from nearby mountains, whereas the smaller trees were grown in farms along the road. They were exported all across Europe. The cost of the trees depended on the size. Trees with a circumference of less than 1 meter were $1,400, and the price rose steadily to $11,000 for 4.5- to 5-meter trees.

It seemed tragic that these living monuments were being torn out of the earth to disappear behind walled compounds in other countries. I was surprised that such a huge rooted tree could be moved at all. Sometimes the shock of being moved or replanted in unsuitable conditions is too much and the trees don't survive the process, but usually olive trees transplant surprisingly well. That doesn't mean the move is easy or cheap; it is a complex and laborious process requiring big machinery and thousands of dollars. Yet despite these hurdles, business is brisk.

Many Spaniards and other Europeans are outraged at losing their heritage, but it has been a difficult business to curtail. The government of Valencia has now banned the sale of olive trees more than five hundred years old, and Catalonia has regulations safeguarding a select group of cataloged olive trees. Still, Spain's policies are relatively weak, especially compared with those of France and Italy, which prevent the removal of any ancient olive trees. The regulations also push the trade underground, and in 2007 Valencia police confiscated a shipment of five hundred illegally obtained olive trees valued at $30 million.

It is difficult to blame the olive farmers, who are often struggling to survive. The windfall from selling an old tree can stave off bankruptcy and allow more productive high-yield olive cultivars to be planted to replace the old trees. Older trees were planted 50 to 100 per hectare instead of 250 in standard modern groves or 2,500 in super-high-density orchards. The older trees are tall and wide, sprawling into unique configurations that make mechanized harvesting impossible. Instead, the olives are picked by hand, a slow and costly process. Another strike against them is their irregular yields. Some years, the trees droop under the weight of their fruit, with as much as three hundred kilograms per tree, whereas other years there may be less than a quarter of that amount.

One of Spain's preeminent olive research labs, the Institute for Food Research and Technology, known by its acronym, IRTA, is trying to preserve these trees using economics instead of legislation. The lab has helped launch the millennium olive oil project, which produces olive oil made exclusively from aged trees. This oil sells for several times as much as generic olive oil, and that added value is enough to encourage farmers to focus on quality versus quantity or quick payoffs. Each millennium tree is certified and undergoes a strict organic growing, harvesting, and processing protocol to create a premium oil. This protocol is more labor intensive than past practices, in which oil from these ancient trees was blended with other olive oils and sold as bulk oil, but the premium price makes it worth the effort and farmers have embraced the project.

Located in the countryside outside of Tarragona, IRTA is an island of offices, research labs, and greenhouses surrounded by a large fence and a moat of olive trees. When we arrived, the gate opened automatically and we parked in a half-full lot. It was silent except for the noise of our feet crunching over the gravel lot and sporadic birdsong. With no busy roads nearby, no sounds of the city, and not a soul to be seen, such an absence of sound was something I hadn't experienced in weeks.

"Sí, te puedo ayudar?" a woman asked, standing in the doorway of a nondescript building we approached.

"*Sí*... we're here to see Ignasi Batlle. We have a meeting to discuss the millennium olive project," I said.

"Un momento."

She hurried up a staircase and reappeared with a handsome man dressed in a white polo shirt and jeans. Ignasi reached out a hand in greeting and introduced himself as the center's director of olives and nuts.

He led us up the stairs to a boardroom bathed in fluorescent light where racks of journals lined one wall and a bookshelf crammed with scholarly tomes stood against another. We settled into stiff chairs around a laminate table.

"Did you notice our greenhouses outside?" Ignasi asked as we waited for the rest of his team to arrive. "We are growing new, experimental strains of olive trees that will offer farmers better olives and hardier trees or perhaps more desirable flavors."

IRTA grew millions of experimental olive trees, first in its greenhouses and then in the surrounding land, but only a few stood out above the rest. The odds of finding a better olive tree were about the same as winning the lottery. But the researchers had already won one jackpot when they discovered the world's most popular olive tree, an Arbequina cultivar that is high in oil and easy to pick, making it popular not only in Spain but also in Argentina, Chile, Australia, and California. Now they were on the hunt for an even more elusive trait, a tree resistant to the olive fly.

Ignasi explained that the olive fly is the Achilles' heel of olive farming; it strikes when the olives are full and nearly ripe, just as farmers are preparing to reap the rewards of their year of work. The fly perches on the olive, curls forward like a bee about to sting, and plunges its ovipositor into the fruit, injecting its eggs. Two or three days later, the eggs hatch, and the larvae tunnel through the fruit, eating, defecating, and thriving. The olive's triglycerides break down, spiking free acidity levels, and unpleasant flavors percolate through the fruit. In twenty days, the maggots will slip into their pupal stage and then burst out as olive flies. The olive is destroyed.

The olive fly has been plaguing olive trees for at least 37,000 years, according to fossil records, and it is the single biggest pest that olive farmers face. Creating a cultivar resistant to the fly would be the greatest advancement in centuries.

But we were here to learn about old trees, not new cultivars. Ignasi introduced us to the rest of his team, including Agusti Romero and Antonia Ninot, who specialized in ancient olive trees. Agusti had been studying early olive trees for two decades and was a certified olive oil taster. Antonia was finishing her PhD on the genetic characteristics of ancient olive trees. They both fit the stereotype of the passionate researcher; their quiet voices rose in excitement when they spoke of their work, and they wore casual clothes hinting of priorities beyond fashion.

"Have you ever seen an old olive tree?" Ignasi asked.

I shook my head. "Only in photos."

Ignasi smiled. "You're in for a treat. When they are a thousand or more years old, they look unlike any tree you have seen before."

He unfurled a map of Spain across the table to show us the region we would be visiting. It was about eighty kilometers southwest of the institute, a corner of Spain near the coast and fed by the Sénia River.

"Are these trees still producing olives?" I asked.

"Yes, they still have very good yields, and this is what we rely on in our efforts to save them."

"The oil we can produce from these trees is actually very good," Agusti said. "It is a very ancient cultivar called Farga, producing oil with a smooth, fruity, sweet, and spicy flavor. It is one of my favorites."

His vivid description reminded me of the wine industry. Just like wine, olive oil was an ancient elixir, but whereas vines can barely reach a hundred years old, the longevity of olive trees allows us to eat and make oil from the fruit of the very same tree that nourished people two millennia ago. I couldn't wait to try olive oil that came from the same trees that may have fed Roman gladiators or Christopher Columbus's crew, olive oil that ancient historian Pliny the Elder called some of the greatest in the Roman Empire.

We piled into two cars and headed southwest. Near Sénia, the land began to buckle as we approached the rugged limestone mountains of Els Ports de Tortosa. In the foothills of these massifs, olive farming is one of the main occupations, as it has been for millennia. We sped along single-track roads with olive trees pressed up against the asphalt, as though trying to reclaim the land that had been taken from them. They spilled over old stone walls and clung to hillsides amid crumbling terracing, some young and spindly, others thick as old cedars and full of sparkling foliage. Except for the vast forests of gnarled olive trees, it was a sparsely populated terrain, with few buildings between villages.

At one of the many dirt tracks leading off the road, we turned and drove into an orchard, bumping over rocky soil and swerving around trees, and then parked under the shade of an olive tree. The trees surrounding our car were unlike any I'd ever seen before. I wandered over to the closest and gazed at its massive trunk. It must have been about six meters in circumference, and roots as thick as logs twisted outward from its base like writhing octopus tentacles frozen in action. It was striking just how short the trunk was. Back at home, giant old-growth cedars of equivalent girth often rise sixty meters or more. This tree, however, was only as tall as it was wide, and the trunk was only about two meters high. It was also deeply corded—as though a giant had twisted together an armful of old burlap ropes—and it terminated in an explosion of branches twisting haphazardly in all directions. The tree looked as though it belonged on a set for *The Lord of the Rings* or *The Hobbit*. I almost expected a few of the folds to shift and shuffle, revealing eyes and a mouth, and for the old tree to start mumbling its secrets.

No wonder these trees were popular as garden pieces. To have one of these living monuments from Roman times suddenly appear in your backyard seemed to defy the very laws of nature. The specimens in front of me appeared to be so firmly rooted to the earth that nothing short of a nuclear bomb could budge them. But a backhoe, a truck, and some other machinery are all that's required to transfer these trees to a manicured estate.

A man in his thirties with deep brown eyes and a chiseled jaw strode over to us and introduced himself as Roma. He was a biologist who inventoried historic olive trees and explained that this part of the orchard was just over a hectare and included thirty-five millennium olive trees, the densest concentration of ancient olive trees in Territori del Sénia, the two-thousand-square-kilometer swath of land that had the largest concentration of old olive trees in the world. The area had been declared an outdoor museum, and interpretive placards written in English, Spanish, and Catalan gave information about the history of the olive in the region and the dimensions of noteworthy trees.

Roma led us over the dry, cracked earth from one giant olive tree to the next. Ancient stone terraces zigzagged between the trees, and a small stone structure that once sheltered farmers abutted one wall.

"This one is called the octopus," Roma said as we approached a tree with exposed roots undulating across the earth.

"And this is the Wedding Tree," Agusti said, pointing toward another behemoth.

"Why is that?" I asked, scrutinizing the shadowy folds and expecting the forms of a bride and groom to materialize.

Agusti slipped through a gap in the trunk and entered the hollow interior cavity. His face suddenly appeared through a V-shaped slot. "Many couples get married here, and this is a favorite spot for taking portrait shots," he said. After a little cajoling, we followed suit and squeezed inside the tree, posing for a picture framed by thousand-year-old wood.

Many of the olive trees had numbered tags tied to branches, marking them as millennium trees. Agusti, Roma, and Antonia had painstakingly identified and cataloged most of Spain's 5,500 ancient trees.

"How do you determine their age?" Colin asked.

"Olive trees are a very difficult tree to date accurately," Agusti said. "You see the inside of the tree; it is hollow. As the tree ages, the inside decays and we lose the oldest part of the tree."

Radio carbon dating is a common method of dating trees and other organic materials. As trees absorb carbon dioxide from the atmosphere through photosynthesis, they incorporate the carbon into their structure. Most of this carbon is in the form of the stable carbon 12 isotope, but a tiny amount is in the form of the unstable carbon 14 isotope. Although a tree absorbs both carbon isotopes, over time the carbon 14 isotope decays, whereas the carbon 12 isotope doesn't. Measuring the ratio of carbon 14 to carbon 12 tells us how long ago the carbon was absorbed and thus the tree's age. When the center of the trunk decays, however, no original wood remains for radio carbon dating. Roots, too, continually decompose and are replaced by new growth, so they are equally unreliable for carbon dating. The third strike against carbon dating is that it is expensive, and dating a grove of olive trees would be out of the question.

Another method used to date olive trees is tree ring analysis, or dendrochronology, in which the annual growth rings in a cross-section of wood are counted. A tree's growth varies throughout the year, accelerating when conditions are favorable, such as in the spring, when there is ample rain and sunshine, and then slowing in other seasons, often in the fall and winter, when the temperatures cool. The wood that is formed during rapid growth is less dense than that formed during slower times, and the variation throughout a calendar year creates a distinct ring. By counting these rings, a tree's age can be determined. A tool called an increment borer is used to take a thin, cylindrical sample of wood stretching from the bark to the core of a standing tree. For trees that have been felled, the rings can be counted on the cross section.

This method also has had considerable success with many types of trees, dating wood back thousands of years, but, again, olive trees pose a challenge. Scientists have to deal with not only the olive tree's missing core but also unreliable growth rings. Olive trees do not always form growth rings annually, and under climatic conditions such as drought or temperature fluctuation, they may form false rings that are indistinguishable from true annual rings. The olive tree's gnarled trunk can also make it difficult to retrieve a core sample. For trees without a center, researchers cannot obtain a complete core sample and they must extrapolate their data to estimate the number of missing rings, adding further uncertainties to the date obtained.

After carbon dating and dendrochronology, the third most common way of dating olive trees—and perhaps the most popular—uses a combination of growth rings and the circumference of the olive's trunk. The rate of a tree's growth is estimated by tree ring analysis, and then the circumference of the tree is measured. The thickness of tree rings is relatively consistent when trees are exposed to similar conditions, and the rate of growth depends on specific climatic and geographic conditions. The growth of an olive tree on rocky terrain in Spain would be much different from that of an olive tree in France but similar to that of an olive tree of the same cultivar on a neighboring bluff. Thus, once a rate of growth is determined for a specific cultivar in a localized area, that information can be used to determine the age of multiple trees. The tree's circumference is measured at a set height, and the tree's age is then determined from that value.

The millennium olive program uses this method to determine which trees may be included in the program. Trees with a trunk circumference greater than 3.5 meters (measured from 1.3 meters off the ground) are considered sufficiently old. Whether these trees are actually 1,000 years old is uncertain, and when ecologists at the Spanish Centre for Ecological Research and Forestry Applications tested fourteen of the trees using tree ring analysis of a cored sample, they found the oldest one to be 627 years old.

"Where is the oldest olive tree?" I asked Agusti, curious to see if he had an insight into this hotly debated subject. From the research we'd done, I knew there were several olive trees purported to be the oldest in the world, some supposedly more than six thousand years old. But most of this information was more legend than science.

"I wish I could tell you, but nobody knows. And just because a tree is small doesn't necessarily mean it isn't old. The olive tree can grow back from the roots if it is cut down or burned or damaged by frost. Some olive trees may look young, but they could be growing from roots that have been around for thousands of years."

In other words, the olive tree can potentially live forever, but we will never know. A tree could sprout back from the same roots countless times. Could such a tree be defined as the original tree? The original organic material from the roots and trunk would be long gone, though it would be genetically identical to the original plant. I suspected the millennium olive team wouldn't spend much time debating this question, since there is no way of identifying ancient trees that don't exhibit their age through size.

The olive owes its remarkable resilience and longevity to a few key factors. For one, it is very slow growing. During its first decade of life, it develops at its fastest, reaching two meters and producing olives in its seventh year, but after that, growth is glacial. The tree will gain another two to three meters in height, sometimes more, depending on the cultivar, and the rest of the growth is horizontal. It is not unusual to find ancient olive trees with circumferences of ten meters or more. The wood is also very hard and rot resistant, allowing the tree to withstand strong winds and other hardships.

"Can I take a sample of this tree?" I asked, pointing to a particularly large and sculpted millennium tree. I wondered what genetic testing of these ancient trees would tell us. Could their originator have been a Phoenician olive tree? Antonia helped me clip some leaves, which I placed in a sealed plastic bag.

"What are those bottles for—to scare away the birds?" Colin asked, pointing to one of the plastic water bottles that hung off this tree and most others. It was perforated with small holes and half-filled with an amber liquid.

"No, it is for a pest much worse than birds," Agusti replied. "It is to catch the olive fly."

I wandered over to a bottle hanging on a low branch. Dozens of tiny carcasses lay inside. They were smaller than houseflies and had thin, translucent wings and caramel-colored bodies. Usually chemical sprays are used to eradicate the olive fly, but in organic groves, bottle traps are the most common method. The bottles are filled with special pheromones that attract the flies, which then become trapped inside.

"It is quite effective, but we are also experimenting with another organic technique," Agusti said. "It was noticed that olive trees next to dirt roads aren't affected by the fly. The coating of dust that settled on the olives discouraged the insect. So we made a spray using water and clay and spray a thin film over the entire tree."

"It works well around here," Roma added. "But in places where it rains regularly, it is very labour intensive. The trees have to be resprayed every time it rains."

Despite the challenges of organic growing, the millennium project is by all accounts a success. The oil is exported to Japan, China, the U.S., and other parts of Europe, and prices range from $25 to $40 for a half-liter bottle. Two years earlier, the project produced five thousand half-liter bottles, and last year that number increased to twelve thousand bottles to meet demand. "There are enough ancient trees to produce forty thousand bottles," Agusti said.

"And if demand exceeds that, I guess you can just plant new trees and wait a thousand years," I joked.

Before the millennium olive oil project began, each ancient tree produced $30 to $40 worth of olive oil a year on average. After the costs of pruning, harvesting, and milling, farmers were left with very little. Some years it cost more to make the oil than they were paid for it. Meanwhile, the going rate for a modest-sized old olive tree is about $16,000. Even if the farmer received just a fraction of this sum, it would be more than he could make selling olive oil from that tree's olives during his lifetime or even his grandchildren's. This project gave farmers an incentive to keep their trees, which, when coupled with the softening market for old olive trees because of the EU's economic struggles, meant more Spanish olive trees would stay where they had been for hundreds of years.

Not only did the olive trees benefit, but the millennium olive oil was very good. Agusti and Antonia characterized the oil using a barrage of laboratory tests along with a sensory analysis by an oil-testing panel of eight experts. The oil from thousand-plus-year-old Farga trees is classified as "green medium-high intensity" with "secondary aromas reminiscent of freshly cut grass, with hints of green almonds and walnuts" and a "good balance between spicy and sweet."

Two years ago, I would never have believed that terms like "freshly cut grass" or "hints of green almonds" could be used to describe basic oil. Terminology like this is well known in the world of whiskies or wine, but were the flavors of olive oil really so complex that such detailed descriptions were required? I would learn over the following months, as Colin and I sampled some of the highest-quality oils produced in Europe, that, yes, the richness and diversity of flavors from these oils require more than standard adjectives to communicate their attributes.

Many European gourmets have a cupboard stocked with a variety of olive oils from different regions. Just as you might choose a fine Bordeaux to complement roast lamb, the discerning foodie would pair an olive oil with the food it accompanied. The millennium oil has a subtle taste, termed a "low sense fatiguing component." It was like the sauvignon blanc of the wine world, delicate and understated, an ideal accompaniment to fish and salads.

But taste is just one of several components. In the lab, tests measured free acidity, polyphenol levels, peroxide value, ultraviolet absorbance, fatty acid profile, saponification value, induction time, moisture content, organoleptics, volatile components, and more. The extensive testing and examination of the oil from the millennium Farga trees provided the first comprehensive analysis of the properties and flavor of oil from ancient olive trees. Ultimately, the testing had been conducted to help market the oil and save the trees, but it also provides valuable scientific information about a resource that will not be around forever.

There was more to saving these trees than making good oil; marketing and selling it were equally important, and Jamie Antich, manager of the governmental organization Taula del Sénia, told us a little about this side. A stocky man with an infectious smile, he wore glasses, a pastel striped shirt, and dress shoes, and looked more suited to an office than an orchard. That didn't stop him from joining us as we continued through the olive grove, where he exuded endless excitement about the oil.

"We have partnered with some of the best restaurants in the region, and we've created a recipe book for the oil," Jamie said, handing us a book titled *Gastronomic Guide—Millennium Olive Oil from Territori del Sénia.*

The glossy coffee table book was the love child of a locavore and a mad scientist. I glanced at a recipe for olive-oil-sautéed sea cucumbers, while Jamie explained that each chef created a dish using the millennium oil. I was keen to try the creations, but I was less confident I could follow the recipes. Whipping olive oil into a foamy emulsion that is then cooled with liquid nitrogen to create lollipops is way out of my league.

Strolling between ancient olive trees felt like stepping into the pages of a fairy tale, where the trees were the bearers of wisdom and guidance, the history of thousands of years of knowledge bottled up inside them. I could have stayed for hours, wandering from tree to tree, marveling at each one's unique and contorted shape. But before long, the relentless August sun drove us to congregate in the shade of a sprawling olive tree canopy. Even here, the heat was inescapable, and when Jamie suggested it was time to try the olive oil, all of us heartily agreed.

We headed to L'Antic Moli, one of the book's featured restaurants. It borders the seasonal Sénia River and is surrounded by farmland, a setting that seemed more fitting for a farmhouse than an upscale restaurant. In fact, the peach-colored manor, encircled by manicured gardens, stone walkways, and old olive millstones, resembled an elegant country estate. But the crowded rustic interior told otherwise, as did the celebrity chef on staff and the Michelin Guide, which describes L'Antic Moli as a restaurant worth the travel.

We settled around a wooden table, and I placed Leif on the ground to explore his surroundings. Although Leif still grumbled or cried when confined, a heartening development was taking place: crawling made him happy. Leif slapped between tables, squealing with delight at his freedom, while Colin and I took turns hovering nearby to ensure that he didn't pull down any tablecloths. No one seemed to mind, and I was grateful that Spain was such a family-centered country.

Jamie ordered our meals, and when the signature dish, Olivart, arrived, it billowed smoke like a stage at a rock concert. The restaurant fell silent, and a roomful of curious onlookers stared at our table. The smoke dissipated to reveal an appetizer that looked more like abstract art than food. But gradually an image emerged from the jumble of shapes and colors.

"It's fall leaves lying in snow and soil," I guessed when Jamie looked at me expectantly.

He nodded and explained that it was an expressionist dish meant to represent autumn. Olive oil was used in every element, from the emulsified oil that created the white foam representing snow to the thick layers of chocolate and oil forming the earth. The mushrooms sautéed in olive oil and the black olive biscuits created the leaves.

The rest of the meal was equally enjoyable, if not quite as flashy, and by the end we had a much greater appreciation for the breadth of cooking that suited olive oil.

IT WAS TIME to cast our lines and make our way up Spain's eastern coast toward France. Our permits for the boat had come through, and we were finally free to begin our voyage.

I was both excited and nervous. Over the last month, Spain had revealed a side of her I had never experienced before, and I was sad to leave. Our time on the Iberian Peninsula was just the appetizer for our olive odyssey, but already I felt I'd learned so much. When I had first arrived, I struggled to discern an olive tree from a cherry. Now I could spot an olive tree from a kilometer away, identifying it by its hue and form. An olive farmer toiling by the roadside was no longer an obscure laborer; I recognized him as part of a brotherhood that stretched around the Mediterranean, united by knowledge and passion. The techniques these farmers used, the difficulties they faced, and the satisfaction they took in a job well done were the same in Greece, Tunisia, or Syria.

As I learned more about the olive, I couldn't help but feel I was learning more about my family's background and, in a way, about myself. And although I was sad to say good-bye to Spain, I looked forward to beginning our long-awaited journey.

3

SEARCHING FOR WILD OLIVES

"Beneath two bushy olives sprung from the same root,
one olive wild, the other well-bred stock.
No sodden gusty winds could ever pierce them . . .
so dense they grew together, tangling side by side."

HOMER, *The Odyssey*[1]

WINDS WERE LIGHT when we left Barcelona, and I felt none of my earlier fear as we glided through rippled waters. The breeze pushed us along at an average speed of eight kilometers per hour, and the autopilot freed us from the monotonous task of steering. I relaxed in the cockpit with Leif in my arms and watched the breakwater walls of Port Olímpic recede into the distance.

With the sails set, our destination plotted in the GPS, and the autopilot keeping us on course, Colin dove inside the galley and clattered through the cupboards. He emerged with a bottle of red wine and two plastic wineglasses.

"This is it. Our big voyage is finally starting—definitely a cause for celebration!"

We clinked glasses and watched Barcelona's glass and concrete towers disappear.

"The flight out, the long search for the boat, and the bureaucracy are all behind us. Now it's just a big exciting adventure with the Mediterranean to explore," I said as I drank in the sparkling waters all around us.

Apart from two sailboats in the distance, we were alone on the water, enjoying an unfamiliar solitude as we drifted away from a city of almost 2 million. The coastal plain allowed easy development near the water, and as we headed northeast, we skirted a bland coastline of cities, towns, suburbs, resorts, and industrial low-rises. The shoreline was pencil straight, with no protected coves or bays to offer shelter or visual respite.

We spent our first night in Blanes, a small town that marks the gateway to the Wild Coast, Costa Brava in Spanish, which stretches to the French border. The town was unremarkable except for the high moorage cost—nearly four times as much as our nightly moorage in Barcelona—and the abundance of concrete resorts, hotels, apartments, and holiday homes that had steamrolled an ancient fishing village.

The following morning, light winds pushed us eastward, past honey-colored beaches buttressed by cliffs and an endless backdrop of green hills. Clouds sped overhead, casting endlessly shifting hues and tones onto the caramel-colored shoreline. Farther north, the Pyrenees and the adjacent mountain ranges plunged into the sea, creating a rugged shoreline of rocky promontories and expansive sandy bays. The challenging topography had curtailed development, and instead, houses and the occasional castle perched on clifftops. Towns and villages were shoehorned into the valleys.

Although ancient Phoenicians had hopscotched along this route and undoubtedly stopped along the way, we hadn't heard of any Phoenician settlements or ancient olive groves in this area and planned to sail steadily to France. We were headed toward a truly wild coast, the calanques, where towering limestone cliffs impeded agricultural development and made road access impossible. Here we hoped to find wild olive trees, cultivars that had grown ten thousand years ago, before people domesticated the olive and long before eastern mariners reached these shores.

Locating wild olive trees isn't as easy as walking into a forest and plucking a branch off a scruffy olive tree. Oleasters and domesticated olives interbreed easily, aided by birds that carry domestic stones into wild areas and the wind, which blows olive pollen long distances. Some scientists even question whether there are any truly wild olive trees anymore and suggest that trees presumed "wild" are merely feral or hybrid plants. One thing we knew with near certainty was that where there were cultivated olives, there were no truly wild olives.

The wild and cultivated olive trees even look similar when they are untended. Wild olive trees are generally shrublike, and domestic olive trees quickly follow suit when they are deprived of regular pruning. Suckers erupt from their roots and fan outward, masking the domestic olive's treelike figure. Where the differences cease, however, is in the size of the olive. Domesticated olive trees have larger olives, which are what they were bred for, and despite neglect, they retain that larger size. In the next generation, however, the size of the olive can quickly change. Like many fruit trees, olive trees that are grown from stones do not necessarily resemble the tree they came from, and that's one of the main reasons olive trees are grown from cuttings or grafted. As a result, it is impossible to determine by looking at it whether an olive tree is truly wild or just feral. Our best bet for finding a wild olive tree was to go somewhere far away from its cultivated relative.

Wild olives, whose small size and petty oil content make them unattractive for human consumption, have been overshadowed by cultivated varieties. But in some parts of the world, it is not unusual for people to pick wild olives and press them into oil for their family to use. And in the past, even when people cultivated olives, they relied on wild olive trees for wood, oil, and olives, and in some cases even preferred the wild tree. The ancient Greeks favored the wild olive tree's wood over the domesticated and used its oil to make their perfumes. In the fourth century BC, the Greek philosopher Theophrastus wrote that the wild olive wood is resistant to decay and "is not eaten by teredon,"[2] the shipworm that destroys the hulls of wooden boats. Since wild trees were thought to be hardier and to "suffer less than the [domesticated] olive from special winds,"[3] their wood was used for shipbuilding, as well as for carpentry tools. The ancient Greeks pruned wild olive trees and transplanted seedlings to encourage productivity, and Theophrastus wrote that the wild olive "produces more fruit than the [domesticated] olive but it ripens less."[4] Wild olive branches were woven together to make the wreaths that crowned ancient Olympians, and the sacred olive tree that stood near the temple of Zeus in Olympia was a wild cultivar. Even in mythology the wild tree was esteemed. Heracles carved his club from a wild olive tree near the Saronic Gulf, and after winning countless battles with it, he dedicated it to the god Mercury, placing it next to his statue in Corinth, where it transformed back into a wild olive tree.

If wild olive trees were going to grow anywhere in the densely populated Mediterranean, we wagered on the remote and inaccessible French calanques. The formidable topography has made it one of the few uninhabited places along the French coast, and it retains much of its original flora. Agriculture is all but impossible on its craggy limestone folds, reducing the likelihood that wild trees interbred with domestic ones. Finding wild local olive trees was crucial for understanding whether domesticated olives were brought here by early seafarers or cultivated from indigenous wild olives. We needed to compare the genetic profile of cultivated trees with that of both local wild trees and domesticated Middle Eastern cultivars to understand which was their closer relative.

WE WERE making good speed, propelled by stronger winds, and a growing confidence allowed me to enjoy the feeling of speed and the gurgling slosh of small breaking waves as we made our way steadily toward France. That ease was shattered in the early afternoon while I was keeping watch and Colin was studying the latest weather forecast. His brow furrowed as he studied the computer screen. With our mobile Internet stick, we were able to surf the web and get detailed reports three or four kilometers offshore; it was vastly better than the Spanish updates broadcast on the VHF radio, which a few years ago would have been our only option.

"They are predicting a tramontane to blow through soon," Colin said, glancing up from the screen.

I looked up at a perfect blue sky. Tramontane is the name given by the French to the frequent gale-force winds that funnel along the Pyrenees and into the Mediterranean, turning the Gulf of Lion into one of the windiest and most treacherous stretches on the Mediterranean.

"When is it expected to begin?" I asked. I was worried about our imminent crossing of the gulf.

"Late this afternoon," Colin said, clicking through pages of arrows depicting wind speed and direction. "At its peak they are expecting forty-five knots."

According to the Beaufort scale, this was a strong gale, producing twenty-foot waves and driving spray. This was not the kind of storm I wanted to be caught out in, especially not with

Leif. Fortunately, our knowledge of the pending storm meant we could pull into a harbor and wait a couple of days for the weather to pass.

We steered *Isis* toward a large sandy bay fronting the tourist town of Palamos. The town had two marinas, but we decided to anchor in front of the beach. Although the anchorage was fully exposed from the south, we would be sheltered from the north tramontane winds.

It was the first time we had anchored, and I marveled at the peaceful solitude. Just a hundred meters from our vessel, thousands of people cloaked the golden sands. The waters in between were dotted with swimmers, air mattresses, and beginners falling off windsurfers, but near our boat the water was empty. I felt removed from the adjacent throngs, as though I were watching it on a huge HD TV. The only sound we could hear on our boat was the gurgle of waves washing up the cockpit drain.

At 4:00 PM a cloudless sky and calm conditions made us question the accuracy of the weather forecast. Twenty minutes later that changed. A thick bank of black clouds scudded over the horizon like a giant wave of darkness drowning the sky. The black wall raced toward us, and the people on the beach ran for shelter like ants fleeing from a disturbed anthill. For a few beautiful moments the entire town was bathed in rich, unfiltered sunlight, framed by a vaporous black hole.

The moment the sun was snuffed by thick clouds, the wind switched from a gentle southerly to a northerly gale blowing with such intensity that our anchor chain jerked taut. The harbor became instant chaos as boats from all directions fled for the safety of the marinas. I was relieved that we were securely anchored in a harbor and not running for shelter. As long as our anchor didn't drag, we wouldn't have any problems.

Leif leaned enthusiastically into the gale, his fine blond hair plastered against his head by wind and rain. Colin was inside the cabin chopping onions for dinner. The boat was starting to feel like home, and my early nagging doubts about the journey were slowly being quashed. I was beginning to realize that through preparation and prudence, sailing could be quite manageable.

A THIRTY-TWO-HOUR nonstop voyage took us 220 kilometers across the Gulf of Lion to the eastern perimeter of the French Riviera, near Marseille. The Massif des Calanques was arguably the most dramatic coastline in France. Towering limestone cliffs jutted out of the ocean, a jumble of talc-colored shapes reaching for the clouds. Spires, serrated ridges like the back of a dinosaur, and stacks of flaking stone created an unworldly clutter of shapes and patterns. Vegetation clung to ridgetops and the less precipitous slopes, and from the water I could see Aleppo pines, Mediterranean oaks, and even a few olive trees. The calanques stretch from Marseille to Cassis, a unique landscape created by the erosion of a thick layer of limestone. Ancient streams and rivers carved near-vertical-sided canyons through the soft limestone, and where these narrow ravines reach the sea, fjord-like inlets have been created. The calanques are named after these inlets; the word comes from a pre-Indo-European term meaning inlet.

We steered our boat toward Calanque d'en Vau, described by our pilot book as the most impressive of the nine or so inlets cutting into these limestone cliffs. The entrance was indiscernible from the sea, and we appeared to be on a collision course with vertical rock. I was beginning to wonder if we'd made a mistake inputting the GPS coordinates when a thin crack appeared in the white cliffs and revealed a narrow inlet about half a kilometer long.

"Wow!" Colin said, staring up at the limestone spires and cliffs. "I knew this area was supposed to be nice, but this is incredible."

We slowed the engine to soak in the panorama surrounding us. A dazzling white beach punctuated the head of the inlet, and sheer cliffs bordered the sides. The sand beneath our keel gave the water the color of a Caribbean lagoon. There were no houses or hotels, and the only access (apart from water) was provided by a trail winding overland through the canyon. Half a dozen people relaxed on the beach, and a few nudists took advantage of the extra privacy offered by swimming-only-access ledges at the base of the crags.

This was the first truly protected anchorage we had encountered since leaving Barcelona, and I was pleased that there were only half a dozen sailboats here, leaving plenty of room for our boat. We chose a spot as close to the beach as possible and dropped anchor. There were ten meters of water beneath us, according to our depth sounder, but the water was so clear it was hard to believe. We could see every detail of the bottom, the gently waving grass, the occasional rock, schools of trout-sized fish. We could even see how well our anchor grabbed the seafloor.

Because of the small amount of space in the inlet, boats couldn't just drop anchor wherever there was space, but lined the cliff, their sterns tied to the rock and an anchor off their bows hooking them to the seabed. This created a neat row of sailboats, as tidy as you'd find in any marina but without the docks. Colin launched our small inflatable dinghy and secured a rope from the bow to an outcrop of rock, while I dropped the anchor and moved us into our final position. Even in wild spaces, Europeans had to know how to park in tight confines. We cut the diesel engine, tensioned the anchor chain, and finally relaxed.

This little fjord, fit for an otherworldly backdrop in the movie *Avatar*, was the perfect introduction to France. Before touching French soil, however, I needed to clear my foggy mind. Slipping on my swimsuit, I climbed onto the cabin and leapt into the clear water. The icy temperature was a shock. This was nothing like swimming in the warm waters off Barcelona; it felt like I'd plunged into a jug of ice water.

As I warmed up back on deck, a Zodiac inflatable approached us. The crew introduced themselves in English as park officials and welcomed us to the calanques.

"Why is the water so cold?" I asked, amazed that the temperature could be so different from that of the waters off Barcelona, just a few hundred kilometers away.

"Two reasons," the young man behind the wheel replied. "The main one is the tramontane that blew through a few days ago. It stirred up the cold water from below. Overnight the water temperature went from twenty-six degrees to eighteen. The other reason is because of a cold freshwater spring that flows into this bay."

"So it was pretty windy here?" I asked, feeling pleased with our decision to delay our crossing.

"*Windy?* It was the worst storm this summer. There was a lot of damage done onshore as well. I wouldn't want to have been out there in a boat."

We chatted a little more about the park's flora and fauna, and then they sped out of the inlet, continuing on what must be one of the best jobs in the world.

The following morning, we rowed our dinghy to the beach and picked our way up the crumbling cliffside, following an animal path worn by countless footsteps. The exposed roots of shrubs offered handrails that I gripped when the footing became more tenuous. Colin, sure-footed as always, effortlessly glided upward while carrying Leif. We passed many pine trees and smaller deciduous shrubs but no olive trees. Our view became increasingly dramatic the higher we climbed, and our boat looked like a toy on the water below.

"Hey, I think I've found one!" Colin shouted from above.

I caught up, panting, and sure enough, he and Leif were standing beside what looked like a wild olive tree. It had multiple gnarled shrublike trunks, each the width of a wrestler's thighs, and a mane of elongated silvery leaves. The tree was thriving despite growing out of solid rock in very arid conditions. Only a handful of pea-sized olives hung from its branches, wrinkled and green. The desiccated drupes reflected the drought conditions the plant faced, but the tree itself looked healthy.

The plant in front of us was as much a shrub as a tree, not uncommon in wild olive trees. The shrublike form and habit of the olive tree have led botanists to classify it as both tree and shrub, and it falls along the spectrum between the two. But that didn't mean this tree was a wild olive, since it is the pruning of cultivated trees that gives more of a tree shape. Olive plants left on their own are generally low and bushy and have multiple shrublike stems, even if they are domesticated varieties. I examined a hard green drupe, noting that it was tiny and probably too small for a domesticated tree. This tree was either a wild olive tree or a feral one.

It is impossible to tell the difference between truly wild olive trees and ones that have sprouted from pits of domesticated trees dropped by birds or that have resulted from the cross-pollination of wild and domestic cultivars. The only way to know whether an olive tree is wild or feral is to look at its DNA. Wild olive trees have certain genetic features that make them less suitable for cultivation and are never found in domesticated trees. Through this genetic fingerprint, we've discovered just how elusive wild olive trees are.

In 2001, a team of scientists published a paper in the journal *Nature* documenting their hunt for wild olive trees. Using criteria such as geographic isolation and growing climate—features similar to those that had led us to the calanques—they found ten forests throughout the Mediterranean that offered suitable wild olive habitat. In each forest they tested forty seemingly wild trees for a total of four hundred trees. Only twelve were wild, and most of those were located in the eastern Mediterranean. The researchers didn't find any wild olive trees in Egypt, Turkey, Syria, Crete, or mainland Greece and hypothesized that it was because olive trees had been cultivated for longer in the eastern Mediterranean. The rarity of truly wild olive trees has been documented again and again, with researchers concurring that genuinely wild olives are found only in a few isolated areas of Mediterranean forests.

Although wild, feral, and domesticated olive trees are generally morphologically indistinguishable, they have significant genetic differences that make retaining wild populations important. Wild trees are much more diverse than domesticated trees and even feral ones. Human selection has sculpted the olive genome to suit our desires, but the wild trees are not subjugated in this manner and therefore have much more variability from one tree to the next. Diversity is the cornerstone of species survival and plays a crucial role in agriculture. When climatic conditions change or new pests arise, a varied population will be better able to withstand those changes. Species that become too homogeneous are at risk of being vanquished by a single pest or stressor, as the potato was in nineteenth-century Ireland, when it was ravaged by blight, leading to the starvation of approximately a million people.

Loss of biodiversity is one of our generation's most pressing environmental concerns, threatening ecosystems, food security, and species survival, and preserving the wild relatives of agricultural crops is one of the most important things we can do to protect our food supply. Wild plants have the potential to contribute a host of beneficial qualities to their more cultivated peers, from pest resistance to hardiness to enhanced fertility, and are routinely used for breeding improvements that have increased crop yields around the world by US$115 billion per year, according to some estimates. The importance of these wild species has received more widespread recognition in recent years, and they have been preserved in seed banks, botanical gardens, and other ex-situ programs. There is also a growing understanding of the importance of protecting them in their natural environment. In 2011, the International Union for Conservation of Nature (IUCN) created a red list identifying 572 European crop wild relatives and classifying them according to their level of endangerment. Nearly 12 percent of those species are threatened, and 3.5 percent are critically endangered. For many, including the olive, not enough data are available to even categorize them.

Was this a wild olive tree? I wondered. Given the scarcity of wild trees, it seemed like too much to hope for, but we were in a wonderfully inaccessible and unfarmable area. The only way to know was through genetic testing. I broke off a short branch from the tree's crown and another one from near its roots and placed them in the plastic bag I had brought along.

"Hey, check this out!" Colin yelled just as I'd finished collecting the samples.

Colin had scrambled farther up the hillside with Leif and was pointing at a gap in the rocks. I climbed up beside him and stared into the opening of a large cave. Cool air wafted from the entrance, hinting at a sizeable interior. I pulled two headlamps from my backpack, and we scrambled up a steep boulder to the narrow entrance.

The floor of the cave was fairly level and quickly opened into a living room–sized space decorated with thick stalactites and spiderwebs caked with flies. It looked perfect for a cave family, but the only signs of human habitation were recent; burnt candles littered the ground and graffiti defaced the walls.

"I bet cavemen lived in here," Colin said, grinning with the enthusiasm of a kid playing Jurassic Park. "Look, it's just perfect—a nice flat living area, the entrance is protected with a small drop, and wow, what a view! I bet this would cost a few mammoth tusks."

He was probably right. Tens of thousands of years ago, early humans occupied this region and used the numerous caverns offered by the karst landscape, a blend of limestone and dolomite that is ideal for cave formation. One of the greatest cave discoveries of all time occurred just 2.5 kilometers from where we were standing, in one of the neighboring inlets, Calanque de Morgiou. In 1985, scuba diver Henri Cosquer discovered the entrance to an underwater cave, now known as the Cosquer Cave, 37 meters beneath the surface. After swimming through a 175-meter tunnel, he emerged into air and a cave art gallery. More than 150 paintings covered the walls, some as much as 27,000 years old. Depictions made from charcoal and clay included horses, bison, penguins (it was much colder in Europe then), humans, and quite a few penises and vaginas, proving that pornography has always been a popular subject.

The art was carbon dated from two periods—27,000 years ago and 18,000 years ago. That was during the last ice age, which peaked 22,000 years ago, and sea levels were about 110 meters lower than now, positioning the cave entrance near the water and not in it. The Cosquer Cave is in many ways as impressive as the well-known Altamira cave, famous for its glorious images of wild horses and bison from 16,500 years ago, but because of its inaccessibility, the Cosquer Cave has remained a hidden gem. Information about the cave and its contents wasn't even released to the public until 1991, when two experienced divers died after becoming lost in the submerged passages. In Cassis, we would visit the Cosquer museum, the closest most people will ever get to these treasures.

"They even had an olive tree in their front yard," Colin said gesturing down to the tree below.

"Well, that depends on when they lived here, doesn't it?" I said. Colin gave me a perplexed look. "If they were living here at the same time the Cosquer Cave was inhabited," I explained, "it would have been too cold for olive trees."

When the last ice age peaked, temperatures here were eight degrees lower on average; it was more like England here than southern France. It would have been far too cold for olive trees; even in today's climate this is the northern reaches of olive habitat. Before that glaciation, more than 100,000 years ago, the olive tree thrived in the Mediterranean, having spread from its origins in Africa some half a million years ago to take advantage of the hot, dry summers and rare frosts in these coastal regions. When temperatures began to drop, the hard frosts decimated olive forests, reducing its population to a few pockets along the Strait of Gibraltar, Aegean area, and Levant, and as the mercury rose, the olive tree spread once again, repopulating any regions it could.

We whiled a couple of leisurely days in Calanque d'en Vau, hiking, swimming, and paddling. We picnicked on food left over from Spain—chorizo, cheese, and tomatoes—and waved to the steady trickle of boats visiting from the nearby town of Cassis, sightseeing vessels top-heavy with camera-toting tourists and brightly colored rental kayaks. In the early mornings, however, the inlet was silent, devoid of boat engines or beach revelers, making it easy to imagine the solitude this region possessed before the advent of tourism.

Our time in the picturesque calanques was the perfect way to convalesce after several days of sleepless sailing. We'd found our wild olive trees, and now it was time to continue to the heart of Provence to learn how olive oil defined this culture.

4 AN ANCIENT FOOD FOR MODERN FOODIES

"Happiness is finding two olives in your martini when you're hungry."

JOHNNY CARSON[1]

SHORTLY AFTER PULLING anchor, we rounded a jagged limestone promontory and sailed into Cassis. Muted pastel buildings contrasted with the white limestone landscape. A crescent beach lay to one side of the town, and the magnificent ocher flanks of one of France's highest cliffs, Cap Canaille, towered over the sea to the east of the town.

We steered for the municipal marina, protected by thick breakwater walls, and slipped through a narrow opening between riprap and the limestone shore. A lighthouse marked the entrance, and three weathered fishermen sitting in its shade glared accusingly as we swerved to avoid their lines, as though international maritime laws didn't apply to them.

The marina was full, but the staff made a spot for us at the end of one of the piers using a delicate arrangement of ropes. It was an ideal location, with an unrestricted view of the bustling promenade, the fishing boats, and the sea. We had what was probably the best vista in town for only $25 per night, a bargain for one of the French Riviera's tourist hot spots.

The French poet Frédéric Mistral once wrote, "Those who have seen Paris but not Cassis have seen nothing,"[2] and a hundred years later that could still be said. Brightly colored traditional fishing boats plied the waters near shore, looking too perfect to be anything more than eye candy for the tourists, while pleasure boats and sightseeing craft lined the remaining docks. Restaurants and shops crowded the waterfront, like books squeezed together on a shelf, vertical ribbons of color with open doors and wrought-iron balconies draped with cascading flowers. Enraptured couples strolled hand in hand along the promenade, and families pushed strollers or led small dogs in harnesses. A fishmonger bartered over a tray of orange scorpion fish and flat turbot he'd caught that morning, while two artists splashed color onto their canvases.

We eagerly disembarked, looking forward to our first French meal. Leif's stroller bumped over polished limestone cobblestones quarried from nearby Calanque de Port-Miou, and we wandered from restaurant to restaurant, studying the posted menus in anticipation. Every carte du jour was dominated by seafood, a mouth-watering selection of dishes that included bouillabaisse, the traditional Provençal fish stew that originated in nearby Marseille, and seafood entrées of eel, bream, turbot, monkfish, crab, hake, mullet, and mussels.

In the interests of preserving our funds, we decided on *moules marinière,* the only seafood that cost less than our night's stay. Settling into seats overlooking the water, we toasted with glasses of chilled Côtes de Provence rosé and dunked slabs of white bread in olive oil and balsamic vinegar. The oil was young and green with delicate herbal notes, the terroir of the French fields: lavender, thyme, grapes, and chalky soil. When the mussels arrived, in big black pots and in copious amounts, they, too, were swimming in a delicate sauce of olive oil mixed with white wine, garlic, and spices.

Although the French are known for indulging in rich, creamy sauces, butter-infused pastries, and hundreds of cheese varieties, these are not part of Provençal cuisine. Instead of butter and milk fats, olive oil has long been the staple here. Nearly a century ago, the politician Jean Charles-Brun remarked, "Every province in France has its way of speaking, its unique sensibility, its literature, its art; it has its tricks and old recipes and gastronomic traditions... You can't force people from the South to gorge themselves on butter or people from the North to use olive oil."[3]

Olive oil first arrived in Provence with the Greeks in the sixth century BC, and its popularity soared during the Roman Empire. But when the empire collapsed, so did olive oil consumption. The invading Germanic tribes ate meat, milk, and butter, a stark contrast to the Roman triad of oil, cereal, and wine. Instead of growing crops, the German tribes hunted, fished, gathered wild foods, and raised livestock. Agricultural land was replaced with pastures, and slowly tastes shifted.

Throughout large swaths of the Mediterranean, olive oil nearly vanished from the kitchen during the Middle Ages. Spanish, French, and Italian cookbooks from the fourteenth to the sixteenth century are notable for their lack of olive oil. It didn't entirely disappear, but its uses were primarily nonculinary, as a lighting fuel, base for perfumes and medicines, and lubricant. This was a stark contrast to the eastern Mediterranean, north

African, and Islamic regions, where olive oil never stopped being a part of daily life.

When Christianity spread westward in the Early Middle Ages, it rekindled a demand for olive oil, not so much out of desire but out of necessity. Monasteries lit their lanterns with olive oil and either planted olive groves to fulfill their needs or bought what they required. But the real impact on the public came from abstinence and Lent. Because people were banned from eating meat, dairy, and eggs for 140 to 160 days a year, olive oil became the obligatory substitute for animal fats. This did not make olive oil a desirable choice, however. Instead, people sought ecclesiastical exemptions. It became possible to buy your way out of eating olive oil, and beginning in the seventh century, church leaders made concessions. The Council of Aix allowed bacon fat to be substituted for olive oil, and Pope Gregory XI followed suit, as did others. People also sought alternative oils. Despite its lack of color and odor, walnut oil became a ready substitute, followed by flaxseed oil in the sixteenth century, and sunflower and grapeseed oils gained some ground. The poor even tried to make oil out of legumes, turnips, and irises.

The disdain for olive oil was because of more than the cultural shift brought by the Germanic invaders; it was mainly the result of the quality and price of the oil. Those outside the olive-growing regions rarely tasted good oil; they were sent the dregs, oil that was old, rancid, and black. An indication of the poor quality was the fifteenth-century English saying "black as olive oil." And for this they had to pay exorbitant prices.

The divide between good and bad olive oils was nothing new. In Roman times, the poet Juvenal mocked the disparity between the rich and poor, describing masters who are served fish doused in fine olive oil from southern Italy, whereas "the sickly greens offered to you, poor devil, will smell like they had oil on them meant for a lamp."[4] Even the quality of oil Romans smeared on their skin at baths differed, and the impoverished Africans used oil that was so putrid it "prevents anyone at Rome sharing a bath with them."[5] It was vile enough to keep animals away, and the fetid oil was said to "protect you from a black serpent's bite."[6]

In Roman times, olive oil underwent strict monitoring and quality controls, but the Middle Ages were a free-for-all of corruption and shoddy standards, resulting in olive oil that was equally vile or worse. The dearth of olive trees ensured a limited supply of oil, and the church's lean-day requirements saw to it that even bad olive oil found buyers. Many Europeans may have never even tasted good olive oil and thus wouldn't have known what they were missing or how badly they were being duped.

This was not so in Provence, where olive trees had grown since at least the twelfth century. In contrast to much of the rest of France, which was flatter, with rich, arable soil, Provence had soil that was rocky, dry, and poor. It was unsuitable for cattle, but olive trees thrived in the difficult earth and under the moderating effects of the sea. By Spanish or Italian standards, there weren't a lot of olive trees, but it was enough to satisfy the local population. A culinary divide formed, one that was so profound that when Provençal people traveled, they carried jars of olive oil with them, rather than risk eating butter, which many believed led to leprosy.

The people of Provence kept the best oil for themselves and exported only the second and third pressings. The French olive oil that arrived in England was not high quality, as the label proclaimed, but came from the third pressing, when boiling water was poured over the olive waste remaining from two earlier pressings to eke out the vile, bitter dregs—or at least that's what the fifteenth-century English traveler Thomas Platter overheard on a visit to Montpellier. Even regions of France that didn't grow olive trees got into the olive oil business, mixing flaxseed oil or poppy seed oil with turpentine and selling it as olive oil. Meanwhile, Venetians mixed high-quality olive oil from the north with plentiful and subpar oil from the southern region of Puglia.

Olive oil fraud was nothing new. It was so popular during Roman times that the fourth- or early fifth-century cookbook *Apicius* explains how inferior oil can be passed off as oil from Liburnia, a coastal region along the Adriatic Sea, now known as Croatia, which was renowned for its olive oil. The recipe reads, "In order to make an oil similar to the Liburnian oil proceed as follows: In Spanish oil put the following mixture of elecampane, Cyprian rush and green laurel leaves that are not too old, all of it crushed and macerated and reduced to a fine powder. Sift this in and add finely ground salt and stir industriously for three days or more. Then allow to settle. Everybody will take this for Liburnian oil."[7]

The Greeks were also no strangers to subterfuge, and the tenth-century book *Geoponika* offers tricks to make Greek oil taste like Istrian oil; Istria was the same region from which the Romans obtained their Liburnian oil. The book also contains tricks to improve rancid, fetid, or turbid oil, as well as what to do "if a mouse, or any other animal, having fallen into the oil, has hurt its flavour."[8] For those curious about what to do if this should happen to you, here are the steps to take. "Suspend a handful of coriander in the oil, and if the unsavoury smell remains, change the coriander."[9] You could also try fenugreek or dried grapes. Let the concoction sit for ten days. Then add warm water and salt, give it a stir, and let the oil rise to the top. Skim the oil off and repeat the water/salt treatment. Add some crushed olive leaves to remove the bitterness, then add a splash of good oil, and call the concoction Spanish oil, presumably to distinguish it from the Greek's own oil.

The stage was set for a ready substitute for olive oil, one that was not rancid, discolored, or overpowering, and that replacement was butter. People had been churning milk into a creamy spread for thousands of years, but in the Mediterranean it had long been shunned. The Greeks and Romans had little regard for butter, avoiding it in their cooking, and the few references to it are disparaging. The fourth-century BC Greek poet Anaxandrides wrote of a Thracian wedding, describing the attendees, whom the Greeks considered barbaric and unkempt, as "butter-eaters with dirty hair."[10] It wasn't until the Roman Empire fell that butter gained a foothold, especially in the north, where the lower temperatures kept it from going rancid and where ample cattle roamed. Still, it was not the commonplace commodity it is now but a lowly food for peasants.

Christianity further curtailed the consumption of butter by banning it on lean days, fasting days that prohibited many foods and other pleasures, such as sex, and included not only the forty days of Lent leading up to Easter but Wednesdays, Fridays, and Saturdays, too, totaling nearly half the year. Given the severity of the punishment—the English were hung for eating meat on the wrong day—the draconian restrictions were widely observed. But the lack of olive oil forced concessions, and in 1500 AD, the archbishop of Rouen allowed his citizens to pay for the right to use butter, collecting enough alms to build Rouen Cathedral's seventy-meter gothic tower known as Saint Romain, or simply the butter tower. Northerners despised the restriction on the use of butter, and Martin Luther bolstered his religious revolution by railing against the restrictions. In *An Open Letter to the Christian Nobility of the German Nation*, he wrote, "For at Rome they themselves laugh at the fasts, making us foreigners eat the oil with which they would not grease their shoes, and afterward selling us liberty to eat butter."[11] Eventually, more sweeping exemptions were made, and people of all classes began to eat butter.

By the seventeenth century, a food revolution consumed France. Butter ousted olive oil, and recipes were transformed, as sauces shifted from sour and robust flavors to delicate creamy bases. Thanks to France's lofty gastronomic reputation, this change soon spread across its borders

By the mid-nineteenth century, the French were consuming so much butter that suppliers couldn't keep up with demand. In response, Emperor Napoleon III sought a cheaper alternative that could feed the less prosperous and be supplied to soldiers. He offered a prize to the successful inventor, and in 1869, it was awarded to French chemist Hippolyte Mège-Mouriès, who patented a mixture of beef tallow and milk known as margarine.

Nowadays, the French use more butter per capita than anyone else in the world—eight kilograms every year, four and a half times the amount of olive oil they consume. And perhaps as a testament to the influence of French cuisine, nearly three times as much butter as olive oil is used throughout the world—8 million tons a year, plus another 9 million tons of margarine.

Olive oil now shares the stage with a crowd of fats, outmuscled not only by butter and margarine but by pretty much every other oil. Of the nine oils listed in the USDA Foreign Agricultural Service database, olive oil is the least abundant. Palm oil tops the list, with 49.92 million tons produced in the 2011–12 harvest, followed by soybean oil, at 41.29 million tons, and rapeseed at nearly half that. Sunflower, peanut, coconut, cottonseed, and palm kernel oils are all produced in greater quantities than the 3.25 million tons of olive oil pressed. Olive oil may have tumbled from its lofty heights when it dominated the market as the only oil, prized more than wine and eulogized by great poets, but being overshadowed by oils that are easier and cheaper to make does not diminish its importance and appeal.

"THE TAPENADES are *magnifique*," Philippe Gion promised as we walked through L'Isle-sur-la-Sorgue to the morning market.

We were in the heart of Provence, a two-hour drive inland from Cassis, eager to learn how to make a meal representative of the region and to better understand the use of olive oil in Provençal cooking. Philippe, a professional chef who runs a Provençal cooking school, is an arresting figure: tall, lean, and strong, dressed in white with a wicker basket threaded over one arm and with short white hair and eyes dark like Kalamata olives.

I first heard about Philippe while doing preliminary research on the history of olive oil in cuisine. I wanted to learn how the masters use this special ingredient, how olive oil is woven into recipes not only in haute cuisine but also in daily cooking. Given France's unparalleled reputation for food, learning from a French chef seemed like a great idea, and when I read about France's top chefs specializing in Provençal cuisine, I kept coming across Philippe's name. *Reader's Digest* included his cooking school in their list of top ten vacations for foodies, and *USA Today* ranked it as one of the top three cooking school vacations in France.

Philippe's culinary background is as impressive as the meals he produces. He has opened and managed restaurants around the world, cooked for Marlon Brando on his atoll in French Polynesia, and was executive chef for Stanford University in California. He has been a professional cellist and a filmmaker, producing military films after he sneaked into the army at age seventeen. Born in Provence, he returned two decades ago to focus on traditional Mediterranean cuisine and is passionate about Provençal ingredients. He believes that food should be simple and delicious, made with the best and freshest ingredients available, and that eating well also means eating healthily. He told us that "food is to replenish the mind and body. I want to make sure mine does both."

When I contacted Philippe to ask about cooking with olive oil, he invited us to meet him in person so that he could show us the importance of olive oil in Provençal meals. But to do that, he explained, we needed to start where Provençal cooking begins, which is not in the kitchen but at the market. The freshest and highest-quality ingredients are the key to Provençal cooking, and so we met beside the L'Isle-sur-la-Sorgue train station and together strolled to the nearby town center.

The Sorgue river carves through town, spinning moss-caked waterwheels, its many channels criss-crossed by wrought-iron bridges, giving the town its nickname, the Venice of Provence. Lining the streets are antique stores—which are crowded with bird cages, wicker baskets, and oversized clocks—and several times a year the town puts on a colossal antique flea market said to be Europe's third largest, after those in London and Paris.

When we arrived, the streets were crowded with Sunday traffic, despite the downpour that had just ended and threatened to return. This may once have been a sleepy little town, but ever since Peter Mayle immortalized this region of the Luberon Valley in his book *A Year in Provence*, visitors have flooded here, and many have stayed, buying old farms and charming manors to live the dream he so persuasively evoked.

We crossed an ornate footbridge and entered the market, where we discovered the truth of Peter Mayles's comment that "the only thing you can't get in L'Isle sur la Sorgue is a bargain." What the market lacks in discounts, however, it makes up for in freshness and quality. Stalls overflowed with mushrooms and cured olives, men sliced chunks of cheese off giant wheels, and a cornucopia of fruits and vegetables covered tables.

"*Madame, bonjour,*" shouted a plump woman, catching my eye from behind a table of sausages. She leaned forward with a sample of smoked venison sausage. I bit into it, savoring its rich and spicy flavor.

Everywhere we looked temptations beckoned: nougat, little more than creamy slabs of honey mixed with roasted pistachios; jars of honey ranging in color from pale ale to Guinness; cheeses in infinite shapes, sizes, and colors; and countless varieties of olives—green and black orbs swimming in oil, some marinated in hot peppers and herbs, others stuffed with anchovies or peppers, and all in a range of sizes, from no larger than a jelly bean to the size of a quail egg.

Philippe nodded or said a few words to acquaintances and vendors as we passed and shared his secrets for finding the best ingredients. At a table of heirloom tomatoes, he described which ones were ideal for gratin. At the figs, he explained that they don't continue ripening after harvesting and that a firm fruit will never become sweet. A perfect fig should feel like a ripened peach and smell delicious, without a hint of fermentation, and in the little hole at its base, there should be a drop of moisture. Touch, sight, and scent—three of our five senses required just to pick a fruit. I doubted that the seller would like it if I added taste to that list.

"Philippe," a man shouted from behind a pyramid of tapenades. He reached his hand across the table and gripped Philippe's. They exchanged a barrage of friendly greetings. A slight blonde woman joined them, and Philippe introduced us to Ruiz Antoine and his wife.

"These are some of the best tapenades in all of France," Philippe said, smiling. "Each one is made with extra virgin olive oil. You can even buy olive oil from them." Philippe pointed to the jugs of olive oil at the end of the table.

Ruiz waved his thickly muscled arms over rows of colorful jars, insisting that we sample them, and pulled out a circular tray crowded with open jars, each one with its own spoon, and a bowl of sliced French bread. There were more than a dozen tapenades, not just the traditional olive, caper, and anchovy paste but ones made with Parmesan cheese, sundried tomatoes, artichokes, truffles, and mushrooms.

Usually considered a Provençal food, tapenade developed over thousands of years. It began as a means of storing capers, the small flavor-packed flower buds that are a popular food around much of the Mediterranean. To preserve the capers, Provençal people stored them in olive oil in large clay amphorae. With time, the capers settled into a mushy paste called *tapenas*, the Provençal word for capers. As the recipe evolved, the black olive surpassed the caper as the primary ingredient. Today, a traditional Provençal tapenade is made from pureed black olives, olive oil, capers, anchovies, and spices, and it is often used as a spread for bread or an addition to vegetables, roasted meats, fish, and hard-boiled eggs.

Long before the French created tapenades, the Greeks and Romans ate an olive paste that was strikingly similar. In 160 BC, the Roman Cato the Elder provided a recipe in his book *De Agricultura* for *epityrum*, a snack of black olives and herbs that originated in ancient Greece. He writes that one should "remove the stones from a mix of green, ripe, and mottled olives, and season as follows: chop the flesh, and add oil, vinegar, coriander, cumin, fennel, rue, and mint. Cover with oil in an earthen dish and serve."[12]

In a book from the first century AD, Columella, a Roman agricultural writer, explains how "a Marmelad of Olives may be made,"[13] a black olive preserve that can be stored for two months. The peasants "gather black olives exceeding ripe, when the weather is fair; and spread them upon reeds for one day, under a shade and separate all the damaged berries from them."[14] The following day, the unbruised olives are picked out and placed in a hemp bag, which is pressed overnight and lightly mashed the following day in a mill, ensuring that the pits stay intact. Fenugreek, cumin, fennel, and Egyptian anise are added, along with a lot of salt ("one *hemina* of salt per *modium* of olives"[15]—about a cup of salt for every eight kilograms of olives) and even more olive oil.

"*Crème d'artichauts,*" Ruiz said, handing me a slice of baguette heaped with a light-beige paste. The artichoke and garlic spread exploded with flavors and richness. Although I felt I must be doing my arteries a disservice, the reality was that olive oil gave it that sumptuousness, and except for the calories, this was eating at its healthiest. I was in heaven. Ruiz handed me another bread slice laden with what he called the family specialty, *crème de noix*—walnuts with mushrooms.

"What kind of mushrooms?" Colin asked.

"It is a mix of three types," Ruiz said, naming chanterelles and two varieties I didn't recognize.

Another spread was inky black, the traditional tapenade from Provence. "The main ingredient is black olives," Ruiz said, "as well as anchovies and capers." The flavor was strong and dominated by fully ripe olives, whereas the *tapenade verte* was exactly the same except made with green olives, which gave it a lighter taste.

France doesn't produce the quantity of olive products its neighbors do, but what they lack in volume they make up for in quality. Each cultivar has a unique taste, firmness of flesh, smell, and color, and the growers pride themselves on their uncommon varieties. Of the olives grown, about a fifth are made into table olives or tapenades, and the rest are pressed into olive oil.

Before beginning this journey, I would have guessed that more olives were eaten than made into oil, but the opposite is true. Of the 22.7 million tons of olives grown around the world in 2012, 88 percent were pressed into oil. It takes on average seven kilograms of olives to make one liter of oil, and the 2012 crop produced 3.25 million tons, or 3.56 billion liters, of olive oil. The remaining 2.6 million tons of olives were prepared as table olives. Most of the table olives were grown in Spain, Egypt, Turkey, Syria, Algeria, and Argentina, and more than half the world's supply is produced in three countries: Spain, Egypt, and Turkey.

Green olives and black olives are not different varieties, as supermarket displays may suggest. All olives start out green and turn black. Olives begin to ripen as early as October, slowly changing from green to black, and by February they are as dark as coal.

As anyone who has tasted both green and black olives can attest, the difference in flavor is pronounced, and this difference can also be detected in tapenades and olive oils. Olive oil made from green olives is spicy and peppery, packing a punch that many connoisseurs appreciate. As the olive ripens and the polyphenol levels drop, the oil it produces is milder and more buttery. Often, olive oil is made from a mix of green and black olives or olives that are a shade in between, creating a balanced oil that is flavorful without being overwhelming in delicate dishes. Tapenades were traditionally made from ripe black olives, though nowadays you can find both green olive and black olive tapenades, each with a distinct flavor influenced by the olive cultivar but mostly by the olive's ripeness, with black olive tapenade offering a gentle, earthier flavor than its younger counterpart. Properly assessing the olive's ripeness is key to producing good food, whether it's olive oil, table olives, or tapenades. Using olives that are too green will result in paltry oil levels and harsh flavors, but when olives become too ripe, the quality degrades as free acidity levels rise, robbing the resultant olive oil of its flavor and fruity scent and compromising the taste of its tapenades and table olives.

We purchased jars of *tapenade noire, tapenade verte,* and *crème d'anchois,* an exceptionally fishy spread that overwhelmed our taste buds in the same way that blue cheese assaults the senses, irresistible to some and repulsive to others.

Thousand-year-old olive trees in the Sénia region of Spain, which has the highest concentration of ancient olive trees in the world.

top left Appetizers in Spain often included olives, anchovies in an olive oil sauce, chorizo, and crostini.

bottom left A typical meal on our sailboat while we were in Provence included fresh baguettes, salad dressing with olive oil, wine, and fresh figs or grapes.

above Leif's first birthday was celebrated in Cannes, France.

top *Isis* anchored in a sheltered bay in Girolata, Corsica.

above Our boat anchored in calm waters in Corsica.

top Mount Testaccio in Italy, which is an ancient Roman garbage pile made of 53 million olive oil amphorae.

above The rugged east coast of Sardinia, near the town of Santa Maria Navarrese.

top left An olive tree growing on a rocky promontory in Sardinia.

bottom left Protected anchorage in southern Sardinia, near Notteri.

above Colin and Leif sailing *Isis* in Sardinia, Italy.

above Sailing *Isis* along the coast of Sardinia.

The gentle drizzle transformed into a torrential downpour. We left the market and followed Philippe to his country home a few kilometers away, a sprawling property, neatly landscaped in the front with a giant plane tree dominating the yard.

"It is converted from a three-hundred-year-old stone barn," Philippe said as we got out of our vehicles. "Horses used to live in my house."

"Wow," Colin said. "They sure treated horses well in France."

The inside of the house was equally beguiling, a seamless blend of charm and tradition inherent to the home's historic architecture, updated by modern conveniences and styles. The living room opened into the kitchen and led onto a backyard patio, giving the house an open, airy feel. Modern art decorated the walls, and an antique organ and cello dominated a corner.

A brown-haired woman wearing chunky white glasses perched low on her nose and a rainbow assortment of bracelets emerged from the kitchen.

"This is Marie-Pierre. She volunteered to assist today," Philippe said. "I don't think she really wanted to help me at all. She just wanted to meet my special guests and hear more about your olive quest."

As we sipped glasses of chilled rosé and chatted about our search to understand the olive, Philippe talked about the olive oils he used and their role in cooking. Marie-Pierre brought an unexpected perspective to the table.

"Did you know both Renoir and Van Gogh painted olive trees?" she said. "Van Gogh was hospitalized not far from here, in Saint-Rémy, and he fell in love with the olive trees that grew there." Marie-Pierre opened her portfolio to show us a watercolor of a grove of gnarled olive trees. "These are the olive trees Van Gogh saw from his window."

After Van Gogh cut off part of his ear, he checked himself into the asylum in Saint-Rémy. He spent a year there, which is said to have been one of the most difficult yet productive times of his life. At least fifteen of his paintings from that time were of olive trees. Two months after leaving the institute, Van Gogh committed suicide by shooting himself in the stomach. He was thirty-seven.

Van Gogh described olive leaves as "old silver... turning to green against the blue." He also wrote that "the rustle of an olive grove has something very secret in it, and immensely old. It is too beautiful for us to dare to paint it or to be able to imagine it."[16]

"They're beautiful," I said, admiring Marie-Pierre's artwork, which also hung on Philippe's walls.

"She is very talented," Philippe said. "Now, you must try the figs." He motioned toward the coffee table, which was crowded with cheeses and fresh fruit. The figs were plump and firm, not much larger than a garlic bulb, and deep royal purple, like the Tyrian purple dye Phoenicians extracted from sea snails.

As I bit into one, the firm flesh gave way and the soft interior melted in my mouth. It was better than any fig I'd eaten before, and I made a mental note to remember the tips Philippe had given us on choosing figs.

"These are different from the figs you get earlier in the season, smaller and sweeter," he said. "We only have these for a few weeks."

The peaches were different, too, paler and flatter than normal peaches, with a top that curved inward to the base of the stem like a miniature pumpkin. Mild and delicate, they tasted like honey-infused peach Bellinis. Next we heaped Brie, gently melting in the late summer air, onto thin slices of olive bread. The rich, pungent cheese was the yin to the fruit's yang, a perfect pairing.

"Today we will make a very simple Provençal meal," Philippe said. "Chicken with forty cloves of garlic, red pepper gratin, and, of course, aioli."

It sounded anything but simple, but I kept my mouth shut. I followed him to the dining table, already set with a cutting board, a sharp knife, and bowls of herbs, and watched him flit about organizing and gathering ingredients with a nimbleness that belied his seventy years. Meanwhile, Colin set up the video cameras to film Philippe, and Leif went upstairs with Marlyn, the young Cassis woman we'd hired to look after him for the day.

"Have you always cooked with olive oil?" Colin asked once he'd turned on the cameras.

"Non," Philippe said. "Before I cooked with creams and butter, typical French haute cuisine, but now I make traditional Provençal food. It is simple food, but it is good and good for you." Given his energy and agility, I couldn't argue. "But you know," he continued in a stage whisper, "it is really the Cretan diet; they brought it here, and in Provence we have kept it."

I had never considered the similarities between the food in Crete and Provence, but now the connection seemed obvious. Both were based on the principles of the Mediterranean diet—lots of in-season vegetables and fruits, fish, and olive oil, with little red meat or dairy. It was the Phocaean Greeks, after all, who settled in Provence 2,600 years ago and founded the city of Marseille, which during their reign was the namesake for all of Provence. The Phocaeans were Greece's first long-distance seafarers, traveling by ship from the Ionian coast in modern-day Turkey and bringing with them Greek customs and traditions, including their appreciation of olives and olive oil. The Greeks have retained their love of olive oil, and today they consume more olive oil per capita than any other population, twenty-six liters per person annually, about fifteen times more than the average person in France.

Sadly, little remains of ancient Greek cookbooks, which were considered unimportant works and therefore lost over the centuries. One exception is the fourth-century BC poem

Hedypatheia (*Life of Luxury*) by the Greek poet Archestratus. The original work was lost, but the Greek writer Athenaeus of Naucratis quoted sixty-two fragments six centuries later in his book *Deipnosophistae* (*Philosophers at Dinner*). *Life of Luxury* was less a cookbook than a comedy about Greek eating habits, a piece of literature that the leisure class, not the chefs toiling in their kitchens, would have enjoyed, and that is probably why so much of it was replicated.

Archestratus traveled throughout ancient Greece—a large swath of Europe that included parts of Italy and Sicily and coastal regions of modern-day Turkey and the Black Sea—sampling foods and reporting on their ingredients and methods of preparation. Despite the brevity of the remaining text, both olives and olive oil are included. Forty-nine of the sixty-two fragments are devoted to fish, about which Archestratus writes, "Now the good fish are naturally tender and have a fat flesh: simply sprinkle these lightly with salt and brush with oil for they possess in themselves the fullness of delight."[17] In another passage he explains how to cook shark: "In the city of Torone, you must buy belly steaks of the karcharias, sprinkling them with cumin and not much salt. You will add nothing else, dear fellow, unless maybe green olive oil."[18] He expresses a disdain for creams and sauces and recommends them only for inferior fish, to hide the off-putting flavor. From his works, we also know that olives were eaten at a meal's beginning and end, along with other flavorful snacks, such as barley breads, small birds, and the less appealing delicacy, pickled sow's womb.

"Smearing themselves with olive oil they sat down to their meal,"[19] Athenaeus writes in *Philosophers at Dinner* when describing a symposium, the popular all-male banquet centered on food, drink, and entertainment. The aristocratic men sat on couches and the food, designed to be eaten with one hand, was set on low tables. The first part of their meal was the *deipnon* (dinner) and consisted of intensely flavored appetizers, which always included brined olives, followed by fish- and meat-based dishes. The symposium followed, a raucous drinking party of wine diluted with water and entertainment, ranging from literary readings, games, and songs to performances by slaves. Outside of symposiums, Greeks ate modestly, and gluttony was frowned on, even mocked by comedic playwrights. Poor people rarely ate fish or meat, sustaining themselves on vegetables and breads, but everyone ate olives and olive oil, though of differing quality.

Brined olives were eaten before, during, and after a meal and as snacks. Considered healthy and nutritious, they were also believed to stimulate the appetite. Olives were an essential seasoning, added to vegetables, meats, and fish along with ingredients such as salt, cheese, thyme, sesame seeds, cumin, cashew nuts, honey, marjoram, chopped acorns, vinegar, young greens, capers, eggs, smoked fish, cress, and fig leaves. The gourmets were particular about their olives. Diphilus, a physician in Sifnos in the third century BC, preferred green olives to black, considering black olives "worse for the stomach and oppressive to the head."[20] Brined green olives, he said, "are more wholesome and act as an astringent on the bowels."

Overripe olives were looked down on, and if you wanted to insult an ancient Greek, you could borrow Athenaeus's denunciation: "Let them serve you with wrinkled, overripe olives."[21] The fifth century BC Greek playwright Aristophanes also disparaged overripe olives, saying, "Do you, master, love the ladies who are over-ripe or the virginal ones with bodies firm as olives steeped in brine?"[22] That didn't mean black olives were wasted. Athenaeus wrote that "black olives are more wholesome if crushed,"[23] and the Greeks used them to create a paste called *stemphyla*, which resembled modern-day tapenade. Little of the olive was squandered, and even olive cakes, the unappetizing olive pulp remaining after the oil has been pressed, were eaten, albeit only by those who couldn't afford any better.

Perhaps even more important than olives was olive oil, which was used in most meals, a vital ingredient used to prepare breads, fish, meats, stews, and vegetables. In *Philosophers at Dinner*, a cook describes how to prepare a stuffed pig by soaking it in wine, boiling it, and then stuffing the partially cooked swine with entrails and gravy. Then he explains, "I plastered half of the pig, as you can see, with a lot of barley meal, having made a batter of it with wine and olive oil." Then he put it in the oven until "the skin had been crisply roasted."[24] The barley meal was then removed, revealing a tender and succulent roasted pig.

More detailed recipes are found in the Roman cookbook *Apicius*, also called *De re coquinaria* (*On the Subject of Cooking*), a collection of Roman recipes compiled in the late fourth or early fifth century AD that were heavily influenced by the Greeks. The book is written in Latin, but the chapter titles are in Greek and the text is full of Greek terminology. And unlike the earlier surviving works, it is a true cookbook, with some five hundred recipes that were used by chefs of the day and for centuries after.

Olive oil is the third most common ingredient in *Apicius*, appearing in three-quarters of its recipes and surpassed only by pepper and garum, a fermented fish sauce. Olive oil was a staple of cooking meats, fish, and stews. It was added for flavor and texture, used for frying and baking, and drizzled on finished foods. To make cuttlefish croquettes, "the meat is separated from the bone and skins, chopped fine and pounded in the mortar," shaped into "neat croquettes," and fried in olive oil. "Chicken forcemeat," the equivalent of the modern chicken sausage, was made by combining minced chicken with olive oil, flour made from ryegrass, stock, and pepper.[25]

Olive oil was just as essential for vegetable dishes as for meats and fish, drizzled on cooked or raw vegetables, added while they baked or fried, or included in sauces. Truffles were eaten in a wine and olive oil sauce spiced with "pepper, lovage, coriander, rue and honey." Peeled beets were boiled, then seasoned with raisin wine, pepper, cumin, and olive oil, and then fried with polypody (a type of fern) and nuts. Other root vegetables, such as parsnips and salsify (an uncommon root said to taste like artichoke hearts that is making a resurgence with adventurous chefs), were boiled with mead, salt, and olive oil until the liquid was reduced and could then be drunk or used as a base to cook chicken. Pumpkin was boiled, then baked with olive oil, pepper, cumin, coriander seed, and green mint. After that, vinegar, date wine, and pine nuts ground with honey, vinegar, and broth were mixed in and the dish was topped with olive oil, condensed wine, and pepper. Pretty much every vegetable the Romans ate—leeks, brussels sprouts, broccoli, cauliflower, squash, turnips, cabbage, celery, nettles, carrots, even lettuce and cucumber—was cooked in olive oil. Salad and raw vegetables were dressed with the highest-quality olive oil, which sat in tabletop glass dispensers, often paired with vinegar or garum. The combination was so popular that some bottles had dual reservoirs and spouts, so that both oil and its accompaniment could be poured simultaneously.

Olives, too, were a popular ingredient. Green olives were added as a seasoning to cooked broccoli, cauliflower, leeks, and other vegetables. Olives were used to hide strong odors, and according to *Apicius*, "if the birds smell, stuff the inside with crushed fresh olives, sew up the aperture and thus cook, then retire the cooked olives."[26] Even milder-tasting fowl, such as chicken, was stuffed with olives.

Another popular dish was brined olives, which the Romans called *colymbades olivae*, meaning olives swimming in brine, a term derived from the Latin word "*colymbus*," meaning "swimming pool." Columella, the first-century Roman writer who gave us the recipe for "Marmelad of Olives," the precursor to tapenades, has a chapter on pickling black olives in his agricultural tome, *De Re Rustica* (*Of Husbandry*). The olives must be picked "by hand, as soon as they are grown black, but are not as yet thoroughly ripe."[27] They are doused in salt in a 1 to 10 ratio, poured into a willow basket, and then covered with more salt. After thirty days, the salt is cleaned off and the olives are transferred to an amphora, along with boiling must (pressed grape juice containing skins, seeds, and stems), vinegar, dry fennel, and honey if there was enough of it. Branches of fennel are placed on top to press down the olives and keep them submerged. In another approach, olives are mixed with salt, fennel seeds, and anise, and stored in amphorae for forty days. Every day, the amphorae are rolled, and every third or fourth day, the vessel is opened and the fluid extracted by the salt, then called lees, is drained. The finished olives are transferred to a clean vessel and stored in a cellar.

To enhance the flavor of brined olives, Columella suggests removing olives from their brine once they start to float; "then cut it in two or three places with a green reed, and keep it three days in vinegar."[28] The olives are then wiped clean and transferred to a new pot containing a layer of parsley and rue, a bitter herb. Concentrated must is poured in and laurel branches are placed on top to press the olives down. The slits halve the soaking time, and the olives are ready in twenty days.

Apicius does not describe brining olives but instead gives us a recipe "to keep green olives," whereby freshly picked olives are placed in olive oil, which preserves them by slowing their oxidation and fermentation. "Having been kept thus for some time the olives may be used as if they had just come off the tree fresh if you desire to make green oil of them."[29]

How much these early settlers influenced Provençal cuisine is hard to say, but many of Philippe's ingredients and techniques would not have seemed out of place in a Greek or Roman kitchen. And like gourmets throughout time, Philippe was obsessed by quality.

"See the red label?" Philippe said, handing me the cellophane-wrapped chicken. "It guarantees the quality."

He unwrapped the accredited chicken and opened its cavity, stuffing a bouquet of lavender, oregano sprigs, and parsley into it. "This is how we add flavor," he said, handing me a handful of garlic cloves and an olive wood shaker filled with *herbes de Provence*, a blend of savory, fennel, basil, thyme, and lavender.

"More, more," Philippe admonished when I set down the shaker. "Inside and on top, you must not be stingy." I sprinkled on sea salt and pepper, placed the chicken in a cast-iron pot, and poured olive oil over the bird.

"The olive oil will keep the chicken tender, but you need to add more," Philippe said again.

I continued drizzling green-gold oil onto the chicken, and when a third of it swam in oil, Philippe motioned for me to stop. "Now the garlic," he said, pointing to a large bowl of unpeeled cloves that had been slightly crushed to help release the flavors. A mischievous grin spread across his face. "Forty cloves and not one more," he added. Before baking the chicken, he squeezed a pencil-wide ribbon of dough made of flour and water between the pot and the lid to create an impenetrable seal. "It will make the chicken moist."

We pushed the chicken into the oven, along with a red pepper gratin we had prepared, and waited.

"You can't dance faster than the music," Philippe said, noting my impatience. "But while we wait, we will make aioli."

"Are you making *le grand aïoli?*" Marie-Pierre chirped from the kitchen.

"*Non*, that would be too much food for just us," Philippe said, a note of regret in his voice.

"*Grand aïoli* is a magnificent dish," Marie-Pierre said. "It is a full meal of fish, artichokes, eggs, chickpeas, and carrots, and is served with aioli."

Aioli, the garlic mayonnaise sauce I dipped yam fries in at home, originated in Provence and is much more refined and versatile than the dish I was used to. Stemming from the Provençal words for garlic and oil, "*alh*" and "*òli*," it is a pungent, creamy mixture of olive oil, garlic, and egg. It is the quintessential French dish, and the French poet Frédéric Mistral even founded a nineteenth-century newspaper called *L'aïoli*. The popularity of the dish spread, and in Greece it was given to soldiers "to give them courage."

We started with a bowl of mashed garlic and egg yolks, each egg carefully washed beforehand to ensure that it was free of salmonella bacteria. Philippe slowly added olive oil, at first whipping it into the mixture drop by drop, then increasing the flow to a slow drizzle. I took over pouring olive oil while Philippe's hand churned like a runaway flywheel until the liquid had emulsified into a thick cream that looked like mayonnaise except that it was pale green. The aioli went into the fridge to allow the flavors to mingle, while Philippe made a paste from the roasted garlic cloves and olive oil, which he ladled over the carved chicken. Accompanied by red pepper gratin and set on colorful plates, it looked like anything but simple food.

"Mmmm," Colin said as soon as he took his first bite. "I can't believe how tender the chicken is."

"The olive oil penetrates the chicken; it keeps it moist and gives it flavor," Philippe said.

I took another bite of the chicken and noted how the subtle taste of the olive oil added fullness to the flavor, as though supercharging all the other ingredients.

Leif also enjoyed the meal, eating more than he had in the entire last week. He wolfed down cut-up pieces of chicken and roasted red pepper with such voracity that Marie-Pierre commented approvingly, "He is a Provençal boy."

5

COVETING VIRGINITY

"Slipped in the bathroom. Put some olive oil in my hair.
Walked in the closet. Tryin' 2 find something 2 wear."
PRINCE, *"There'll Never B (Another Like Me)"*

BY OUR THIRD NIGHT in Cassis, we had bought a month's worth of groceries, signed up for a French mobile Internet plan, and changed the engine's oil filter. We were ready to continue on to the French Riviera when Colin announced, "I'm afraid I've got some bad news."

His head was buried in the engine compartment, where a fine slick of oil coated everything.

"It's leaking," Colin said, rubbing his oily hands on a rag. "I think it's the gasket, but there's no way to know until we replace it."

The marina's chandlery didn't have a gasket, so it had to be ordered directly from the Spanish manufacturer. It would take a few days to arrive, but I could think of worse things than being stuck in Provence. Instead of sailing on, we wandered through the semiweekly market, crowded with families slinging wicker baskets and tables heaped with everything from fresh fruit to shoes and, of course, olives—lots of olives.

We bought fat green Picholines stuffed with slivers of anchovy and small emerald Salonenques doused in pesto. The merchant explained that the *olives cassées au pistou* were freshly picked Salonenque olives gently pounded to soften the flesh and speed up the curing process and then slathered in pesto. They were picked as table olives now and throughout the rest of September, and in two months, when they had ripened further, they would be plucked for oil.

I was interested to learn that some olives were equally good cured or pressed. Until now, the olives I'd heard about were used for either one purpose or the other. The olives destined for oil are usually smaller, weighing less than 3.5 grams, whereas table olives are about twice as large and some varieties weigh as much as 17 grams. Table olives are meatier than olives used for oil, with smaller stones relative to the flesh, but they are also less oily. Olive cultivars destined to be made into oil generally contain at least 16 to 18 percent oil, and some are as much as 35 percent oil at full maturity. Olives used for both lie in the middle. For example, Sevillano olives, large olives often called Queen olives, have a very low oil content, ranging from 12 to 17 percent, and are primarily eaten as table olives. In contrast, Koroneiki olives, which are tiny and made up of as much as 28 percent oil, are almost exclusively made into oil.

The French varieties we bought sat in the middle of this spectrum. Picholine olives are moderately oily and make excellent oil, but it is difficult to extract and the cultivar is primarily used for table olives. Salonenque olives also produce good oil and have an even higher oil content, but in France they, too, are primarily used for table olives.

I bought olive oil soap from a vendor who sold dozens of varieties, many infused with herbs and floral scents, and even one from Aleppo, where olive oil soap has been made for thousands of years. The soap reminded me of the last time we were in Aleppo, when we had bought bricks of the forest-green olive oil soap in the bazaar, letting my uncle haggle over the price. Given the growing unrest in Syria, I wondered if this would be my only chance to buy Aleppo olive oil soap.

Olive oil soap production once was a great empire in both Provence and Syria and continues to fuel both economies. Forms of soap using animal fats and ash have been in existence since ancient Babylon, and according to legend, Syrians have been making olive oil soap since the Roman times, when Syria's third-century Queen Zenobia bathed with it. Returning Crusaders brought Aleppo soap to Europe in the eleventh century, and thereafter soap manufacturing blossomed throughout the Mediterranean. The following century, the Spanish cities of Alicante, Malaga, Carthagene, and Castile produced olive oil soap, as did the Italian centers of Naples, Savona, Genoa, Bologna, and Venice. In the fifteenth century, soap production came to Marseille.

Traditional Aleppo soap was made of olive oil, laurel oil, and potash. Olive oil comprised the bulk of the soap, between 60 and 98 percent, and the more expensive laurel oil constituted the remainder of the oil. Olive oil and potash were boiled together, and just before the oil separated into glycerine and sodium, laurel oil was added. The green mixture was spread onto a flat surface, and workers with wooden planks strapped to their feet smoothed it by walking on it. The mixture was then cut into squares and stamped with the maker's logo. The soap was air-dried and then stored for six months, a process that breaks down the remaining alkaline and further dehydrates the soap. In the end, the soap is pale green, somewhat darker inside, and extremely hard and long lasting. To me, it smells earthy, even slightly repugnant, like a garden freshly augmented with compost.

The smell of Aleppo soap reminded me of my childhood, when my Syrian aunt sent us packages of it and my father brought it back from his visits to Syria. I hated it then, preferring perfumed soaps that came in perfect shapes, and was embarrassed when friends washed their hands at my house. But now when I visit my parents, I scrounge extra olive oil soap from their closets and bring it home with me. What I hated about the soap as a kid I appreciate now. Devoid of any perfumes or additives, it is a gentle hypoallergenic soap that never irritates or dries my skin and is so mild that I've used it on Leif since he was born. Like olive oil itself, the soap has a long list of ailments it can be used for, though these have not been put under the same rigorous scrutiny as the oil. The soap is used to treat psoriasis, dermatitis, eczema, acne, and even hair loss, as well as to rejuvenate skin and reduce signs of wrinkles. Olive oil's ability to deeply penetrate and moisturize skin is credited for these benefits, and its antioxidants may protect the skin by combating free radical damage and stimulating cell regeneration.

The last time I visited Aleppo, the soap we bought in the fourteenth-century souk seemed timeless, as though nothing had changed over two millennia. Aleppo soap is now often cold-processed, and lye is used instead of potash, but it is still mostly olive oil and is made by dozens of small soap manufacturers who sell it in the same market that has been used for seven hundred years. The Aleppo soap in Cassis wasn't quite as pungent as the bars I remembered, and I wondered whether higher-quality soap was exported or if extracts were added to soften the scent.

A nearby stall sold cubes of Marseille soap, nearly identical to the Aleppo soap except that it was more golden than green and even more delicately scented. Marseille began making olive oil soap in the fourteenth century, and in 1688, Louis XIV issued a set of strict guidelines governing soapmaking, including outlawing the use of any oil or fat other than olive oil. The Edict of Colbert stated that "in the fabrication of soap... no fats, butter or other materials other than pure olive oil, and without blending other fats, is allowed, or the merchandise will be confiscated." The edict threatened that violators "will be condemned and punished, and if they recommit and found guilty of infraction four times, they will be banished from Provence."[1] *Savon de Marseille* became renowned throughout Europe for its luxurious quality, and by the early twentieth century, more than 100 Marseille soapmakers were producing 180,000 tons of soap. Now only a handful remains.

"We won't have room for all this on the boat," Colin joked when I added another two bars of soap to my basket, followed by a cutting board and a *herbes de Provence* spice mill, both made of olive wood.

"It's all in the name of research," I said. But I knew he didn't buy it, and if we stayed much longer in Cassis, we wouldn't have any room in our boat for us.

That afternoon, we milled about Cassis, strolling along narrow lanes and peering into warmly lit bakeries rich with the smell of fresh baguettes. We played in a small playground and rode on the carousel full of horses and cars. But it wasn't until we found the church that Leif became enthusiastic. He raced along the aisles, hands slapping the marble tiles, and climbed endlessly up and down the altar stairs while I hovered nervously, ready to catch him. People came and went, sitting on benches and perusing placards on the wall, while we stayed like the devout Christians we weren't. I couldn't help but think how delighted my mother would be if she knew how much time we were spending in church.

SINCE WE HAD another few days in Cassis, we made arrangements to visit an olive mill, and one of the scientists we met at Spain's IRTA put us in touch with Christine Ceylan at one of France's largest olive farms. Château Virant is in the heart of Aix-en-Provence, a Provençal paradise with thirty hectares of olive trees thriving on sun-drenched hills and rocky soil. Christine led us through her family's olive groves, inspecting trees as we passed. With piercing blue eyes, shoulder-length curly hair, and a slim figure dressed in jeans and a T-shirt, she looked more like a delicate tomboy than the CEO of one of France's most acclaimed olive oil companies.

"This is a good year for olives," she said, holding up a branch for us to inspect. "See how many olives there are and how healthy they look. Voilà."

"It's a beautiful farm," Colin agreed. "How long has your family been growing olives?"

"My grandparents grew olives," she said. "And then my parents bought Château Virant because they wanted to be—how do you say?—independent."

"You see that rock?" she said when we reached a clearing in the grove with an expansive view of neighboring hills and distant fields. The garage-sized boulder she pointed to lay on a nearby hilltop. "That is Virant. They had to buy that rock to keep the name; otherwise, they could not have called it Château Virant."

Back in the three-hundred-year-old château, in the cavernous tasting room where huge stainless steel tanks loomed, Christine explained that it took thirteen years to transform the castle from a ruin to the stylish place it is now. "Our first wine was produced in 1987, and nine years later we had our first olive oil."

Christine laughed when I asked her if she had always wanted to make olive oil. "No, not at all," she said. "I never wanted to get into the olive oil business." Instead of staying in France when she graduated, Christine moved across the Atlantic to Montreal, where she completed a PhD in human resource management. But on a visit home, her father proposed adding an olive oil label to their winery, and she couldn't resist.

"I wanted to have independence," Christine said as she guided us through the showroom. Her foray into olive oil hinged on the condition that she have full control of the olive oil production. She set up the mill and began pressing the family's own olives, and now Château Virant is France's largest olive mill, producing 15,000 to 22,000 liters of olive oil a year and employing thirty-four full-time people.

Although large for France, this mill is tiny on a global scale, and its focus on quality has garnered Château Virant praise from around the world. Its oil has won gold for a number of years running at the Paris competition, where a panel judged Christine's oil to be the best in all of France. Several years ago, she took home Madrid's gold medal for the best oil in the world. Meanwhile, the olive oil guidebook *Flos Olei* gave the oil a ranking of 92 out of 100.

I wasn't surprised to learn that French olive oil has won such praise; after all, the French are renowned for exquisite gastronomy. Even the British had to agree, I thought, recalling a phrase I'd read in the 1931 book *A Modern Herbal* by English horticulturist Maud Grieve. "Provence oil is the most valued and the most refined,"[2] she writes. It seemed that not much had changed in eighty years.

"We make good oil, but it is not easy," Christine said, opening the door to the olive mill. "Our costs are four times higher than what most wholesalers will pay for oil."

The unaffordability of producing olive oil was a theme we'd hear again and again. In every country, olive farmers struggled to press their olives and make a living at it. Château Virant's costs were higher than many, but its oil was also a premium product that sold for more, and that was a good thing. Farmers who sold their olive oil in bulk were getting prices that were a fraction of what they had been more than a decade ago. In 1997, bulk olive oil was $5.67 a liter; today it is $2.61. If you take inflation into account, that means the prices have dropped nearly threefold in the last fifteen years. And they would continue to plummet; 2012 prices were so low that many farmers abandoned their year's crop.

It cost Château Virant approximately $10 to make a liter of olive oil, far more than most farmers get paid and even more than many extra virgin olive oils sell for in the supermarket. The costs are so high that when I discussed olive oil production with a Greek olive farmer, he joked, "Do they shine the olives by hand?"

But when you see the farm and the facility and learn about the particulars of making olive oil in France, you begin to understand why it is so expensive to make French oil. It begins with the type of olive. Château Virant grows mostly Aglandau olives. These olives cling to the tree, allowing them to withstand the powerful mistral winds but making machine-harvesting impossible. The olives must be handpicked, and French labor costs are much higher than in many olive-producing countries such as Morocco, Tunisia, or Algeria. The olives are also grown according to the standards of *culture maisonnée*, a time-consuming process that rarely uses pesticides and returns all waste from the milling process to the olive fields as fertilizer.

But the financial challenges do not compare with the fear of being on the northern edge of the olive-growing belt.

"We have had a very bad experience, and every winter we are afraid," Christine said. "When my grandfather told me about it, he cried."

In 1956, frost killed all their olive trees and almost every olive tree in France. Olive trees can withstand the cold, but they can't take a rapid change in temperature, and on this February day the mercury plummeted from twelve degrees Celsius to minus twelve degrees Celsius. Olive trees throughout France froze and perished. Farmers were devastated, and many switched to grapes or cherry trees. Some replanted olive trees, whereas others, including Christine's grandparents, waited for the dead olive trees to regrow from their roots, which were insulated from the frost by the soil.

"When the trees grew back, this is how they came," Christine said, pointing to olive trees that were clustered in groups of four instead of evenly spaced. "It took eight years until the olives returned."

Given the challenges of growing olives in France, it is not surprising that the French produce only 5 percent of the olive oil they consume. Since the eighteenth and nineteenth centuries, when French olive tree cultivation reached its zenith, olive farming has declined precipitously. With only 4 million olive trees (there were 26 million in 1840), France produces less than 0.5 percent the oil that Spain does. Yet despite being one of the smallest olive oil–producing nations, France makes some of the world's best oils. As Christine explains, "to compete, we have to focus on quality."

To clarify what constitutes a great olive oil, Christine began by describing the different grades of olive oil. Her oils are extra virgin, which means they come from the first pressing of the olives, done only by mechanical means, and using no heat or chemicals. The oil also has to have an acidity level of less than 0.8 percent and has to pass a rigorous taste test. If an oil shows hints of defects such as rancidity, mustiness, fustiness, or sourness, it isn't extra virgin.

If the first pressed oil falls short, it may drop into the next category, virgin olive oil. This oil can have an acidity of up to 1.5 percent, and the taste merely has to be good. However, if an oil is really foul, which 50 percent of the oil produced in the Mediterranean is, it will plummet to the lampante virgin category, a name that reflects olive oil's historic use as lamp oil. This oil has an acidity greater than 3.3 percent and is considered unfit for human consumption; instead, it is used for industrial application or refined using chemicals that strip it of its flavor and then sold as cheap supermarket olive oil.

Like many of the olive experts we met, Christine emphasized the importance of understanding olive oil's complex naming conventions and the vast chasm between extra virgin olive oil and the confusing menagerie of monikers used to describe refined olive oil. "Light," "pure," "extra light," or even "olive oil" were all names given to refined olive oil, sometimes with a swig of "virgin olive oil" thrown in for flavor. It was enough to perplex even the savviest foodie.

"Just remember, if it's not extra virgin or virgin, it has been refined," Christine said.

Refining strips away much of olive oil's taste and many of its nutrients, leaving behind an oil that is a poor cousin to the original. Charcoal, chemical, and physical filters are used to remove the bad taste from inedible oils and drop their acidity to 0.3 percent or less. Many people consider refined oil unfit for consumption because of its lack of flavor. For the most part, it is safe to eat, but having been stripped of its flavor, odor, color, and health-boosting polyphenols, it's about as bland as your average vegetable oil.

"I've bought light olive oil before," I admitted. "I thought it was lower in calories."

Colin laughed. "I don't think they make low-calorie oil."

It was an easy mistake to make, and I wondered if the labeling was purposely misleading. After all, "extra light" and "pure" were appealing descriptors and were perhaps more appropriate than "virgin" or "extra virgin." "Virgin" seemed more fitting as a term to describe nonalcoholic versions of cocktails, like a Virgin Caesar or Virgin Mary. Other food products manage to differentiate their grade with self-explanatory terms. Top beef in the United States is graded prime, and then it drops down to choice, select, and finally standard, whereas U.S. maple syrup grading is even more self-explanatory, with the best labeled grade A, followed by grade B, and finally grade C for unpalatable syrup.

"At least you didn't buy pomace oil," Colin said.

Pomace oils are so bad that they're rarely found on supermarket shelves, but they are a staple of pizza parlors and restaurants. These oils are made from the pulp, or pomace, left over from the virgin oil extraction, a mix of skin, stone, and flesh that still contains 5 to 8 percent oil. Château Virant spreads this pomace over their olive groves to fertilize the soil, but others extract the remaining dredges of oil using chemical solvents and high heat.

Both pomace oils and virgin oils that do not meet the standards for virgin status are refined using a process that can contain toxic and carcinogenic compounds. One of the main solvents used to extract oil is hexane, a component of gasoline and glues that causes brain damage in solvent sniffers and can be fatal in extreme cases. Using a potentially lethal liquid in food manufacturing isn't as unusual as it sounds, and hexane is used in extracting almost all seed oils, including canola, sunflower, soy, and vegetable. Hexane is removed using heat—like gasoline, it has a low boiling point and readily evaporates—but trace amounts remain. The high heat used during oil refinement poses additional health hazards, producing benzopyrene, the potent carcinogen that forms on charred steaks and burnt toast, and in

2001, several countries placed a temporary ban on pomace oil as a result of high levels of this toxin.

But even among the vast selection of extra virgin olive oils there is an abyss of difference between the flavorless pale liquid many supermarkets sell and the limpid golden oil that wins competitions. There are many factors that set the great oils apart, including the variety of olives, how they are picked, how quickly they are milled, and the type of equipment used to press the oil.

"Modern machines changed the quality of olive oil," Christine said as she led us into Château Virant's mill, a cavernous room with a row of towering stainless steel tanks and a complex collection of heavy-duty equipment, pipes, control panels, vats, and centrifuge tanks, all gleaming with operating-room sterility and overlooking the olive orchard through large curved windows.

She walked us through the process, describing how in an hour and a half their mill transforms more than three thousand kilograms of olives into oil. The freshly picked olives are poured onto a conveyor belt that separates out the leaves and stems and moves them upward and into the washer, where they are rinsed clean with water and then strained. The washed olives are shunted into the hammer crusher, where hammers pound them into a rough paste that is transferred to a vat resembling an industrial deep fryer. A large horizontal blade like a washing machine's agitator slowly mixes the paste in a process called malaxation that cajoles globules of oil out of the paste and pools them together into larger drops that are easier to separate. The paste is then shunted into a large centrifuge that spins at 4,080 rpm, separating the oil, which makes up 20 percent of this olive cultivar, from the solids and water. The olive remnants, or pomace, are shunted outside, where they will be returned to the fields to fertilize the trees for another season, and the oil flows into a second, even faster, centrifuge that clarifies it. Afterward, the oil is stored in the large stainless steel tanks, which are filled with inert gas, because, as Christine explained, "oxygen is not a friend to the olive." When the oil is ready to be shipped, it is filtered and bottled.

Making olive oil is both an ancient craft that has changed little and one that embraces modern technology. When you glance at olive presses around the world, you'll see there are nearly as many ways of making olive oil as there are olive cultivars. In some places, families continue to mash olives by hand and decant the olive oil that rises to the surface, a method as old as olive oil and even older than cultivated olives. Traditional olive oil mills crush olives using millstones and then press the mash between mats of woven hemp or coconut fiber or in burlap sacks until oil dribbles out.

The millstone is turned by hand, mule, or motor, whereas the presses could be lever, screw, or hydraulic. The screw and lever presses are the oldest, exerting pressure either by a large screw that is twisted down onto the stack of mats or a long, heavy wooden lever pulled down by a system of pulleys and heavy stones. The modern version uses hydraulic pistons to compress the mats and often uses mats made out of synthetic fibers instead of natural. The pressure is intense, reaching as much as 5,800 psi, or two hundred times the pressure a car exerts on the ground beneath it. Warm water is poured onto the press to help extract the olive oil, often for the first press and always for the second and third, and sometimes talc is added to enhance oil extraction. Some modern traditionalists include a malaxation step, in which the crushed olives are kneaded before pressing to help extract more oil. Others add a final vertical centrifugation step to separate the oil from the water instead of relying on gravity to separate the two. Meanwhile, other mills completely avoid the pressing part of olive oil production, using the *affiorato* process, whereby the crushed olives sit in a specialized container until the oil rises to the surface.

In contrast, modern facilities rely on stainless steel machines to crush the olives and separate the oil from the rest, but there is a range of choices for each step, including variations in machines, temperature, time, amount of water added, and more. Olives can be crushed—usually whole but sometimes destoned—using a hammer mill or metal-toothed grinder. The paste is then malaxed, usually horizontally but sometimes vertically, often in sealed containers that may contain an inert gas to enhance quality. Water may be added or even heat; both will increase yields but at the expense of quality, as will increasing the malaxation time beyond an hour. The olive paste and olive oil are then separated by a centrifugal system, with either a three-phase or two-phase centrifuge, or less commonly by cold dripping. The decanting centrifuge spins horizontally, separating the material according to weight. Vegetative matter is the heaviest and slips to the outside, water is next and creates the middle layer, and oil, which is the lightest, creates the innermost layer.

The three-phase and two-phase centrifuges differ in output, quality of oil, and environmental impact. The three-phase releases three items—oil, water, and pomace—whereas the two-phase produces only oil and a sludgy mixture of water and solids. The two-phase centrifuge is newer and was designed to overcome the shortfalls of its predecessor—namely, water consumption and the challenges of disposing of the aqueous waste. In addition to being generally considered more environmentally sound—though one problem is that its soft pomace is more difficult to process than the hard cakes spit out by the older models—it produces a high-quality olive oil with more polyphenols.

oil to the use of large machinery whereby a revolving millstone crushed olives and a long wooden lever and heavy weight compressed sacks of olive paste against a stone base. For the next three thousand years, there were minor advances; the screw press replaced the lever during Roman times, and there were tweaks to the grindstone and press. Machinery was modified so that it could be powered by animals, water, and, during the industrial age, steam and diesel engines. But it wasn't until the centrifuge was turned to olive oil production that the industry made another dramatic shift.

Centrifuges have been used in agriculture since the mid-nineteenth century, when they separated cream from milk, and in the 1970s they were applied to olive oil production. This innovation had a revolutionary impact, decreasing the processing time and labor while increasing the yield. Spain embraced the technology, and by 1970, 10 percent of its mills used centrifugal separation. Thirty years later, nearly all Spain's mills replaced their presses with stainless steel drums. This technology did not have the same runaway impact throughout the 25,000 olive mills in the rest of the world, though by the twenty-first century, modern presses were responsible for more than half the olive oil production in a number of countries, including Greece, Italy, Cyprus, Croatia, and Malta.

The reduction in processing time helped improve the quality of olive oil, and the sealed system minimized exposure to oxygen and restricted olive oil degradation. But it was necessary to add water to extract the oil, which decreased the oil's polyphenols and produced waste water high in nitrogen and phosphorus. The two-phase centrifuge eliminated the need to add water and reduced waste, making an olive oil that was high in polyphenols while reducing the environmental impact of olive oil production. Today, many of Europe's mills are two-phase, including all of Spain's and half of Greece's, and tightening environmental regulations are forcing more and more mills to make the conversion.

OUR FOOTSTEPS echoed throughout the empty plant, the machinery quiet, cold, and idle since the last harvest. But when the olives are ripe, still mostly green but shining like waxed apples, it will be frantic.

"From October 20 to Christmas we will harvest the olives," Christine said. Forty additional olive pickers will be hired, and the machinery will thunder around the clock with little rest. A hundred hands will rake the trees and gather their fruit in nets, piling olives in plastic crates and bringing them to the plant, where every eight kilograms will produce a liter of oil that will eventually make its way to French stores as well as specialty shops in distant countries, including Canada, the U.S., and Norway.

"We make two kinds of oil," Christine said. She opened the spigots on two hulking tanks and filled a bottle from each. "Both are green and fruity, but one is intense and the other medium. They are identical except the olives for the medium oil are picked a month later."

Christine compared their scent to artichoke and green grass and said, "There is a bitterness and pepperiness, but just a little to prove the fruit are fresh and there is an engagement in life."

She poured a shot glass amount into small plastic cups, and invited us to try them and to distinguish between the two kinds. To a professional taster like Christine, who spent years perfecting olive oil and chairs an international olive oil competition, there was a vast difference in the flavors, but we had only recently realized olive oil was supposed to even have a flavor.

"There are 250 types of flavors in olive oil," Christine explained. "Wine has 450."

I doubted I could pick out five, and I was relieved when Colin asked, "Could you give us a few tasting tips?"

"Of course," Christine said. "First you warm the oil." She clasped the cup with one hand, placed her other over the opening, and gently swirled it. "This helps release the aromas. Then you smell it." She lifted her hand off the oil and inhaled deeply. We did the same. It smelled like spring, freshly cut lawns, and flowers about to bloom.

"It smells like grass," Colin said. Christine nodded and smiled.

"To taste the oil," Christine continued, "you must sip it like this. Voilà." She lifted the cup with her usual grace and then slurped, sucking loudly and deeply, the type of rude noise children get chastised for. She swirled it like mouthwash and swallowed it. "Voilà, now you try it."

I was a little apprehensive about slurping in public, but I knew that slurping intensified the flavors. The loud sucking draws in air along with the oil, and the resulting emulsification coats your mouth more thoroughly. The oil is even drawn up into your nasal passages, which are extraordinarily sensitive to aromas. Wine tasters use a similar approach, and the Italians call it *strippaggio*, "stripping" in English. Afterward, you swirl the oil in your mouth, coating all the surfaces from the tip of your tongue to the roof of your mouth. When you swallow the oil, you should feel its pepperiness, a much-desired trait that stems from antioxidants and extends the oil's longevity.

We followed her lead, pursing our lips and loudly sucking in oil. I must have done the *strippaggio* right because the oil sprayed into my mouth, coating my tongue and reaching the back of my throat, where it burned like freshly cracked pepper. Even my nose tingled. The oil softened my lips, but in my mouth I could barely feel its oiliness.

The flavor was complex and difficult to describe, robust and full, falling on my taste receptors in layers, like a symphony. I struggled to remember the flavor attributes associated with olive oil and to pick out the ones that applied here. Like the smell, the taste was fresh, green, and fruity. Unable to come up with anything more profound, I swallowed the oil and got the real surprise. It burned like whiskey, and the sensation lingered, my throat and even my nose warmed by the pepperiness of the oil.

Colin coughed. "Wow," he said. "That packs a punch. It tastes like wheatgrass with a dash of Tabasco."

"The pepperiness comes when the olives are picked young," Christine said. The mature oil, picked from the same olives but a month later, was equally flavorful but gentler on my throat.

Flos Olei, the who's who guide to olive oil, describes Christine's oil as having an aroma that is "rotund and strong, endowed with ample fruity notes of unripe tomato, white apple and dried fruit, especially fresh walnut and almond," and a taste that is "definite and complex, with a distinct aromatic flavour of basil, field balm, black pepper and vegetal notes of celery, lettuce and artichoke." I would have a hard time picking out those flavors, but I could easily imagine pairing it with "marinated salmon, grilled vegetables, ovoli mushroom soup, risotto with artichokes or baked lamb" as the guide recommends.

"We also make a third kind," Christine said, placing two more cups in front of us, "but we do not sell this one or enter it into competitions."

The oil was dark, almost murky, and had a strong, unpleasant smell that reminded me of a sweaty locker room. "This is more like how olive oil used to taste, and some people are used to the flavor," she said. Christine called it "black fruity," and it was made only when farmers requested that their olives be pressed this way. The oil was made from black olives that sat and rotted for four to eight days before pressing, unlike the other oils, which were pressed as soon as the olives were picked.

The taste was revolting, and I could understand why Christine had said she didn't like it. Pungent, foul, and rotten, it was too putrid to swallow, and I spat it back into the cup. I couldn't imagine why anyone would prefer this oil. Even two thousand years ago, Cato the Elder wrote that olive oil had to be pressed the same day olives were picked. "The more quickly you work them up the better the results will be, and you will get more and better oil from a given quantity," he wrote in *De Agricultura*. Christine theorized that in difficult times, the strong flavor of the oil was a benefit because just a little was required to impart a distinct flavor.

Although I couldn't distinguish between two great oils, the bad one certainly stood out, and all three were a world apart from the flavorless supermarket oils I was used to. With time and practice, I hoped my palate would become more attuned to olive oils, and now that I knew what one of the world's best olive oils tasted like, I'd know what to look for.

BY THE TIME our boat gasket arrived, we'd been in Cassis for eleven days. Colin carefully slipped the giant O-ring into place and began reassembling the engine, while Leif and I went to the marine work yard to see if it had a torque wrench we could borrow. But because it was Monday, the work yard was closed. Instead, I borrowed a wrench from a kayak rental shop with a well-stocked workshop, but when I brought it back to the boat, we realized it couldn't measure torque.

"It will be hard to find this tool in Cassis," the man said when I returned the wrench. "You could try the garages, but I do not think they will want to lend their tools."

I tried two garages, along with the dive shop, and Colin visited a superyacht and hardware store. We walked all over town, feeling hot and disillusioned. For all we knew, the engine might not even work. There was still one garage on the outskirts of town, and we trudged up the hill toward it until the sidewalk disappeared and the road narrowed into a shoulderless highway that was dangerous to walk on let alone push a stroller up. Colin waited with Leif at a pull-off while I continued upward.

"Avez-vous d'une clé dynamométrique?" I read from my crumpled paper.

"I've never lent my tools before," said the shop's owner. But perhaps sensing my despair, he smiled and pulled down a large baseball-sized wrench and handed it to me in exchange for my passport.

We jogged back to the boat, and Colin buried himself in the engine hatch. Fifteen minutes later he emerged. "Well, that's it. Now we'll see if she runs."

Colin turned the key, and the engine sputtered. On the second try, it roared to life and our faces split into huge grins. We were on our way to the French Riviera.

ILLUMINATION AND INSPIRATION ON THE FRENCH RIVIERA

"And the dove came in to him in the evening; and, lo, in her mouth was an olive leaf pluckt off: so Noah knew that the waters were abated from off the earth." GENESIS 8:11

"Kindled from a blessed tree, an olive neither of the East nor of the West, whose oil would almost glow forth though no fire touched it." KORAN, 24:35

SAINT-RÉMY, SAINT-TROPEZ, CANNES, Côte d'Azur—the names of these playgrounds for the rich and famous rolled off my tongue. Yet here we were, a family in a thirty-year-old boat bought for the price of a secondhand car.

We weren't after the glitzy cities and mile-long beaches but rather the less-frequented islands. The hidden side of the Riviera—well, as hidden as one of the world's most popular tourist destinations can get—was an important stepping-stone in the olive's popularization throughout Europe. Olive trees had grown on the islands since the Greeks first colonized them, and hundreds of years later, when monks claimed these outposts, they created monasteries and planted groves of olive trees.

The olive tree flourishes throughout Judaism, Islam, and Christianity as a symbol of peace and prosperity, its oil cherished and its growers respected. The word "Christ" is derived from the Greek word "chrism," meaning "to anoint with oil," and "Messiah" means "anointed one" in Hebrew. There are more than 180 references to olives and olive oil in the Bible. In Genesis, the dove returned to Noah and the ark with an olive leaf in its beak, marking the end of the great flood. In early Christianity, a dove holding an olive branch was associated with baptisms and death and was portrayed in images and on tombstones as a harbinger of everlasting peace. Psalm 128 pledges prosperity to believers, promising, "Your children will be like olive shoots around the table."[1] Moses exempted olive farmers from military service, and the book of Deuteronomy instructed them on charitable actions, stating, "When you beat the olives from your trees, do not go over the branches a second time. Leave what remains for the foreigner, the fatherless and the widow."[2]

Some hypothesize that the Garden of Eden's Tree of Life was an olive tree. In the *Apocalypse of Moses*, a Greek version of the story of Adam and Eve, when Adam fell sick after being expelled from Eden, he asked Eve to return to the garden with their son and plead for his life. "Perhaps He will have pity upon you and send His angel across to the tree of His mercy, from which flows the oil of life, and will give you a drop of it, to anoint me with it."[3] The tree of mercy is the tree of life, and although the oil is not explicitly identified as olive oil, it is the only ancient oil associated with anointing and healing.

Olive oil was a revered liquid, probably used in biblical times for healing, anointing, lighting lamps, and religious purposes more than for food. "Command the Israelites to bring you clear oil of pressed olives for the light so that the lamps may be kept burning,"[4] states a passage in Exodus, and orthodox Christians continue to use olive oil in their vigil lamps. Olive oil was prized for its healing powers, and wounds were "softened with oil" or treated by "pouring on wine and oil."

But it is consecrated oils that receive the most play, and olive oil is the base of the three sacred oils. "Take the flask of oil and pour it on his head and say, 'Thus says the LORD, "I have anointed you king over Israel,"'"[5] the Bible states. The Holy Chrism, or anointing oil, as it is often called, is a scent-infused olive oil that has been used for anointing for more than two thousand years. Oil of the Catechumens coats the bodies of baptized babies to strengthen them against the struggles life will bring, consecrates churches, blesses altars, and ordains priests. And the third holy oil, Oil of the Sick, also called Unction, is used to heal, and the Bible is peppered with its uses.

Judaism shares Christianity's reverence for the olive tree, and many of the olive's key references reside in the Old Testament, teachings that are found in both the Bible and the Torah. The importance of olive oil is seen in the menorah, the seven-pronged lampstand that may be fueled only by olive oil. The gold lamp lit the Tabernacle during the exodus from Egypt and later the Temple of Jerusalem, and it has been a symbol of Judaism for thousands of years. It appears on Israel's coat of arms, with an olive branch on each side. When God told Moses how to design the lamp, He said it should burn only olive oil. "And thou shalt command the children of Israel, that they bring unto thee pure olive oil beaten for the light, to cause a lamp to burn continuously."[6] But during the second century BC Syrian Greeks invaded Jerusalem, outlawed Judaism, and desecrated the Second Temple of Jerusalem, snuffing out the continuous flame. Two years later, the Jewish people reclaimed their temple and lit the menorah again. There was only enough oil for one day; yet it lasted eight days, allowing the lamp to burn continuously until more oil was ready. This was seen as a miracle and led to the creation of Hanukkah, the eight-day festival of lights celebrated every fall.

Rabbis have long identified with the olive tree as a symbol of Israel or of the Jewish people, and in the Mishnah, a book of Jewish oral traditions compiled in the third century, Rabbi Yohanan asks, "Why are the People of Israel compared to an olive? To teach you that just as an olive does not give its oil except when crushed, so too the Jewish people do not repent and return to God except after being crushed by suffering."[7] Another rabbi says that "just as the leaves of the olive tree do not fall off either in summer or winter, the Jewish people shall not be cast off, either in the world or the world-to-come."[8] For the Jewish people, the olive and the olive tree represent strength and resilience, and the oil is equated with luminosity: "Just as olive oil brings light to the world, so do the People of Israel bring light to the world."[9]

In Islam, the olive tree is also holy, revered for its medicine, wood, and light. Prophet Mohammed was reported to have said that olive oil cures seventy ailments, and in a hadith he says, "Eat the olive oil and massage it over your bodies since it is a holy tree."[10] From piles to leprosy, olive oil was an elixir. Prophet Mohammed rubbed olive oil into his beard, eyebrows, and hair and instructed his followers to oil their bodies. The Koranic passage that extolls man as God's noblest achievement begins "By the fig and the olive, and the Mount Sinai, and this secure city"[11]—a reference to the importance of the olive. As in Judaism and Christianity, oil as a source of light is also a powerful metaphor, and the Koran states, "God is the light of the Heavens and the Earth; the likeness of His light is as a niche wherein is a lamp—the lamp in a glass, the glass as it were a glittering star—lit by a blessed olive tree, neither Eastern nor Western, its oil almost glows, even without fire touching it, light upon light."[12]

The olive tree blanketed the lands in which these three great monotheistic religions flourished, and became as important to the soul as it was to the soil.

TWO DAYS after leaving Cassis, we reached the Îles d'Hyères, a cluster of four islands east of Toulon that the locals call the Porquerolles, after the largest island. We slipped between Porquerolles island and the coast, avoiding the craggy cliffs sandwiching us in the narrow channel. A lighthouse stood sentinel on a rocky outcrop leading into a quiet village of modest houses, a swath of urbanity on a mostly wild island. Compared with the mainland—dotted with stately mansions and manicured gardens and teeming with rainbow-sailed hobie cats, kayakers, and dive boats—the islands were quiet. Only the bays, crowded with sailboats, their masts like candles on a centenarian's birthday cake, alluded to the popularity of the island, which is crowded with mainlanders on weekends and in the summer.

A moat of water has an enormous impact on a place, even when it is only a couple kilometers wide and can be easily traversed by a ferry. If we go back in history, the effect is even more striking. Throughout the Middle Ages, these islands were lawless domains commandeered by pirates, corsairs, and hooligans. Eventually, France wrested control of them, and saddled with the problem of how to get settlers to farm these outposts, officials came up with an unusual incentive: they granted asylum to criminals who relocated here. It was a popular decision, and felons flocked to the Îles d'Hyères. To the authorities' surprise, some felons retained their lawless leanings, and piracy once again flourished.

In the last two hundred years, the islands have been invaded by the English and the Germans, artists have retreated here, as have the sick, and a man with the unfortunate name of Dr. Poo tried to build a resort for the wealthy. That plan, however, was flushed down the toilet, so to speak.

Besides isolating people, these islands also became bastions of ecological uniqueness. Olive trees, which readily cross-pollinate with other olive cultivars, are not exposed to the same variety of olive pollen that trees on mainland Europe are. Only pollen that is blown across expanses of water can influence an island's olive trees. For this reason, these olive trees are more likely than trees elsewhere to resemble the original trees, and sampling these trees could tell us which varieties monks planted nearly two millennia ago.

We began our search for olive trees on Port-Cros, the highest and wildest of the islands. Because it is mostly parkland, fishing is prohibited in the surrounding waters, and anchoring is allowed only in the harbors of Port-Cros and Port-Man. We rounded Île de Bagaud, a tiny crescent-shaped island completely off limits to boats, and slipped into the natural harbor of Port-Cros. Craggy green hills enveloped the emerald bay, and a scattering of French sailboats anchored in the sheltered waters. We dropped our sails and found a spot amidst the boats to spend the night. Colin lowered the anchor and pulled out the chain and rope, and I set the anchor by reversing the boat. When we finished, I placed Leif in the cockpit to play, and before I could stop him, he yanked the keys out of the engine, setting off our engine alarm. A piercing air raid siren sounded, and by the time I shut it off, we had announced our arrival with the subtlety of a sledgehammer.

In the morning, we rowed our tender, a small inflatable boat, ashore and pulled up onto a pale sandy beach that merged into a sugarcane plantation, beamy green stalks swaying in the morning breeze. With our dinghy tied onto the farmer's fence, we picked our way across the beach and onto a rugged path that cut through thick forest and vegetation. It hugged the coastline, winding its way up to the clifftop Fort de Port-Man, a hulking fifteenth-century fortification built to protect the island from piracy.

We searched for the silvery sheen of olive leaves amidst the green of oaks, pines, and holly. Near the crumbling remains of a factory that once produced soda ash, a limestone deposit used in construction, we spotted our first olive trees. Tall and gangly, with a smattering of hard, blackening olives clinging to their branches, they stretched above the forest to glimpse the sun.

"These trees look so different," Colin said.

They were nothing like the plump and productive trees we'd seen in Spanish groves or the squat wild olives in the French calanques. I jumped up and snatched an olive that was just barely out of reach. It was the color of a fig, slightly elongated, and as big as an almond—and pockmarked with bites from olive flies and other pests. I bit into it, not for its taste, which I knew would be bitter, but to see the size of the stone.

"The olive stone is quite small," I said, showing the ruptured olive to Colin. The flesh was a pale purple and the pit no bigger than one you'd find in a typical supermarket olive.

"That's more like the cultivated trees than the wild ones," Colin said.

We had noticed that wild olives were more stone than flesh, whereas the cultivated ones were much meatier. Even though this tree was untended, it appeared to be a domesticated olive tree. Either someone had planted and abandoned it, or it had seeded itself from other cultivated trees and retained the ability to produce large olives. We clipped two branches from each tree, one from as high up as we could reach and the other from the base of the trunk, and slipped them into ziplock bags along with a few olives.

A few minutes farther along the trail, we discovered a group of squat, round olive trees, silvery bushes with a mass of branches erupting from the ground instead of a single trunk. They were also studded with olives, which were smaller, rounder, and sparser than those on the tall trees. We took samples and continued on to the fortress, stopping at the top to lounge on the stone fence, where heat beat down and lizards sunned themselves. The interior of the fortress was closed to the public, so we resigned ourselves to exploring its perimeter.

In the late morning we sailed on, tracing the northern coast of Port-Cros and its neighbor Île du Levant, an island split between a military base and a dedicated nudist camp. On one side, people tested rockets, and on the other, people worshipped the sun in their birthday suits. It was hard to imagine more disparate neighbors, but the island provided the one thing they both wanted: privacy in one of the world's most populated places.

From the quiet solitude of islands, we sailed past the posh Saint-Tropez, where a trio of colossal cruise ships anchored in the harbor, and continued on to a sheltered bay near Saint-Rémy, joining stately yachts flying flags from France, Britain, and Germany. The anchorage was so popular that in the summer an enterprising person made the rounds and took orders for croissants and baguettes to be delivered the next morning. But September was too late for this service, and we ate our usual cereal and coffee.

"I'll get us out of here. You can stay in here with Leif," Colin said as he climbed the companionway steps. It was barely light, and a thick fog hung in the air, but we wanted to make the most of the slight breeze, which we knew from experience would dwindle by afternoon.

Pulling up the anchor, hoisting the sails, and maneuvering out of a crowded anchorage is not an easy thing to do alone, but we were becoming adept at handling the boat on our own, especially Colin. We had to. It was impossible to leave Leif alone.

"We're faster than the luxury yachts," Colin yelled as we left the anchorage. I looked out the window at the two yachts that had been readying for departure while we breakfasted and still hadn't moved.

The wind filled our sails and Colin cut the motor. It was silent as we glided along the coastline, the fog parting to display a jumble of red cliffs glowing like Australia's Ayers Rock. By late morning, the sun burned in the cloudless sky, but a slight breeze kept the temperature perfect and pushed us along. As predicted, the wind faded in the afternoon, and by the time we'd reached Cannes we were motoring.

Across the strait from Cannes is Île Sainte-Marguerite, a three-kilometer-long island made famous by its seventeenth-century Fort Royal, a massive fortress with narrow windows, a high fence, and a watchtower perched on a forested cliff. The Man in the Iron Mask, who wore a mask for three decades to conceal his identity, had been imprisoned within its walls. Voltaire and Alexandre Dumas wrote about him, and Leonardo DiCaprio played him in the Hollywood blockbuster *The Man in the Iron Mask*.

No one knows who the man in the iron mask was, but there are many theories. Marie-Pierre, whom we had met in Provence, told us that he was the brother of King Louis XIV and had been imprisoned to keep him from the throne. While imprisoned, he fathered a child, who was sent off to Corsica to be raised by foster parents, and decades later, Napoleon Bonaparte would claim that boy was his grandfather. Other theories say he was King Louis's identical twin, illegitimate son, father, or doctor; a traitorous Italian diplomat; or even the illegitimate son of England's king. What is agreed upon is that he was someone important and that the mystery is too irresistible to let go.

Île Sainte-Marguerite's anchorage bustled with multimillion-dollar megayachts and tenders worth more than some houses, let alone our boat, and we dropped anchor next to a sleek three-level superyacht. Leif threw stale bread to the fish until a flock of seagulls frightened him, and Colin and I took turns swimming. We rowed ashore and pulled our tender onto a beach near a set of wooden lounge chairs, skirted a sandy pit scattered with heavy metal Boules balls, and wound past empty patio tables adorned with straw umbrellas. The fort sat atop the hill, accessible by a steep stone staircase carved into the cliff. The ticket booth for the museum was closed, but the grounds were open and we wandered in. They were neat and orderly, clean stone walkways leading to well-maintained buildings. If it weren't for the thick iron bars covering the windows, it could be mistaken for a boarding school or government housing.

Outside the fenced fortress, nature reclaimed the grounds. Planted trees—oaks, chestnuts, hollies—had been overtaken by wild Aleppo pines, eucalyptus, and dense shrubbery. A few olive trees sprouted, looking nothing like those in the well-groomed groves. Years without pruning had caused them to morph into bushy orbs. I wondered whether these trees were descended from those the monks planted 1,500 years ago.

From the fifth century onwards, monks lived on and visited this island and the neighboring Île Saint-Honorat, where they built a monastery that influenced Christianity throughout the Western world. A fifth-century writer had called it the Metropolis of Learning. Bishops and saints, including Ireland's Saint Patrick, were educated there, and for a thousand years it was dubbed the Isle of Saints. As in many monasteries, olive trees were planted to provide oil for religious purposes, lighting, and food. Although olive trees still grow on the island, the thirty Cistercian monks who now live in the monastery no longer make olive oil.

It is likely that the monks made several grades of olive oil but that only the first pressing was used to create tinctures or for anointing and the rest lit their lanterns. The holy tincture was one of the most sacred uses of olive oil in the church, and from the Bible we know exactly what went into this sacred anointment. "Take the finest spices of liquid myrrh... and of sweet-smelling cinnamon... and of aromatic cane... and of cassia... and of olive oil... and you shall make of these a sacred anointing oil," reads the Book of Exodus.[13] Holy tincture, called Holy Muron, is still made today, by Armenian priests following the same recipe that has been used for 1,700 years. Every seven years, the priests gather in the world's oldest state-built church, Armenia's Cathedral of Etchmiadzin, and mix dozens of herbs and flowers with olive oil. The tincture is baked, covered with a veil, blessed on an altar for forty days, and finally topped off with a gallon of holy oil from the previous batch to create a connection to the original Muron. Each priest receives a tiny vial from which he can never be separated, and it must last him seven years, until the next batch is made.

THE FOLLOWING morning we chugged across the bay to Cannes to celebrate Leif's first birthday. Cannes's old quarter churned with tourists milling around displays of olive oils and gourmet cheese and racks of tablecloths embroidered with fields of lavender. I weaved the stroller around patio tables, gently bumping over the cobblestones, searching for a cake and present for Leif. He started snoring before I reached the bakery, and his gentle rumblings drew a smile from the kerchiefed woman who boxed our raspberry tart. In the supermarket I found birthday candles and a windup helicopter with spinning blades.

Leif was still sleeping, so I continued along the hotel-lined waterfront, watching bronzed men spike volleyballs in netted courts and kids plunge off pontoons anchored in shallow waters. I climbed to the hilltop fort and the nine-hundred-year-old Chapel of St. Anne, built by monks from the nearby Lérins Islands. The Musée de la Castre was free today but didn't allow strollers, so I circled the courtyard, weaving among ambling tourists and bored-looking school groups, enjoying the panoramic view of Cannes's old quarter and downtown, including Port de Cannes and a tiny speck of blue I thought might be our boat.

When we returned to the boat, Colin was chatting with our neighbor, a tall man with a gray crew cut and weathered skin.

"I hate the English," William said in a strong British accent. Until then I had thought he was British, but soon we'd learn he was from Marseille, visiting Cannes for a boat race with his wife, a waif with angles like a woman in a Picasso painting. He laughed and continued, "No, that's not true. Some of my best friends are English, and it is the English who made Cannes famous."

"How's that?" I said. What followed was a lesson in local history.

Cannes had been inhabited since Roman times, but it was little more than a fishing village and a port for the Lérins Islands. It wasn't until a cholera epidemic stranded Lord Brougham, the lord chancellor of England, and his daughter en route to their holiday in Italy that Cannes's status skyrocketed. The chancellor built a villa here, as did his friends, and by the time he died, in 1868, the population had tripled. People came for the mild winters, but it wasn't until 1936, when French workers were given vacations, that it became a summertime destination. Now 2 million people live on the Côte d'Azur, 75,000 people in Cannes alone, and many more vacation here, helping to make France the world's most popular tourist destination.

For a long time this port was considered "a dangerous harbor, without shelter... open to the southwesterly sea, where the ships are in constant danger,"[14] as Guy de Maupassant once wrote. But now LCD screens line the piers, reporting weather forecasts, and rows of superyachts gleam and bustle with bronzed staff in crisp white polo shirts. One of the flashiest and most popular marinas on the Riviera, the Cannes harbor caters to the uber-rich, who flock there in droves. Each year, half of the world's superyachts cruise this part of the Mediterranean.

According to the girl in the *capitainerie*, the harbormaster's office, we were lucky to get a spot. Between the duty-free conference—cases of liquor and electronics were parked in front of many yachts—and the upcoming Royal Regatta, considered "one of the most prestigious regattas of the French Riviera,"[15] it was a busy place.

The marina is a short stroll away from Le Festival, the restaurant Marie-Pierre had suggested for lunch. When we arrived, Marie-Pierre was waiting and rushed over to greet us. She was just as ebullient as when we first met her in Provence, and she engulfed us in hugs and kissed our cheeks in typical *faire la bise* greeting. She squeezed Leif and called him "my little skipper," the nickname she and Philippe had coined.

"There are many restaurants here that are for the tourists," she said as we settled into our patio table, "where the food is expensive and not so good." This restaurant was her choice, and despite "not being trendy," it was stylish and packed, mostly with locals, I guessed from the number of people she recognized. It felt very French, elegant and sophisticated, and I could imagine a glamorous movie star sauntering in after a festival screening without anyone batting an eye.

"Renoir lived near Nice," Marie-Pierre said, picking at her chicken Caesar salad. "The house is not much, but the garden—that's where he painted—is full of olive trees."

I took another bite of my lamb, and the deliciously roasted meat melted in my mouth. Colin ate with equal zeal. We had both ordered the daily specials, but his lamb was long gone and only a few bites of his quinoa salad remained. Even Leif had eaten modestly, and for once he sat throughout the meal. Perhaps he had matured, I mused, now that he was a year old. Marie-Pierre's plate was the only one not scraped clean, her attention now devoted to Picasso and the call of Provence.

"The light is magical here," she continued, beaming as though it flowed through her pores. "Monet and Matisse came here for the light, too." The sun shone here three hundred days a year, and the light had a magical property—or so the artists believed.

The waitress cleared our plates and returned with coffee and dessert. On Marie-Pierre's recommendation, I ordered the *café gourmand,* a plateful of miniature desserts alongside an espresso. Marie-Pierre sipped her coffee, drawing out a plan for our afternoon, while I devoured my crème brûlée, chocolate soufflé, fig biscuit, and two brightly coloured cream-filled macaroons. If I stayed in France much longer, I'd have to start exercising or follow Marie-Pierre's modest eating habits.

It was only a half-hour drive to Nice, but our meandering route past pretty beaches and expensive villas was full of stops. A dozen colorful fishing boats were anchored in a sandy bay called Plage de l'Olivette, where families picnicked on the beach. The rocky promontory past the bay was Cap d'Antibes and the most expensive hotel on the French Riviera, Hôtel du Cap-Eden-Roc. Built in 1869 for writers seeking inspiration, it once housed famous writers, artists, and politicians, including F. Scott Fitzgerald, Ernest Hemingway, Marc Chagall, Winston Churchill, and Elizabeth Taylor.

"Sounds like a good spot to write your book," Colin quipped.

"Right after I win the lottery," I said.

Many of history's great writers and artists had come to the Mediterranean for inspiration, and the ubiquitous olive tree had ignited countless masterpieces. Van Gogh fervently pursued the olive and created more than fifteen paintings of olive trees in the year before his suicide. André Derain, who moved from Paris to the Mediterranean village of Collioure and worked alongside Henri Matisse, portrayed olive trees in glowing grays and silvers against the color-drenched Mediterranean landscape. "White, black, terra verde—Derain's rendering of the gray tree is complete,"[16] writes Aldous Huxley.

Henri Matisse painted olive trees in diverse styles. His 1898 *Olive Tree* is done in Postimpressionist style, and the trees are a cross between realistic and abstract, great flames of green foliage swooning upward. *Promenade among the Olive Trees,* painted in Collioure, is categorized as one of the most important works of his Fauve period, an abstract style he invented alongside André Derain, with trees that are mere splashes of color. Later in his career, he depicted olive trees as reaching trunks with billowing clouds of silver foliage, more like cotton balls than individual leaves.

When British novelist Lawrence Durrell moved to Corfu, he wrote in *Prospero's Cell* that "the entire Mediterranean seems to rise out of the sour, pungent taste of black olives between the teeth. A taste older than meat or wine, a taste as old as cold water. Only the sea itself seems as ancient a part of the region as the olive and its oil, that like no other products of nature, have shaped civilizations from remotest antiquity to the present."[17] More than a hundred years earlier, British poet Lord Byron also forsook England for the Mediterranean, and the olive tree peppers his works. In *The Curse of Minerva,* he writes, "The Olive Branch, which still she deign'd to clasp, / Shrunk from her touch and withered in her grasp,"[18] symbolizing the destruction Britain's Earl of Elgin caused in Greece. In *Don Juan,* the olive tree represents Eden: "There the large olive rains its amber store / In marble fonts; there grain, and flower, and fruit, / Gush from the earth until the land runs o'er."[19] Lord Byron's appreciation of olive trees is reflected in the countless hours he spent meditating under olive trees at the monastery on St. Lazarus island in Venice, a pose so familiar that it is captured in a painting and the trees were renamed the "Olive Trees of Lord Byron." Even in his final days, as he struggled to overthrow the Ottoman Empire in the Greek War of Independence, he was surrounded by olive groves, and one of his last acts before dying was to ride his horse through those trees.

Even those who lived in oliveless climes wrote about this tree, and in Shakespeare's works the olive is a symbol of peace, juxtaposed against violence and standing as a symbol of purity. "The time of universal peace is near: / Prove this a prosperous day, the three nook'd world / Shall bear the olive freely,"[20] Caesar says, expressing his hope for peace in *Antony and Cleopatra*. In *Timon of Athens*, Alcibiades promises, "And I will use the olive with my sword,"[21] reflecting his intention to show both mercy and strength. In *Henry VI*, Clarence says, "Adjudged an olive branch and laurel crown, / As likely to be blest in peace and war;"[22] contrasting the desire for peace (the olive branch) and that for victory (laurel). Shakespeare's frequent use of the olive as a sign of peace solidifies the importance and deep-seated significance of this symbolism during the Renaissance period, further enriched by the olive's longevity, as in the sonnet line, "And peace proclaims olives of endless age."[23]

THE CAPE of Antibes is bookended by Juan-les-Pins and Antibes. Juan-les-Pins is a leafy oasis full of narrow-trunked trees with a canopy that explodes outward like a parasol. In the 1920s, Juan-les-Pins helped grow the jazz movement, and many superstars played here in their early days. Inhabited since 500 BC, Antibes contains the fortifications of bygone eras and is older and more staid than Juan-les-Pins.

"You can feel Italy a little more," Marie-Pierre said as we passed some pale pink and purple buildings, a reminder that Antibes had been Italian up to the early nineteenth century. We pulled into a marina with some of the biggest superyachts in the world, which according to Marie-Pierre were owned by wealthy Arabs. We saw cruise ship–sized yachts with an arsenal of toys—Jet Skis, powerboats, and even a helicopter—but it wasn't until we reached a dilapidated boat held together with plywood, tarps, and duct tape that Marie-Pierre said, "This is my favorite."

"You see the sign?" she said, pointing to a piece of plywood with "*ça me suffit*" spray-painted on it. She translated it for us: "That's enough for me."

Renoir's house was inland, just past Cagnes, on a bucolic country lane, atop a hill with views of the sea and the medieval village of Haut-de-Cagnes. Les Collettes is a 3.5-hectare estate that Renoir lived on for the last eleven years of his life and that inspired more than six hundred of his works. His grandson wrote that Renoir "sought to envelop himself in an aura of peace and tranquility,"[24] which he found in an olive grove. One hundred and forty-eight aged olive trees stood on a grassy field, casting long shadows and an air of eternity, shimmering despite the overcast day. "Look at the light on the olive trees," Renoir once said. "It shines like a diamond... it's pink, it's blue... and the sky that plays across them... it drives you mad!"[25]

It is thanks to Renoir that these five-hundred-year-old olive trees still stand. He bought the property on impulse in 1907, when he heard developers were going to clear the land. Renoir said they were the most beautiful trees he had ever seen and he couldn't bear the thought of their being turned into "napkin rings, paperweights and wooden spoons."[26] He kept the olive grove as a working farm. Each fall, olives were harvested and pressed into oil, while olive-wood prunings stoked the fireplace.

Olive trees inspired Renoir. He painted in the olive grove, in a specially built wooden studio with a corrugated roof and a large window, and called the olive harvest one of his favorite times, in part because he scouted for muses among the village girls who came to pick drupes. He painted the trees, often as backdrops to his portraits, but like Van Gogh, he struggled to capture them.

"The olive tree. What a brute!" Renoir once wrote. "If you realized how much trouble it has caused me. A tree full of colors. Not great at all. How all those little leaves make me sweat! A gust of wind and my tree's tonality changes. The color isn't on its leaves, but in the spaces between them."[27]

Aldous Huxley concurred with Renoir's embellished depiction of the olive tree. "It was not in his nature to be content with a black, white and earth-green olive," Huxley wrote of Renoir's painted olive trees. "His gray trees have shadows of cadmium green, and where they look toward the sun, are suffused with a glow of pink."[28] Huxley was an astute observer and admirer of olive trees. He titled one of his books *The Olive Tree* and in it wrote, "If I could paint and had the necessary time, I should devote myself for a few years to making pictures only of olive trees."[29]

Near Renoir's boxy stone villa and formal garden, designed by his wife, Aline, is a reproduction of Renoir's *Paysage des Collettes* (*Landscape at Collettes*), in which two stately olive trees frame a view of the hillside below. It is placed in the same spot he would have sat to paint it, and my eyes darted from the painting to the view, marking the changes that ninety-seven years had brought. The two olive trees had grown a little; the valley below was still blanketed in olive trees, pines, and wild herbs; and the mountains remained a faint corrugation in the distance. The biggest difference was in the village. Today, Haut-de-Cagnes has grown beyond a watchtower and cluster of red-roofed homes.

Even if the world around Renoir's garden had changed, here time stood still, his gardens and house frozen as he left them. The olive trees echoed this sense of timelessness, their long lives linking generations, connecting the future to the past, and offering a reassuring continuum in a rapidly changing world.

Most things in the French Riviera don't stand still for a century, and soon we were back in the car hurtling toward Monaco with Marie-Pierre, trying to cram a semester's worth of French history into an afternoon. From the idyllic countryside, we whipped past France's second-busiest airport and pebbly beaches, following the waterfront walkway Promenade des Anglais all the way into Nice. France's second-largest seaside city explodes with color, courtesy of its years as an Italian dominion. We drove past fuchsia buildings with yellow trim and blue shutters and through a central square checkered with gray and white stones like a giant chessboard, while Marie-Pierre rattled off obscure facts and stories.

"Look at the shutters," she said, pointing to a colorful building. "See how they open from the bottom; nowhere else are they like that." The shutters were divided into thirds, and the bottom flap hinged outward to let in air. When we passed Le Negresco, France's last private luxury hotel, Marie-Pierre said, "They tried to buy it many times, but Madame Augier left it to her staff." It was palatial and would have sold for a hefty sum, but instead the octogenarian owner created an endowment to ensure that her "260 colleagues are not sacrificed on the altar of profit"[30] when she died.

We went as far east as Monaco, spiraling upward to its medieval center, home to the Prince's Palace and the hundred-year-old oceanographic museum. You needed a special pass to drive here, which Marie-Pierre had, and the guards monitored the vehicles, ensuring that they kept to the proper roads and didn't stop. Monaco's constitutional monarchy governs from here, but it wasn't until we crossed the harbor to Monte Carlo that we saw where the real power lies. Its gilded casino propelled the world's second-smallest country from bankruptcy to haven for the rich, with more millionaires per capita than anywhere else in the world. And olive oil played a small but important role in that success.

In the past, most of Monaco's tax revenue came from agriculture, mainly olive oil and fruit, and went into Grimaldi family coffers. The Grimaldis had ruled Monaco since the eleventh century, when François Grimaldi, a Genoese leader, captured the Rock of Monaco. It was, according to Marie-Pierre, "a country founded by crooks," and without blue blood until Hanover royalty married into the family in 1999. In the mid-nineteenth century, farmers stopped paying taxes to the Grimaldis, and two towns broke away and were annexed by France. The ruling family lost 95 percent of its country and was on the brink of bankruptcy. To stave off disaster, the prince's wife, Princess Caroline, built Monaco's first casino, Monte Carlo Casino.

We paused in front of the opulent building, bejewelled with lights, fountains, and palm trees, a regal version of Las Vegas, and briefly contemplated spinning the roulette wheel or pulling a slot machine handle. But we decided it was too late and returned to Cannes, where Marie-Pierre offered to make dinner for us.

Marie-Pierre's apartment is in a restored nineteenth-century building with a manicured courtyard and marble entrance. Art—hers and others'—covers the walls, and there are books piled everywhere. It is a toddler's utopia, and Leif, who was well rested after napping for most of the drive, crawled everywhere, exploring rooms and yanking doors open.

"He's such a good baby," Marie-Pierre cooed as he threw her shoes across the floor. I looked at her for a hint of sarcasm, but she was serious. "So happy to play by himself and so imaginative."

We nibbled on toasted bread with anchovies and sautéed onions, which Leif also enjoyed. Even though he didn't eat much, I was happily surprised at what he did like and hoped that it was a sign of good things to come—at the least an adventurous palate and at the best a free-thinking mind. Leif ate several pieces of anchovy-laden toast, and Marie-Pierre beamed once again. "He is a Provençal boy."

For dinner we ate cod poached in a creamy wine sauce with delicate undertones of ginger and Asian spices, pureed celery root, and roasted vegetables, and for dessert lemon tart with braised peaches. Marie-Pierre brushed off our praise saying, "It is nothing," before shyly pulling out a scrapbook containing an article praising her as one of the top one hundred chefs in the world. "I am not a chef," she said, "but I used to own a lodge and I made the meals there."

She was full of surprises, and with a few questions we teased out the troubled past that fostered her culinary talents. The lodge had been a hunting retreat that her father rented, but one year he was accidentally shot and killed. Afterward, her mother bought the lodge, and eventually, Marie-Pierre took over and transformed it into a retreat. Stories like this kept us riveted, and it was nearly midnight by the time we left. Leif was fast asleep, and we said good-bye with lots of hugs and promises to stay in touch. Marie-Pierre said we convinced her to embark on a round-the-world trip that she had been planning for decades, and a few months later she would e-mail to say she had started and was in Australia.

"THE MEDITERRANEAN is a dangerous sea," William warned as we readied our boat, nestled next to his in the Cannes marina. The winds blew at force 4 and swirled into the marina, jostling our boat and making the halyards scream like shrieking owls.

We said good-bye and motored out of the marina until there was space to unfurl the mainsail and foresail. The wind inflated our sails and we screamed along. It was a beautiful day, bright and sunny, and as I adjusted the sails, I realized how comfortable I was at the helm. Gone were the moments of trepidation, when my stomach lurched as the wind gusted or the boat heeled. I was still acutely aware of each of these details, but they were no longer dark shadows to fear.

We planned on sailing to Villefranche, a small village near Nice where the day before we had drunk tea in a waterfront café with Marie-Pierre. I had instantly fallen in love with its mazelike streets and storybook buildings. Its sheltered harbor was one of the deepest natural bays in the Mediterranean, making it popular with large boats, including those of the U.S. Navy, which was stationed here for nearly two decades following World War II. Like all of Europe, every building had a story, and when Marie-Pierre told us about Mère Germaine, I was determined to return to the restaurant for a belated celebration of our anniversary, which we had spent scrubbing the boat. It was an excellent seafood restaurant, Marie-Pierre said, but more enticing was the story of "Mom Germaine." The original owner, she treated the troops stationed here during the war as her boys, earning her the nickname, an official honor from the U.S. Navy, and a feature role in a film and book.

"At this speed, we should be there in four hours," Colin shouted over the wind. Villefranche was only twenty-five kilometers away, a comfortable afternoon sailing if the winds remained. "I'm going to pull in the foresail. Can you turn the autopilot on?"

I took Leif inside the cabin and shouted, "It's on," after flipping the appropriate switch. Then I scanned through the radio stations until I found one that was clear. It was blasting the pop music Europeans seem to love so much. Leif bounced enthusiastically and I sang "Moves Like Jagger," which, despite my best intentions, I seemed to know quite well.

"It's broken," Colin yelled, interrupting our party. I turned down the music. "The motor's churning, but it's not doing anything."

Without an autopilot, it would be challenging if not impossible to sail solo, and Villefranche was too small to have much of a chandlery, if any. We were a few kilometers from Antibes, Europe's biggest marina, and decided to pull in there instead. It housed 1,700 boats and megayachts that stretched to 165 meters, but when I went to the *capitainerie*, the harbormaster said they had no room. I stressed the small size of our vessel and our mechanical plight, and he spent what felt like an eternity flipping through computer screens before finally announcing that he'd found a spot.

The stores were closed by the time we walked downtown, but the following morning we took our autopilot to the nearest marine electronic store. A tall dark-haired man with a football player's physique unfolded himself from his chair and greeted us. He looked vaguely familiar, but I couldn't quite place him.

"Are you Philippe's son?" I asked, suddenly remembering that the French chef we met in Provence had said he had a son who worked in the yacht industry in Antibes.

He looked startled. "Who are you?"

Alexis laughed when I explained our connection and immediately began examining our autopilot. After several minutes, he deduced it was beyond repair and suggested we get a new one. Since it would not arrive until the next day, we had a chance to explore one of France's oldest towns.

The Phocaean Greeks founded Antibes in the fifth century BC. Under the Roman Empire, it became the region's largest city before it dwindled under the attack of Ostrogoths and Visigoths in the Middle Ages. It was an important port city, and Phoenicians had traveled here in their galleys, trading olive oil, wine, and other goods with the inhabitants.

An imposing twelfth-century wall had protected the town from maritime invaders, but it did nothing to stop the recent flood of English invaders. Places like the Colonial Pub, the Irish Pub, Beer n' Curry, and Geoffrey's of London jostled against stone buildings, making this town more un-French than any others we'd been to. But it retains its archetypal love of art and history.

The Picasso museum is housed in a heavily fortified castle that Picasso once lived in, and crammed with ceramics, sketches, and paintings, it is one of the most complete collections in the world for any given period of his life. I wasn't that enamoured of the paintings of dancing goats and stick figures with oversized genitals, but the museum of archaeology was another story. Also housed in an ancient fortification, it was full of amphorae, oil lamps, and perfume bottles that offered an insight into the early trade in olive oil.

"What did they carry?" I asked, gesturing to a wall lined with amphorae.

"Wine, olive oil, fish sauce," said a dark-haired woman with fiery red fingernails who was leading a school group. She pointed to an amphora elongated like a missile. "You can tell what they carried by their shape." There were slight and not-so-slight differences in size and shape, some bases were flat and others rounded, and the spouts were different, as were the handles—some were rounder, others flatter. "That is also how you know where they came from—Africa, Greece, Spain."

"Are any of them Phoenician?" Colin asked.

"Yes, I believe so. The oldest are 2,200 years old," she said.

"And would those old ones have carried olive oil?" I asked.

"Olive oil was one of the earliest traded goods, so it's likely. But if you are interested in olive oil, you must also see the lamps and perfume bottles we have in the other room."

The lamps ranged from simple shapes in terra-cotta to ornate iron works with intricate carved figurines. All that was needed was a vessel to hold the oil and a place for the wick, and the rest depended on the era, the civilization, and the prosperity of the owner. The one thing they had in common was olive oil, which has been the main fuel for lamps for much of the last three millennia. The perfume bottles were equally diverse and also united by olive oil, which has been a common perfume base since the Egyptians first created perfumed oils, originally for rituals and then for use in the broader community.

"I'm glad we ended up in Antibes," Colin said as we ambled back to the boat.

"I couldn't imagine a better place to break down," I agreed.

The following day when Alexis handed us our new autopilot, I was once again reminded of how lucky we were that our malfunction had occurred in front of Europe's largest marina. Now it was time to leave the mainland and begin the overnight sail to France's largest island, Corsica—a place that still sporadically sheds blood over its desire to separate from France—which is home to an abundance of wild olive trees and has an ancient megalithic site nestled in an olive grove.

7

ANCIENT CIVILIZATIONS, ANCIENT OIL

"Pass then through this little space of time conformably to nature, and end thy journey in content, just as an olive falls off when it is ripe, blessing nature who produced it, and thanking the tree on which it grew."

MARCUS AURELIUS, ROMAN EMPEROR (161–180 AD)[1]

GIROLATA'S STEEP ocher cliffs are dusted with wild herbs, shrubs, and olive trees. A Genoese watchtower crowns one of the cliffs, and stone homes cling to the mountainside, a fishing village frozen in time. On either side, reddish mountaintops, like flocks of rooster combs, plummet into the sea, and spires of granite erupt near the shore like frozen geysers. It was this wild, fiery landscape that inspired some of the scenes in Dante's *Inferno*. The only ways to get here are either by sea or a ninety-minute trek along a goat trail.

A young man in a Zodiac shot toward us as we entered the harbor and beckoned us to an empty buoy. I climbed onto the bow, carrying Leif with one arm, and readied the lines that would secure us to the buoy. Colin maneuvered the boat, squeezing through a narrow gap between a sailboat and the shore and gliding over translucent waters that made them seem shallower than they were.

"You can stop," I said when we had slipped past the empty buoy. The woman in the sailboat ahead of me looked up and squinted into the sunlight as we approached.

"*Stop!*" I shouted as we continued toward the yacht. I leaned off the bow and stretched my foot out. Fortunately, my foot offered enough resistance to push off the other boat and prevent our hulls from touching.

"I'm so sorry," I said, embarrassed and shocked at what had just happened. "Our boats didn't touch," I added as I leaned over to examine the spot where I'd put my foot to ensure the boat wasn't scuffed.

"The engine wouldn't go into reverse," Colin explained when I returned to the cockpit and he'd turned off the engine.

We'd just finished a thirty-hour crossing from France, and besides being exhausted, we were worried about our motor once again. Two-thirds of the way into our crossing, the motor's gearbox had started slipping, making it difficult to start the engine, and Colin had jerry-rigged a system that held us until we reached land.

"Madame, Monsieur," the French couple yelled, waving from their cockpit. I cringed, expecting a rebuke, but instead the man said, "We have an engine mechanic with us; he can help you."

In the end, we didn't need their help, and Colin fixed the engine within the hour. After rowing ashore and registering at the thatch-roofed hut, we followed a stony trail that led from the beach past a cluster of houses that was the town and into Scandola Nature Reserve. Rosemary, juniper, sage, wild olives, oaks, and wildflowers engulfed the cliffside trail. Herbaceous scents flourished in the hot afternoon sun and mingled with a fresh ocean breeze, making it clear why Corsica is nicknamed "the scented isle." This scrubland, known as maquis, gave Corsica's olive oil, as well as its honey and wine, a distinctive taste, its terroir.

Wild olive trees have grown on Corsica since the last ice age and have been harvested for millennia, or at least since the Phoenicians set up their colonies. The civilizations that followed—Etruscans, Carthaginians, Greeks, and Romans—were all avid growers and consumers of olives and olive oil. Olive trees were not as abundant then as they are now, and when the Roman philosopher Seneca was exiled to the island, he lamented that it was a bleak, savage desert, where "no winter-olive grows."[2] Although it is not true that Corsica was barren of olive trees during Roman times, it wasn't until the 1600s that olive groves flourished. Genoese rulers ordered farmers to plant olive trees; by 1820, 12 million trees covered the land, and nineteenth-century travel writers remarked on the abundance of olive trees. Now the island is dominated by three main olive cultivars: Picholine, a squat olive originally from France; Germaine, also found in northern Italy; and Sabina, pretty much exclusive to Corsica.

Corsica is also blanketed with "wild" olive trees, but most of these are feral, cultivars that spread from their original orchards, or wild trees interbred with domestic variants. An island offered more segregation than the mainland, but it was like throwing groups of purebred dogs onto an island; after a few generations, they'd all be mongrels unless one breed was isolated from the others. Geographical isolation was the only thing that could accomplish that, and it was only in remote and inaccessible places, like this rocky outcrop, that we could hope to find a truly wild olive tree.

We undulated with the trail, speeding downward and trudging back up. Leif crawled at a flattish section, while Colin bushwhacked to sample a spindly oleaster that towered over the neighboring oaks. Exhausted after our sleepless night, we collected a few more samples and returned to our boat. We'd barely slept in the last forty-eight hours, and even though it wasn't yet dark, I yearned to fall into bed. I looked at the boats around us and suspected the anchorage would be quiet enough for that. It didn't look like the party atmosphere we had occasionally encountered on the French Riviera.

Despite being a part of France, Corsica felt a world apart, and glancing at the flags hanging from the boat masts, you'd be forgiven for thinking you were in a different country. Ours was the only boat flying a French courtesy flag; all the others displayed the *tête de Maure*, a Moor's face with a white bandana, and we would have too had we been able to find the flag in Girolata. Even though Corsicans have their own language, which is more like Latin and Italian than French, and geographically they are closer to Italy than France, Corsica has never been independent, except for a brief stint in the eighteenth century. It isn't for lack of trying, and the most recent movement, spearheaded by the National Liberation Front of Corsica, grabbed headlines by bombing hotels, public buildings, and banks in major cities throughout mainland France and Corsica beginning in the 1970s. Today, support for the extremists has waned, but most people still see themselves as Corsicans first and French second or not at all.

In the morning, we began our sail down Corsica's rugged western edge and our search for patches of remoteness promising truly wild olives. In Cargèse, a hilltop village settled by Greeks three hundred years ago, we anchored next to a sailboat skippered by a naked man and trekked up a road sandwiched between olive trees, sugarcane, and prickly pears laden with fermenting fruit. The town was full of olive trees, growing like palm trees in Florida—some as landscape features in gardens, others stuffed into backyard gardens. Men rolled Boules balls on a stone patio, and skinny cats flitted through long grass in ragged fields. Two nineteenth-century churches faced each other like gunslingers in a showdown—both Catholic and built by descendants of Greek colonists, but one was Greek Orthodox, the other Roman Catholic. At the Roman Catholic church, I plucked an olive from the stocky tree; it was black and pockmarked, and inside I could see the larvae of the olive fly, burrowing and destroying the olive from the inside.

Our search for Corsican olive oil took us through town, a charming place full of brightly colored flowers and shops selling books, clothing, and fresh bread. In a ramshackle house advertising Corsican foods, a man with long hair and flowing clothes gave us a sample of his olive spread, little more than chopped black olives in olive oil. It tasted like a coarse tapenade but bland.

"Is this Corsican olive oil?" I asked, after biting into the bread.

"I make it myself," he said, pointing to the gallon jugs of Greek olive oil and giant cans of Greek black olives behind him. Not the Corsican oil we were searching for.

We continued southward, across Ajaccio canyon and past Ajaccio, tucked into its craggy armpit—Corsica's capital and Napoleon Bonaparte's birthplace. Steep cliffs eased into rounded mountains, and foothills rose to the towering range that pierces the island's center. Turquoise waters and honey-colored beaches with sand fine enough for an hourglass gave the island a tropical feel. After anchoring in the gentle swell of one of these oases, we whiled the evening away onshore, picnicking on green bean salad, tuna, bread, and wine and searching for wild olive trees.

Olive trees rarely grow near sandy beaches, but here we spotted a spindly olive growing just above the high-tide mark. Later, we would learn that it is rare to find olive trees growing so close to the ocean and that these trees are of great interest to researchers. Olive trees growing near the ocean may have adapted to use saltier water, and those trees could help reclaim vast tracts of land that can't be farmed because of high salinity often caused by irrigation or agricultural practices. The olive orchards would help draw salt out of the soil, returning it to an equilibrium that is hospitable to other vegetation. Researchers are working to develop salt-loving olive cultivars, and finding one in the wild would be a huge advantage.

On our third day after leaving Girolata, we neared Corsica's southern tip and cut into a river estuary to the Figaria marina. It was flat and marshy, a typical delta, and lacked the stark beauty we'd come to associate with Corsica. But its location and price made it an ideal place to moor our boat while we explored the island.

"I heard this is a popular place to overwinter," I said as we slipped past a pier of rental catamarans.

"It looks more like a sailboat graveyard," Colin said, pointing to a sailboat that had torn free of its anchor and lay on the shore like a beached whale.

Other boats, not quite as bedraggled, were anchored in the shallow waters. We tied up in the modest marina, where the only other overnight guests were a glum Austrian couple and a quintet of drunken Poles.

The tiny town—with little more than a cemetery, church, and bakery—was a two-kilometer hike up a mountain of cork oaks, olive trees, small red-berried shrubs called mastics, and otherworldly rock formations. House-sized boulders, shaped like giant marbles, were scattered through the forest, and it looked as though a sculptor had chiseled faces into the cliff—a natural Mount Rushmore. That night we ate onion tarts, quiche, and olive bread in the bakery, and the next morning Colin ran ten kilometers to the airport to pick up our rental car, a tiny two-door Renault Twingo hatchback.

Our search for ancient and wild olive trees would take us around the island in a clockwise direction, and eventually we'd circle the Mediterranean's fourth-largest island. Beginning on the west side, we retraced our maritime route, carving along tortured mountain roads overlooking the waters we'd sailed. At Sartène, a somber village of fortresses and ruined castles, we asked our waiter if he knew where we could find locally made olive oil.

"*Non,*" he said as he set our pizza and salad down. Then, after a pause, he added, "Maybe in the north."

"*Merci bo-o-coop,*" Colin said.

The man gave us a bemused smile. "It's not *merci bo-o-coop*, but *merci beaucoup.*"

"*Merci bo-o-coop,*" Colin repeated with a French accent.

"*Non, non. Merci beaucoup.*"

"*Merci booo-oo-coop,*" Colin said and shrugged his shoulders apologetically.

"You are saying nice..." The waiter turned around and pointed to his backside. "Nice ass."

We laughed and wondered if he was playing with us. After the meal we said "nice ass" and continued on to Filitosa, an ancient town nestled in an olive grove.

If you're looking for old olive trees, it makes sense to start with the oldest signs of civilization, and in Corsica that is the megaliths. The island has been inhabited for nine thousand years, and its early dwellers erected giant carved stones called menhirs that sit in the ground like a randomly arranged Stonehenge. One of the best collections is in southwestern Corsica, a few kilometers inland on a quiet farm road.

Vendors at outdoor tables were selling clay mini-menhirs and olive-wood spoons, but we headed straight for the entrance. Most of the museum was outdoors, but there was a dimly lit building filled with flint arrowheads, stone pendants, and clay vases in glass display cases. Evidence of the people's livelihood implied that the inhabitants herded sheep, fished, and gathered edibles from the wild. I wondered if that included olives.

In an airy forest of ferns and wild olive trees, dozens of menhirs—shoulder-height statues carved with faces—sat like giant Pez dispensers. No one knows with certainty why they were created. Perhaps they were a way to seek dominion over their enemies or talismans to bring good weather for their crops. The ancient megalith religion faded by the first millennium BC, and all we have is their remnants to provide us with clues. Relics of stone houses outlined the dwelling's form like a blueprint, and a curved boulder in the shape of a giant question mark provided more primitive shelter. On the other side of the hill lay a lush valley with grazing cattle and more olive trees.

"This tree is supposed to be two thousand years old," I said as we approached an impressive olive tree surrounded by an arc of menhirs.

"I wonder who planted it."

"Maybe the Romans," I offered. Romans started coming to Corsica in 250 BC, and if the tree was two thousand years old, that would have been during their heyday.

"It'll be interesting to get the DNA analysis for this tree," Colin said as he searched for a suitable twig. "The Phoenicians could have planted it. Who knows how old it is."

Wild olive trees disappeared from Corsica during the last major ice age, but as temperatures warmed, they returned, recolonized from areas that remained warm enough to support the olive tree. Only a few regions were able to offer refuge to the olive during these frigid times, and some speculate that olive stones or pollen were brought from Sicily, where temperatures were less hostile. Sea levels were lower at that time, and it is likely the olive would have spread via the nearby island of Sardinia. Whether these trees were then domesticated is disputed, and some have suggested that the trees were independently domesticated here five thousand years ago. It is more likely that when traders arrived, they brought olive stones or saplings with them. These trees would then have crossbred with local trees, leading to increased diversity.

In Filitosa we had seen one of Corsica's oldest olive trees, but I hoped we would find more giants in the olive-dense regions of Balagne in northern Corsica. But by nightfall we were still an hour away from Balagne, the tortuous mountainous roads amplifying the 180 kilometers that separated Corsica's north and south. To escape the coastal route, we turned onto the N193, a highway that angles through the island's deeply forested and mountainous interior. Besides being more direct, it highlighted just how underpopulated Corsica is. There were few towns and fewer people. With only 300,000 inhabitants, the island has one-quarter the population density of the rest of France.

"Maybe we should just camp," I said as the sky darkened and Leif fell asleep. "It doesn't look like we'd have any trouble finding a quiet spot."

At a bus stop spray-painted with *"per l'Indipendenza,"* Corsican for "independence" and one of the common catchphrases we saw graffitied elsewhere, we turned onto a dirt track and wound our way through dense forest down the mountain. On the other side of a river, a signpost marked the start of a trail and a widening in the road that was just large enough for our tent.

"Do you think it's safe?" I said. It was dark and we were in a remote spot, and I felt a twinge of uncertainty. "I mean, there are extremists on the island. Maybe they don't appreciate rogue campers."

Colin walked around for a quick reconnaissance of the area and concluded, "It looks good."

We pitched our tent, inflated our Therm-a-Rests, and rolled out our sleeping bags. The chill of the mountain air and the absence of the ocean's tempering effect made it colder than any night we'd experienced so far, and I hoped Leif would be warm enough. We tucked him between us so that our body heat would keep him warm.

The night was eternal, and in the morning I said, "Sleeping with Leif is like being next to an alarm clock that goes off every fifteen minutes."

"Did he get up a lot?" Colin asked innocently, having slept through all of Leif's nursings and wakings. I watched Leif crawl around the tent exploring corners and gurgling contentedly while Colin rolled up his air mattress. Both of them looked rested and happy. I pulled my sleeping bag up around my shoulders. "I feel like I could sleep for days," I said.

"THERE IS NO district throughout the whole of Italy where the olive attains such a size as it does in the Balagna,"[3] writes the nineteenth-century traveler Ferdinand Gregorovius. Known as the "orchard of Corsica," Balagna has seen a resurgence in olive cultivation, and there are several orchards where inky black olives are picked and pressed into an oil that is known for its unique flavor, a mild herbaceous taste attributed to the marquis and the ripeness of the olives. But the olive trees we were searching for didn't grow in these orchards; we were looking for ancient wild trees.

Our hunt began at Saleccia Park, a three-hectare private garden with dozens of olive trees amidst cypresses and rhododendrons. It had once been an ancient olive grove, but nearly forty years earlier, a fire had ravaged the land, leaving only five olive trees, which we discovered were out of sight, in a private part of the garden. Disappointed and overwhelmed by the heat, we trudged back to the refreshment stand and a grassy kids' play area at the entrance. I bought some drinks and asked the auburn-haired woman who served me about old olive trees.

"I do not know, but I will ask," she said, handing me two pops and a milk.

She translated my question to another woman, who knew where we could find the oldest olive tree in Corsica and drew us a map to the nearby location. As for wild olives, she explained that many people picked wild olives and pressed their own oil. Their coworker did this, and if we came back tomorrow, we could talk to him.

I thanked them, and the auburn-haired woman smiled with a slight hesitation, as though she was contemplating telling me something else. "You may find it hard to find people to talk to," she said. "We Corsicans are..." She paused, searching for the right word. "We keep to ourselves, but you have to keep trying."

Her directions led to L'Île-Rousse, an ancient seaside town shaded by plane trees and date palms. We ate lunch on a park bench and then continued on roads so narrow and dusty they could have been goat trails. The road spiraled upward. We passed crumbling mausoleums and ancient stone houses, and gazed down at a forested valley that dipped to the ocean with hawks circling on updrafts above it. Near the top, we passed a handful of tiny communities and groves of ancient olive trees, wrinkled like wizened old men and carefully tended.

Caleri was an empty hamlet perched on a hillside; old mill-stones lay against stone houses, and lavender flowers cascaded from window boxes. As in the rest of Corsica, the homes were fortified, with small windows crisscrossed with wrought-iron bars, heavy wooden doors, and gated courtyards. It was a reminder of the fury of Corsica's vendetta, revenge killings and lawlessness that had killed 350,000 Corsicans since the fourteenth century—more people than the current population of Corsica. "The law cannot protect the individual,"[4] a nineteenth-century traveler wrote of Corsica. Europe had reined in its lawlessness, but in Corsica, "everyone carries his double-barrelled gun and I have found half [the] village in arms."[5]

The ancient olive tree was supposed to be here, but where? We strolled throughout the town looking for someone to ask, but no one was there. There were two shops in town, a pottery store and a post office, but both were closed for lunch. The church was empty. Finally, we spotted a gray-haired man with a bronzed face and eyebrows as bushy as a squirrel's tail leaning out of his second-story window.

"S'il vous plait," I shouted. *"Ou se trouve l'olivier de trois mille ans dans le village de Cateri?"*

He shrugged with incomprehension and inched down to meet us, eventually concluding that we made no more sense up close and focusing his attentions on Leif instead.

There were olive trees everywhere, on the hillside flanking the town and leaning against crumbling backyard fences, and most looked old, with arthritic branches and pockmarked trunks. But which was the oldest tree? And would we recognize it? On the outskirts of town, a fit couple in their sixties strode toward us, and when we asked about the tree, they pointed up the hill. "You'll know when you see it."

It was perhaps the biggest olive tree we'd yet seen. A mountain of roots bulged out of the earth like a pile of boulders, and two trunks spread outward in a V formation, one larger than the other and both topped with thick silver-green foliage shaped like a mushroom cap. The tree sat in the fenced front yard of somebody's house, but besides a leashed-up dog, no one was home. Did we dare hop a fence and steal olives in the land of the vendetta? In the past, a person could get killed for such an indiscretion, but we'd come too far not to return with a sample, and a coin toss relegated the task to Colin.

Our drive back took us through ancient olive groves, and in one orchard, we saw a handwritten sign advertising olive oil for sale.

"We have to try it," I said. "It's the first Corsican olive oil we've seen."

We backtracked to a pale plaster house that doubled as a pizzeria in the summer. Antique olive presses and millstones sat in the front yard, and there was an oversized garage near the back. A woman with black-rimmed glasses and a gray bob led us through a disheveled garage crowded with tools, bottles, and olive-pressing equipment to the back, where three shiny metal vats sat. She poured olive oil into a one-liter glass bottle, wrapped it in newspaper, and handed it to me. This was oil from the millennium trees that blanketed this region, pressed in this garage, and made for locals. I couldn't wait to try it.

As soon as we returned to the car, I took a swig. It was strong and pungent and tasted of overripe olives. It reminded me of the oil we had tried in Château Virant, not the award-winning varieties but the fruity black style they pressed only on request for the locals, oil that was made from ripe olives that had sat for days before being pressed, growing moldy and fermenting. Colin didn't share my strong dislike, and concluded, "It's not that bad, and with food it wouldn't be so strong."

Again, I wondered if this is what olive oil used to taste like. In many ways, Corsica was an island frozen in time, and I suspected the olive oil was, too. The traditional olive press, stone grindstones, and clay jars had become museum pieces, replaced by stainless steel, but the process was unchanged. In many places, olives were picked when they fell, and there was no rush to press them. The people followed tradition, creating an oil that satisfied an age-old palate. Or did it?

More than two thousand years ago, Romans had strong opinions about how olive oil should and shouldn't be made. In 160 BC, Cato the Elder wrote, "When the olives are ripe they should be gathered as soon as possible, and allowed to remain on the ground or the floor as short a time as possible, as they spoil on the ground or the floor."[6] He acknowledged that this was not the easiest method and that the farmer would face resistance. "The gatherers want to have as many windfalls as possible, that there may be more of them to gather; and the pressers want them to lie on the floor a long time, so that they will soften and be easier to mill."[7] But that would not lead to the best oil, and he stressed, "olives which have been long on the ground or the floor will yield less oil and of a poorer quality the olive."[8]

Our route back followed the east coast, flat and populated with mobile pizzerias. Despite stopping only twice, once for dinner and another time to pick wild figs, we didn't return to the boat until 10:30 PM, and twelve hours later, we left for Sardinia. By late afternoon, we were inching into force 5 headwinds along the southern coast, Sardinia still a vague outline in the distance. Colin dropped the sails and revved the motor, but we barely crept forward. Leif and I braced ourselves in the cabin's V-berth, bouncing up and down as waves charged past us. I couldn't leave Leif alone, and Colin had no choice but to deal with the challenging seas alone.

"There was a point where I wasn't sure we'd be able to make it," he said after we rounded a cape and pulled into a sheltered fjord where we'd anchor. "We'll have to leave early tomorrow before the winds build."

As the sun rose, we ghosted past Bonifacio, the ancient city where giant cannibals destroyed Homer's ships. It towered above us like an impenetrable fortress, a jumble of narrow medieval apartments, with tiny windows in shades of beige, like the limestone promontory they sat on, a legacy of turbulent times, when the sea didn't bring tourists in sailboats but raiders and pirates.

A shiver of apprehension came over me as we inched away from Corsica, the westerly wind filling our sails and the morning haze burning off. The crossing to Sardinia wasn't as long as crossing the Gulf of Lion or reaching Corsica, but winds funneled through the twenty-kilometer passage, making it much more dangerous than an open crossing.

The day before, we had tested *Isis*'s limits. The distance we intended to cover today was much greater, and there were no safe anchorages to duck into. If the winds overpowered us, we might be blown past the islands and have to make landfall somewhere else.

Sardinia's northern tip, the Emerald Coast, or Costa Smeralda in Italian, is separated from Corsica by twelve kilometers of islet-dotted waters. Colin and I took turns at the sails, watching the "mountain in the sea" fade away. The ridges of the sheer limestone cliff blurred and became indistinguishable from the rock that was Corsica. The wind blew briskly but not overpoweringly, and we made steady progress. By late afternoon, we had reached the archipelago of islands that lay between France and Italy, and the biggest crossing was behind us. From here, we could skirt the dozens of tiny islands and islets, seeking their leeward side, and safely make our way to Sardinia. The islands, La Maddalena archipelago, are little more than bare granite mountains etched with green maquis and white sandy beaches—stunning parkland that is Sardinia's best sailing ground.

"I can't believe we're missing this," Colin said as we sat in the cockpit, sails full and lines drawn tight as a cello string. "This is the last good sailing we're going to have on this trip."

"What about the south, near the Phoenician ruins of Nora?" I said.

"It's nothing like this. The whole way down is mountainous and exposed, and there are few islands in the south."

I knew Colin was right, but I loathed admitting it. "Maybe in Malta," I tried.

Leif rolled the winch handle on the floor of the cockpit, oblivious to the tension building between us.

"That'll just be a long crossing. We probably won't even have time to cruise."

"Well, if you wanted to stop here, you should have said something," I said a little too brusquely.

Colin bristled and turned his gaze to the sail, and I stewed. I had pushed for a brisk pace through Sardinia to make up for earlier delays, but it was more than that. After months of indecision, we had decided that it was too dangerous to travel to Syria. Since it had joined the Arab Spring, months before our departure, the violence had escalated and the hope that President Assad would quickly step down, as the rulers in Tunisia and Egypt had, was fading.

Syria's port town of Latakia, where we once imagined arriving, was thick with gunboats and weapon shipments from Russia, and the country was in turmoil. Thousands of innocent people had been killed, villages burned to the ground, families slaughtered by machetes, peaceful protesters shot dead by snipers, and children tortured, their dead bodies returned to intimidate dissidents.

We were disheartened at not being able to return to my family's olive farm, the place that inspired this journey, but above all we were worried, for the Syrian people and for my aunts, uncles, and cousins. Most of my family lived in Aleppo, Syria's largest city, which thankfully was not yet one of the hardest-hit areas.

But the violence was escalating. A bomb had exploded near my aunt's apartment, and armed guards patrolled the streets. Heating fuel was in short supply, and roving blackouts and water shortages were commonplace. There were checkpoints everywhere, and travel was dangerous. My family struggled to reach their olive groves, and other olive groves had been burned to the ground in murderous violence.

Even if we wanted to go to Syria, I doubted we could. Foreign journalists were banned, and a journalist with Canadian citizenship had been held hostage for weeks. I doubted writers would be viewed much differently. I might be able to use my Syrian citizenship—automatically conferred on children of Syrian fathers—to ease our way into the country, but that might subject us to additional scrutiny and risk.

Instead, we decided to travel to Syria's neighbors, Palestine and Israel. We would sail as far as we could before the winter storms set in and then travel the rest of the way overland. This way, we could still visit the key places on our itinerary and culminate the journey at the birthplace of the domesticated olive.

"I'm sorry," I said, watching Colin deftly adjust the sails. "It's just that I'm worried."

"I am, too," Colin said, leaning down to give me a quick kiss. "But there's nothing we can do."

I tried to push my worries away and focus on our beautiful surroundings. The islands were striking, but so was Sardinia's northern coast. Mountains of pink granite laced with verdant marquis gave way to wide bays of pale sand and an occasional swath of holiday homes. Once wild and unpopulated, this fifty-five-kilometer stretch of coastline is now one of the ritziest places in the world, where a night in a hotel room can cost more than most people make in a month and spotting Hollywood's A-list is as easy as fishing a stocked pond. In the 1950s, Karim

Aga Khan IV, a wealthy prince and the spiritual leader of 15 million Ismaili Muslims, came here by yacht and, after falling in love with this stretch of coastline, bought it along with a group of investors, branded it Costa Smeralda, and created an oasis for the uber-rich.

"We can stay an extra day here," I said. "But there are no ferries running on the weekend. We'll have to wait until Monday to go to Rome."

"No, we should continue. Besides, we've already passed the best places," Colin said as we squeezed between an island and a white lighthouse on a promontory. "Porto Cervo is on the other side of this headland."

Porto Cervo marked the eastern edge of the Emerald Coast and the end of gentle sailing. From here, the coastline was an "unbroken chain of impassable mountains," as the Greek geographer Pausanias wrote two thousand years ago. He warned, "You will find no anchorage on this side of the island, while violent but irregular gusts of wind sweep down to the sea from the tops of the mountains."[9]

After Cape Figari, a wall of rock that juts out like a swordfish's dorsal fin, we turned into a long, narrow inlet lined with marshland and shipping yards. Olbia was at its base, a bustling city of fifty thousand that was a key Phoenician port and is now one of the island's main ferry hubs. Navigating by our pilot chart, we skirted oyster farms and passed the two behemoth ferries berthed at the terminal, including the one we'd catch to mainland Italy that night.

At Marina di Olbia, a tanned man in khakis led us to an empty dock that gleamed like freshly polished hardwood floors without a footprint or stray hose in sight. The marina was new and immaculately maintained. Walkways of pale stone, islands of golf-course grass, and clusters of tidy shrubs led to a simple outdoor café. A security booth guarded the entrance.

"These cleats are made of stainless steel," Colin said, pointing to the T-shaped hook we'd tie our boat to. "I've never seen that—do you know how much that would cost?"

"I hope the rate they gave us wasn't a mistake," I said, recalling that I'd read just tying up to a buoy can cost $100.

Of the few boats in the marina, we were by far the humblest, and the stately stone and glass office did nothing to alleviate our concern. We planned to stay here for a week while we traveled to Rome and Perugia, but the way things looked, I doubted we'd be able to afford a day.

"I guess that's the benefit of sailing in the off-season," Colin said after we left the office and had paid one of the cheapest moorage rates yet on our journey.

It was October 1, long past the heady months of July and August, when just getting a slip was challenging, irrespective of the cost. We'd heard of Italian marinas turning away modest yachts, not because they were full, but because they were holding out for wealthier customers. A French sailor had cautioned us, "In Italy only the rich sail," but so far, Italy was nothing but hospitable.

The marina was an oasis of quiet, with marble bathrooms and hot showers. After our eleven-hour sail, all I wanted to do was lounge in our cockpit and relax with a glass of wine. Instead, we inhaled pesto noodles, packed hastily, and waited for our taxi, a late-model black Mercedes with leather seats and a gray-haired driver who whisked us through the suburbs and onto a sleek highway to the ferry terminal.

Fluorescent lights flooded the terminal, which pulsed with activity like a miniature version of New York's Grand Central Station. We wormed our way through the crowd to collect our prepaid tickets and found our ship, looking as tired as it was colossal, with fading paint and rust dripping from its windows. We were ushered into a lounge with all the appeal of a tired seniors' center. Passengers were draped over worn couches, families on blankets checkered the floor, and television sets blared Italian reality shows. I couldn't imagine anyone being able to sleep here.

"There must be somewhere else," Colin said hopefully.

I shook my head, only now realizing that the basic tickets I had purchased did not include a seat. We squeezed between two ample women on a sagging couch. Leif explored our neighbors' shoes and purses, and they greeted him with equal enthusiasm. It could be worse, I consoled myself, imagining what it would be like if Leif was crying. Given that it was nearly midnight, I suspected it would be only a matter of time before Leif's tiredness caught up with him and grumpiness set in. But I was wrong; he was more content than he'd been all day. I was the one getting grumpy.

"I think we should risk it," I said.

"Risk what?"

"I can't sleep here," I said. "Let's go."

We gathered our things and crept upstairs to reclining chairs in a nearly empty room, where the only noise was a television set quietly humming in the distance. I felt a pang of guilt at breaking the rules and was nervous that we would get caught, but my desire for a little sleep overrode both feelings.

SARDINIA IS farther from Italy than it is from Africa. Our 225-kilometer crossing is the closest point between the island and the mainland, and it would take seven and a half hours for the ferry to get us there. By sailboat it would have been at least five times longer, and I was glad we had left our boat in Sardinia. Despite the significant span, these waters have been zigzagged for thousands of years. Phoenicians, Etruscans, and Romans all had ports along these coasts. Our destination, Civitavecchia, had been a port before the Romans moved in. Fifty kilometers farther south was Rome's main port, Portus, where just last week archeologists had discovered the largest Roman shipyard to date. Bigger than two professional hockey rinks and five stories high, the shipyard had allowed ships weighing as much as 350 tons to be built and repaired in it.

These ships were the lifeblood of meeting Rome's considerable needs, and olive oil was Rome's most important imported commodity after grain. Romans consumed on average two liters of olive oil a month—just the city of Rome, which had more than 1 million inhabitants at its peak, consumed 24 million liters of olive oil a year—and most of that oil came across the Mediterranean from Spain or Africa. It was not easy to meet these needs, and transporting olive oil had its own unique challenges. It required timely delivery to ensure freshness, spill-proof nonporous containers that were easy to move, protection against tampering and corruption, and smooth passage through customs and middlemen.

Leif had finally fallen asleep, curled up next to me on the floor, his head on my arm and a sleeping bag covering both of us. But just when I had fallen asleep, he woke looking for milk. He ate, fell asleep, and repeated the cycle again and again. I spent the night awake, envying Colin's ability to sleep through noise and discomfort and wishing for morning.

Civitavecchia was still asleep when we arrived, the night sky soft with predawn light and glowing street lamps. The port is the Mediterranean's third largest, with more than 2 million passengers a year, and even at this early hour the cavernous station bustled with weary travelers. We ate a pastry and drank coffee before walking downtown to the car rental office, passing the medieval wall that once protected the town against invaders, an imposing sixteenth-century fort, and hardened fishermen on stumpy stools mending fishing nets. Even on our short tour, it was easy to understand how the city got its name; Civitavecchia means "ancient city" in Italian.

Rome is eighty kilometers away, along a coastal highway that cuts through flat farmland with tattered greenhouses and scraggy towns of graffiti-covered townhomes, low-rise apartments, and used mobile home dealerships. We didn't have a solid plan for Rome, not even a place to stay. I had been here fifteen years before, when I was an exchange student studying at an English university, and I knew a few places I wanted to show Colin. But our main purpose was to understand the importance of olive oil in ancient Rome.

After visiting St. Peter's Basilica on the first day, we spent the second day at the world's grandest garbage dump. Monte Testaccio—the name is a fusion of the Latin *testa* and Italian *cocci*, both meaning potsherds—is a two-thousand-year-old trash pile made up entirely of broken olive oil amphorae. It is the size of a small ski hill and supports the adage that you can tell a lot about people by their trash. This is how we know ancient Romans used twenty-four liters of olive oil a year, more than just about anyone nowadays.

Five kilometers south of Vatican City in an unassuming community next to the Tiber River, Mount Testaccio is dotted with trees, shrubs, and patches of dried grass and fringed with restaurants, bars, and houses. It doesn't look like anything special from afar, and besides us, there were no tourists. A group of hormone-fueled teenagers strutted and smoked in front of a youth center, and we parked in a nearly empty lot across the street, hiding everything in the trunk.

From a closer vantage, I could see that the beige peeking out beneath the shrubs and grass wasn't soil but shards of amphorae. Colin was excited and eager to explore, but getting onto the mountain wasn't easy. Although the top is untouched by development, every inch of the base has been developed. Bars with rooftop patios or restaurants dug into the hillside line the perimeter. There is an auto garage and houses with backyard chickens. A gated road leads to the hilltop, but it was locked, and when someone finally arrived, he refused to let us in.

The hill is made up of as many as 53 million amphorae, and it takes half an hour to stroll around its one-kilometer base. The amphorae shards are meticulously arranged, cut into pieces and stacked so that they fit into one another, creating layers and terraces dusted with lime to neutralize rancid olive oil dregs. You can still see this organization, and red terra-cotta shards overlapping like roof shingles poke out between shrubs and grasses. Each amphora held around seventy liters, about the size of a keg, and was shaped like a vase with a teardropped base and two handles. Most of them were from Spain, a type called Dressel 20s, after the archaeologist Heinrich Dressel, who excavated the site in 1827. The other 15 percent came from north Africa.

What is striking about this hill, besides its size, is that it contains only amphorae used for olive oil, up to 6 billion liters of it. Amphorae were also used to hold wine, grain, fish sauce, and more, so why aren't there comparably high mountains for wine amphorae or a few other types thrown into this heap? One possible reason is that olive oil amphorae could only be used once. The terra-cotta absorbed the olive oil, which eventually became rancid, and it would taint future contents. Another reason might be that it was cheaper to make new amphorae than ship these back to the olive presses.

When amphorae weren't reused for their original purpose, they were used as drain pipes or flower pots or were pounded into small fragments and made into *opus signinum*, a cement-like paste used for houses and aqueducts. But the Dressel 20 didn't shatter well, breaking into large shards that were difficult to reuse. These olive oil amphorae are like today's Styrofoam, not fit to reuse or recycle and instead dumped into the landfill.

Romans began using this garbage dump around 10 BC, and it remained active for 270 years. Ships arrived at Rome's main port, Portus, where the amphorae were transferred to river-going boats or carried overland to Rome. The amphorae were unloaded in warehouses, the olive oil was transferred into smaller containers to be distributed to the populace, and the dirty amphorae were brought here by donkey for disposal. Remnants of nearby warehouses have been found, and last year archaeologists discovered a ninety-meter-wide canal—that's nearly the length of two Olympic-sized swimming pools—connecting Rome's main port to Ostia, on the Tiber River, allowing Romans to use boats to easily carry olive oil from far-off places all the way into Rome.

"Imagine living here," Colin said as we rounded the far side of the mountain and passed a row of dilapidated, graffiti-covered homes. "You're living on two-thousand-year-old Roman artifacts."

"I know. I thought it would be completely off-limits," I said. "Back home, finding an arrowhead can be enough to derail a development project."

But in Europe, thousand-year-old artifacts are common, and for most of its history, this midden did not receive any special treatment—at least not the kind intended to preserve it. When the Romans stopped dumping their amphorae here, a move triggered by the construction of a wall between Monte Testaccio and the river, the area was abandoned and reclaimed for other purposes. The pope led pilgrims to its summit in a festival called Way of the Cross, and in another celebration cartloads of pigs were pushed down the hill and, when they smashed at the bottom, were attacked by revelers intent on roasting them for dinner. Monte Testaccio has been a place for joists, picnics, city-wide parties, rabbit hunts, heroin addicts, a nineteenth-century gun battle against the French, and wine storage in cellars that were dug into the amphorae, which stay remarkably cool during hot Roman summers.

Monte Testaccio is the largest midden in the world and offers the best insight into ancient Rome's food distribution system—the engine that drove their remarkable expansion, fueled their armies, and sustained them at home. What makes this site so remarkable is not only its continuity—it was consistently used for 250 years, beginning in the time of Augustus, Rome's first emperor—but its meticulous record keeping.

Each amphora was labeled with enough data to satisfy a census taker. Before the amphorae were kiln fired, the name of the amphora maker or olive oil producer was engraved into the handle. Afterward, markings known as *tituli picti* were inscribed on the jug in red or black ink, detailing the production, transfer, and regulation of the oil. This meant a typical amphora might have the following particulars written on it: empty and full weight of amphora, places of export and inspection dates, as well as names of custom agents, traders, oil producer, shipping companies, and storage warehouses. It was a system of organization that today's olive oil producers could be envious of, and these data offer an unparalleled glimpse into the secret behind Rome's success.

Olive oil drove Roman society in the same way oil drives today's economy. In fact, the word "petroleum" is Latin for "olive oil from stone"; *"oleum"* means "olive oil," and *"petra"* means "stone." The government controlled much of the olive oil trade, and all the amphorae in this heap came from government coffers. There were also private sales, ballooning Rome's olive oil consumption to more than the 1.75 billion liters found here. Olive oil was used for food, lamp fuel, medicine, and industrial lubrication, just as petroleum is used today not only for gas but also for toys, clothes, computers, and heat. And just like governments today, governments in ancient Rome flourished or foundered on their oil policies.

Roman satirist Juvenal coined the phrase "bread and circuses" to describe the political strategy of first-century Rome and its reliance on food subsidies and free entertainment. A placated public and happy army was a stay-in-power strategy. Subsidies known as *annona* were distributed to plebeians and the military. When Septimius Severus, an olive oil baron from Africa, came to power, he made olive oil a subsidized commodity and ordered it from his home town, Leptis, a strategy that enriched the town and kept him in power until he died from gout. At his death, he bequeathed to Italy enough olive oil to last for five years.

The government didn't always buy its olive oil but often procured it by taxation or retribution. After Julius Caesar defeated Africa's king Juba, he fined the town of Leptis more than 1 million liters of olive oil a year to pay for supporting the enemy. Rome's provinces were taxed on the agricultural goods they produced, and that tax was often paid in kind, pouring into Rome in amphorae.

To see the bread and not the circus, as Juvenal might have said, seemed unbalanced, and so before leaving Rome we spent the afternoon at the Coliseum, Rome's largest building and a testament to Roman showmanship. Stone bleachers that once held fifty thousand boisterous spectators stared down at the vast stage. Its wooden floor deteriorated long ago, leaving behind an elaborate structure of tunnels and cages that would have held lions, tigers, rhinoceros, panthers, leopards, and gladiators. It was impossible not to marvel at the Romans' impressive engineering and meticulous organization—and at how their need for oil changed the Mediterranean.

THE SCIENCE OF OLIVES

"I like them all, but especially the olive. For what it symbolizes, first of all—peace with its leaves and joy with its golden oil."

ALDOUS HUXLEY, *The Olive Tree*[1]

"WE THINK THE Phoenicians were the first that brought not only olive oil but olive plants all around the Mediterranean," Dr. Luciana Baldoni said, raising her voice to be heard over the whirl of industrial equipment and graduate students in her Institute of Plant Genetics laboratory.

She is tall with wavy brown hair tucked behind her ears, dark eyes, and a distinguished-looking Roman nose, and she looks casually elegant in a white ruffled tunic and jeans. With a PhD in olive propagation, she now leads one of the world's foremost olive research laboratories and grows olive trees, just as her family has done for generations.

I first discovered her work while researching the early history of olive trees and reading an *Annals of Botany* publication with the unexciting title of "Genetic Structure of Wild and Cultivation

Olive in the Central Mediterranean Basin." Using DNA analysis, she concluded that the domesticated olive trees in Sicily and Sardinia were not local but imported from elsewhere. It had been years since I finished my genetics degree, but I wondered if DNA forensics could determine whether Phoenicians were the original exporters of the olive tree. When I e-mailed to ask, she wrote back enthusiastically. Not only was her laboratory interested in this topic, but they were already studying ancient Italian trees as well as Roman and Greek olive remains from archaeological sites in Pompeii and Palermo.

"Is there any genetic proof that the Phoenicians brought olive trees with them?" Colin asked.

"There is no strong evidence," Luciana said. Their contribution had been masked by more modern civilizations, she explained. "For example, Sicily has been under domination by many civilizations, and everyone brought different varieties. Phoenicians brought cultivars from the eastern part of the Mediterranean. Then Greeks brought other varieties, then the Spanish people."

"What about testing ancient trees?" I asked, reasoning that that would negate the effect of modern cultivars.

"That will allow us to discover the DNA profile of the original trees," Luciana said. "Olive trees can grow for hundreds and even thousands of years, so the original tree may only be one or two generations back."

In her office, a square room crowded with desks and overflowing bookshelves, we emptied our collection of olive samples, each carefully stored in a ziplocked bag, onto a desk. Could the contents of these bags hold the elusive proof? We were full of excitement and hope.

"Tell me where you found this one," Luciana said lifting a bag with two silver-leaved twigs and a handful of green olives. "Do you have GPS coordinates? What about photos?"

We showed her photos of the trees and their locations on Google satellite maps. I was sorry we hadn't compiled the information and promised to send it. Compared with rigorous scientific methods, our crumpled ziplocked bags scrawled with messy handwriting might have traumatized some, but Luciana and her graduate students were unfazed. They catalogued each sample and queried us for missing information.

Fiammedda, a young woman in her twenties with long, straight hair and an olive leaf pendant necklace around her neck, and Roberto, a jovial man with twinkling eyes, chattered in Italian as they carefully opened each bag and extracted the contents, turning over branches and olives with gloved hands.

"Did you sample the base of the tree?" Luciana asked.

"When we could," I said. Luciana's instructions on taking olive samples included clipping one twig from the tree's crown and another from the base. This was important because grafted trees had different rootstock, so we'd be able to tell which trees were grafted. "There are a few trees where we couldn't get rootstock samples."

"Yes, that happens," Luciana said. "When there are no suckers, you can take a piece of the bark. We can get the DNA sample from that."

It was harder to extract DNA from dried leaves and bark than from fresh leaves, which required only half a leaf. But we had collected at least a dozen leaves from each tree, and they seemed to think the samples we'd collected were fine. Using that DNA, they would look for tiny differences.

The olive nuclear genome is made up of 1.7 billion letters, which are called base pairs (bp), organized on twenty-three pairs of chromosomes. It is like two sets of encyclopedias, each with twenty-three books containing 1.7 billion letters made from an alphabet that contains only four letters: A, C, G, and T.

The encyclopedic sets are almost identical, and the cumulative information creates the blueprint of the olive.

Coincidently, humans also have twenty-three pairs of chromosomes, and since 2003, when the thirteen-year $3 billion publicly funded human genome project was completed, we've known what each of those letters are. This information created a plethora of medical advances, from cancer diagnostic tests to gene therapy to pharmacogenomics. The olive's genome would be equally revolutionary for agricultural research, and Luciana explained that researchers were on the verge of completing this multi-institution ten-year project. "The next five years will be an exciting time for us," she said.

Luciana and her team would not only examine the nuclear DNA from our samples but also the DNA contained in the olive's plastid, the organelles responsible for photosynthesis. Plastid DNA is much smaller than nuclear DNA (150,000 bp versus 1.5 billion bp), and it is inherited maternally (haploid versus diploid). Instead of being on a collection of chromosomes, the DNA is arranged in a circle. And unlike the olive's nuclear genome, the plastid DNA of several olive cultivars has been fully sequenced.

Many researchers prefer to study the plastid DNA because it is maternally inherited and passes virtually unchanged from one generation to the next. Nuclear DNA has a faster rate of evolution, as pairs of maternal and paternal chromosomes swap information with each other in a process called recombination. The mutation rate in olive plastid DNA is further suppressed, perhaps a result of the olive's long life span, and is tenfold lower than that of the typical plastid genome. These features make plastid DNA more accurate at detecting evolutionary events, and they are a preferred tool of olive geneticists.

Luciana's team would extract the DNA from our sample's olive leaves and then amplify specific regions using a process called polymerase chain reaction. The researchers would focus on eleven molecular markers, six in nuclear DNA and five in plastid DNA. The markers are regions that have high variability and are either simple sequence repeats or single nucleotide polymorphisms. The variation in simple sequence repeats is like a stutter; the same phrase is said over and over again, but there are differences in how often it is repeated. Whereas a single nucleotide polymorphism is a change in a single letter, as in the words "defected" and "detected."

To understand where the olive tree originated, Luciana would compare the DNA of the ancient trees we collected to that of the wild trees we sampled and of other trees throughout the Mediterranean. If an ancient tree came from somewhere else, it would be less similar to the wild trees and more like distant trees. A strong similarity between ancient trees and those in lands that were once Phoenicia would provide solid evidence to support our theory that Phoenicians carried olive trees with them on their ships.

UMBRIA IS A landlocked region the size of New Jersey that lies next to the more famous Tuscany. Historically called "the green heart of Italy," it is a collage of verdant hills, olive orchards, vineyards, and castles. Luciana's lab is near the center, in Perugia, a three-thousand-year-old city that is the capital of one of Umbria's two provinces. It was an ideal location from which to explore Umbria, and for the next two days, we crisscrossed the region with Luciana, visiting ancient olive groves, storied olive trees, one of Italy's top olive mills, and an olive museum.

In the town of Bovara, an hour south of Perugia, we examined an ancient tree that had split into three thick trunks like a trident's spears. Each twisted and knotted limb culminated in a mane of frosted leaves and green/black olives. Cordoned off by wooden beams and commemorated with a plaque, it was a significant tree.

"It is called Olivo di S. Emiliano," Luciana said, "after the saint that was tied to it and beheaded in 306 AD."

Saint Emiliano was the patron saint of Trevi, the hilltop town that overlooks this farmland. Every year on January 27, Saint Emiliano's feast day and likely the anniversary of his death, a golden life-sized statue of him perched in a throne is paraded through the street in the Processione dell'Illuminata. There are no other old trees nearby, and this one probably owes its survival to its macabre history. Not far away sits a Benedictine abbey, and its monks cared for the olive tree and ensured that it was not felled.

"Sometimes we know how old a tree is because of historical records, but it is difficult to prove," Luciana said. The earliest record of Saint Emiliano's beheading is in a tenth-century book, but for a scientist, that is not conclusive enough. "We carbon-dated this tree in collaboration with another group," Luciana continued, "but our results did not match. One laboratory dated it at 800 years old, the other at 1,500."

How could the results be so disparate and provide such a young age?

"It's because olive trees are very difficult to date," Luciana said. "There is nothing left from the original trunk; it has rotted away. The challenge is to know what part of the olive tree to test and how much older the tree is."

Although carbon dating olive trees is still a formidable task and tends to be inaccurate, real progress has been made with genetic testing. "We have discovered much about the ancient olive trees across Italy," Luciana said. "Some varieties are still grown, but the funny thing is that others do not look like any other cultivars. We do not know where they come from."

Could they have come from the Middle East? And could our samples help answer that question?

Luciana continued, "The trees in southern Italy and here are different. In the south they are grafted, while here they have been directly planted."

"Why is that?" Colin asked.

"Not all cultivars can root, and a grafted tree will bear fruit much faster," Luciana explained.

Sometimes trees were grafted in the wild, as in Sardinia, where cultivar scions were spliced onto wild rootstock and left to grow in the forest, untended except at picking time. In Italy, wild trees were more often transplanted in nurseries and the grafted trees replanted in groves. At other times the domestic cultivar was rooted and directly planted. It all depended on the tree type, the soil conditions, and the farmers.

In Trevi's olive museum, an airy two-story building on the town's main street, Luciana pointed out different grafting techniques, all variations of roping a spindly tree to the severed trunk of an established tree. It was a technique that the Romans had popularized, and grafted trees were found throughout the Roman Empire. Even the Bible uses olive grafting as an analogy, reversing the normal technique by grafting a wild olive tree onto a cultivated one to make a point. "If some of the branches have been broken off, and you, though a wild olive shoot, have been grafted in among the others and now share in the nourishing sap from the olive root."[2]

We inched past displays of oil lamps, barnacle-coated amphorae, a replica of a Phoenician ship, vases, perfume vials, and a bronze strigil that had once scraped oil off athletes. At a replica of a Roman olive mill, we corralled Leif in the mill's stone bowl, next to the hulking grindstone. He found his stone playpen less amusing than we did and strained to return to the marble stairs, which he worked like an athlete training to climb Everest. Instead of looking at exquisitely painted alabastrons, Colin and I took turns hovering over Leif, ready to catch him if he slipped.

"He's your kid," Colin joked.

"We all know who he looks like," I retorted. Leif trained his blue eyes on Colin and shook his head with delight, blond hair whipping back and forth, like a dog drying off after a swim.

"Sometimes I think you must have had an affair with a Scandinavian man or an albino."

"Be nice. Otherwise, I'll have to get out the olive leaves and see if you really love me." I explained to Colin that I had just read a placard saying that to find out whether a man loved her, a woman would put olive leaves into a hole in her hearth ashes. If the leaves turned and the tips pointed to the woman, the man loved her. "Watch out," I said, narrowing my eyes in mock threat.

"Oh, yeah? Well, if you think you can intimidate me with that evil eye, I have news for you," Colin said, for he had just read that olive oil cured evil-eye hexes. The healer, usually an elderly woman, would drop an odd number of olive oil drops into water. If the oil coalesced, the person was fine, but if the drop spread out, he or she was cursed and needed to be exorcized—yet another ritual using olive oil.

I'd heard dozens of uses for olive oil, trees, and leaves, from lubricating the gears of Rome's military machines to creating soap to anointing kings, but it seemed there were still more, as varied and often as preposterous as tabloid headlines. Olive oil was rubbed onto pregnant women's bellies to protect babies against frights their mothers might receive, used in wax statues and "holy dolls" presented as gifts at weddings and births, spread over stiff linen and wool fibers before they were woven and placed on nursing mothers' nipples to reinvigorate their milk supply. Burning olive leaves could deter hail, divine your longevity, and divulge whether your wish would come true.

Children wore amulets to safeguard them made of olive leaves, salt, incense, and sacred artifacts called *brevi* or *abitini.*

Olive oil was a staple of the medicine cabinet, used alone or with special ingredients, and often applied with a prayer. A mixture of snow and oil called "oil of snow" treated burns, as did a salve made of wax and oil. Three rusty nails boiled in olive oil made "ferrous oil" to treat respiratory problems and eye pain. A lizard boiled in olive oil cured baldness and ringworm, "toad oil" helped with tuberculosis, and "scorpion oil" healed wounds—but only if the scorpions were caught during a full May moon and drowned in the oil. May was also the month for boiling bats in oil to make hernia medication. Olive oil treated joint pain, sore throats, styes, chest pains, and conjunctivitis, whereas the leaves and bark stopped bleeding and cured whitlows.

LIKE PROVENCE, northern Umbria was at the edge of olive-growing territory. The countryside was filled with farmland, tilled fields dark with rich soil, hilltop villages, and groves of sprightly olive trees. What the trees lacked in size, they made up for in number. Olive trees grew where nothing else could take root; a rocky hill was covered with hundreds of seventeenth-century half-moon terraces, each one jutting out like an opera house balcony and protecting a single olive tree. The terraces were old, but the trees weren't. Northern Italy's olive trees are hampered by brutal winters, which annihilate olive groves every few decades. The trees regrow from their roots or farmers replant them, but they are destined to stay eternally small.

It is the exceptions that tweak the curiosity of Luciana and her team, and at a grove of five ancient olive trees, with hollow centers and trunks entangled like limbs in a game of Twister, Luciana explained how these trees could change where we grow olive trees.

"These are the oldest trees in the area," Luciana said as we walked through the grove. She carried Leif, while Colin and I snapped photos and took a video of the trees, capturing the stunning size difference between these five and the rest of the grove. "They are able to survive the cold that kills all the other trees."

The trees of Villastrada were aided by the moderating effects of nearby Lake Trasimeno, where fishermen rowed their boats standing up and hauled pike and eel from its shallow waters. But that wasn't enough to explain their tenacity.

"Some trees are more cold-resistant, such as Rigali and Nostrali," Luciana continued, "and in northern Europe, places like Germany, they are beginning to grow cold-resistant strains."

"Could we grow these trees in Canada?" Colin asked, pocketing a handful of olives.

"Canadian olive oil," I mused. I had heard of a few brave farmers on Vancouver Island and in the Gulf Islands trying to grow olive trees, but it was a struggle. It wasn't until you went farther down the coast to California that olive trees grew with vigor.

To search for olive trees that could grow in cooler climes, Luciana crossbred these ancient trees with another cold-hardy variant called Pendolino. Back at her laboratory, we saw this experiment unfolding in rows of greenhouses—plastic domes arcing over potted olive trees and fluttering in the afternoon breeze—and a forest of young olive trees. The trees ranged from delicate seedlings no bigger than a flower to trees that stretched overhead and were lush with silver leaves and green olives.

"Maybe you'll find a strain that we can grow in Canada," Colin repeated.

Luciana laughed. "Maybe, but you will have to be patient." The trees had been planted only this year, and researchers wouldn't know anything until the trees started producing olives, which took years.

top A mountaintop village in the Mani Peninsula, Greece.

above Leif sitting on a Greek widow's lap in a small village on the Mani Peninsula.

above A Byzantine chapel built on top of the Greek temple that held the Poseidon death oracle at Cape Taenaron on the Mani Peninsula.

top right Biolea olive oil production facility in Crete, Greece.

bottom right Freshly washed olives moving on a conveyer belt at an olive oil mill.

top left Olive oil pouring out from woven mats squeezed together using a hydraulic press.

bottom left Ancient olive tree in Crete, Greece.

above Olive tree pickers in Crete using mechanical rakes to drop olives onto nets below.

above Colin and Leif replicating how early civilizations may have first made olive oil.

top right Halutza olive orchard in Israel's Negev desert.

bottom right Reconstructed lever-based olive oil press from the first millennium BC, found in Israel.

top Colin and Leif in the salty waters of the Dead Sea.

above Phoenician letters carved into a cliffside along an ancient trading route in Israel. One of the few remaining signs from the civilization that gave us many things, including our modern alphabet.

"Only 15 percent of these trees have olives," Luciana said as we walked through a grove of five-year-old trees. These two hundred trees came from an earlier crossbreeding program involving two Italian cultivars, Leccino and Dolce Agogia, but it would still be years before the experiment was complete. The trees were so different that it was hard to believe they were all olive trees, let alone from the same cultivars. Some were taller than me, others waist high and bushy. There were differences in leaf shape, thickness of trunk, size of olives—pretty much every attribute that matters. Some barely looked like trees but had reverted to their wild phenotype, scruffy and squat as a shrub.

Breeding programs like this are rare, and they are the main reason that today's olive cultivars are very similar to those grown hundreds of years ago. When farmers obtain new cultivars, it is through clonal selection, where shoots of a single cultivar are propagated to search for slight variations. Crossbreeding olive trees creates much greater variability, as we could see by the trees growing here, but it is more challenging and not for the impatient. It takes at least seven years before a reasonable number of the trees are producing olives, and you need a lot of space. Most of the trees will not be as good as the parents, but some might be better. If so, they could result in new-tasting olives and olive oil or minimize the challenges of pests, cold, rain, drought, salinity, and low yield, as well as the dozens of other challenges olive farmers face.

We had come to Luciana because she used DNA forensics to understand the history of ancient olive trees, but in her olive grove we realized that ancient olive trees hold secrets not only to the past but also to the future. Much of her team's work focused on solving pressing problems the olive industry faced, and so when Colin asked about fraudulent olive oils, I was not surprised to hear that they were also working on this.

"We have created markers that detect where the olive oil comes from," Luciana said. "Sometimes a label says the olive oil is from Italy, but it is really from Spain or Tunisia. Sometimes it is not only olive oil but mixed with other oils: soybean oil, hazelnut, sunflower, and corn."

I had heard a lot about corruption in the olive oil industry. In his book *Extra Virginity: The Sublime and Scandalous World of Olive Oil*, Tom Mueller exposed the underbelly of what he calls the most corrupt food industry in the world, and investigators have prosecuted olive oil scams across the globe. In 2011, Spain's "Operation Cholesterol" imprisoned two olive businessmen for two years for selling hundreds of thousands of liters of olive oil that was mostly sunflower oil. Another nineteen people were arrested in Spain in 2012, for selling a mix of avocado, palm, sunflower, and vegetable oil as olive oil, along with money laundering and $4 million in tax evasion. The Italian "Operation Golden Oil" found that nearly a quarter of the 787 producers investigated were selling fraudulent extra virgin olive oil.

Things in North America are not any better. According to a 2010 University of California, Davis, study, 69 percent of olive oils imported into California did not meet the standard for extra virgin olive oil. But the U.S. FDA doesn't have any meaningful testing program for olive oil; nor does it have a record of prosecuting offenders. Canada has an accredited government lab that tests olive oil, and the Canadian Food Inspection Agency regularly evaluates oil, but the fraud is also rampant up north. In 2009, three Canadian companies were fined nearly $200,000 for adulterating tens of thousands of liters of olive oil. Mueller calls the U.S. "an oil criminal's dream" and contrasts it to Canada, which he says does an "excellent job of policing the market."[3]

Olive oil charlatans have been around since before Roman times, and their techniques have become increasingly sophisticated, allowing them to elude regulators, cheat honest producers, and deceive customers. DNA forensics is the next step in that battle, offering a way to confirm whether an oil only contains olives as well as the identity of those olives. The price you pay for Tuscan olive oil could be tenfold that of Tunisian oil, but people do not always get what they pay for. As we heard again and again, Italy is the biggest olive oil importer; the reality is that olive oil from elsewhere gets shipped here and bottled as Italian.

In the laboratory, we had seen benches of high-tech equipment and samples in tiny plastic tubes—olive forensics in action. Extracting DNA from olive oil is challenging enough, but discovering the provenance of the oil in that bottle would seem to be even more difficult. When Colin asked Luciana about this, she agreed. "Getting the DNA is difficult because of the small quantity, and it is highly fragmented. We use nested PCR and chloroplast markers."

Luciana and her team used PCR, which stands for polymerase chain reaction, a technique used to make thousands of copies of a piece of DNA, like photocopying a page, to examine chloroplast DNA, also called plastid DNA, looking for specific patterns in the DNA, known as chloroplast markers. Chloroplast DNA is great for this type of forensic work, because unlike nuclear DNA, it is small, with only a few thousand bp, and there are dozens of copies in each cell. The small size and larger quantity of chloroplast DNA make it easier to get an intact copy when the sample has been exposed to harsh conditions, such as being pounded with a stone hammer, being centrifuged, or sitting for months in a bottle.

Tests like this provide concrete proof of compromised oil, but for now, professional olive oil tasters are still at the forefront of rooting out fraud. Saverio Pandolfi, a stout man with shaggy salt-and-pepper hair and goatee, was the lab's taster and also had a PhD in plant sciences. Luciana called him the king of olive oil testing, and he rated olive oils for the slow food movement's annual olive oil guide, which he brought for us at dinner.

"It is a gift for you," he said, handing us an apple-green book with 479 pages of tightly typed columns rating 1,106 Italian olive oils. It was the second olive guidebook we had received that day, and I sensed a bit of friendly competition when Saverio explained the differences between it and *Flos Olei*.

As we sipped Grechetto di Todi, a sweet white wine, and nibbled on codfish and chickpeas creamed in olive oil and topped with cuttlefish ink, Saverio talked oil. He threw around the names of olive varieties as though they were wines, praising some and calling others cat piss, and confided that the best Italian oils came from Umbria and Tuscany and the worst from the south, regions that used to produce lampante oil during Roman times and maintained a taste for wretched oil.

When Luciana brought Saverio olive oil she made from her family's Moraiolo and Frantoio olives, he denounced it as terrible. "I will take it to a different mill this year," Luciana said, undeterred.

Although his critique was often scathing, there was little doubt as to who he thought made the best oil. Not only did quality depend on the cultivars and how the olives were grown, but the olives had to be picked without bruising, carried to the mill immediately, transported in shallow layers in crates to avoid damage, and then pressed with modern equipment that was highly regulated and controlled.

"Do you know what olive oil most Americans use?" Saverio asked.

"Italian?" I ventured.

"No, it's not even olive oil. They use refined oil with only a small amount of olive oil added for flavor." Saverio said this with the incredulity of someone who has discovered that dog crap is a delicacy in a foreign country.

"That's called pure or light olive oil," Colin said.

With a mouth full of farro pasta, deliciously chewy and sensuous against the delicate saltiness of the pork and trasimeno bean sauce, I nodded at the preposterousness of it. Here I was, eating a bean that had been saved from extinction with a dedication usually reserved for fuzzy animals. If the Italians could create a protection of the trasimeno bean agricultural consortium to save a legume, shouldn't we care whether we used extra virgin olive oil or some overly processed, flavorless substitute?

As the waitress brought our fourth dish, ravioli dusted with salted fish eggs, Leif vigorously tugged at my shirt and Saverio asked, "Do you know olive oil has the same fat composition as a mother's milk?"

"Really?"

"The ratio of essential fatty acids, linoleic, and linolenic acids is nearly identical. Italian mothers feed their babies olive oil," he said.

I would later learn that not only was olive oil good for infants but that pregnant and lactating mothers who consumed olive oil had bigger and more coordinated babies. When rats were fed fish oil instead of olive oil, their offspring were smaller and less developed because of the lower levels of a key omega-6 fatty acid called arachidonic acid. Maybe instead of taking a fish oil pill every day, I should be swigging olive oil.

Getting Leif to drink olive oil would be about as easy as convincing him to consume anything besides milk. For now, I resigned myself to nursing him in the bathroom, and afterward, I paced downtown Perugia's streets to lull him to sleep. As I cradled him, I ducked the pools of light spilling from streetlamps and sped past restaurants jostling with merry diners, while he stared blankly up at me, forcing his eyes open with the same resoluteness with which I willed them shut. It wasn't until my arm had fallen asleep that he closed his eyes and his breath deepened, and I returned to our table and the collection of dishes that awaited me.

I was still sated the next morning when we breakfasted at our cabin, surrounded by vineyards and horses, one of the agritourism businesses that were becoming increasingly popular. As we drove back to the Mediterranean, skirting hillsides of silver-leaved trees and plunging through fecund farmland, I could understand why the slow food movement was born here and how scientists could dedicate their lives to understanding a single tree. We'd seen a passion and a profound respect for the land in all the olive researchers and farmers we'd met. Luciana had picked her grandfather's olives as a child, sparking a lifelong love that went to the core of her personality. Olive trees did that to you.

9 HOW TO LIVE LIKE A CENTENARIAN

"The olive tree is surely the richest gift of Heaven."

THOMAS JEFFERSON[1]

AN OVERCAST SKY loomed and wind played our halyards like a harp. Even in the sheltered marina, *Isis* rocked and tugged against her lines, and beyond our breakwater, the sea seethed with whitecaps, which churned and spilled over each other like foam sprayed from a fire extinguisher. The ferry had soldiered through the wind and waves and easily returned us to Sardinia after our weeklong sojourn on the Italian mainland, but *Isis* was tiny in comparison, and we were grounded by yet another storm cooked up in the Gulf of Lion.

"We might as well make the best of it," said Colin, who was perched at our kitchen table writing in his notebook. He ripped the page out and showed me a long list of overdue chores and errands.

"I'll get the groceries," I volunteered, eager to postpone scrubbing the decks or cleaning the head.

Colin trekked to the laundromat with two backpacks' worth of dirty clothes, while Leif and I strolled to the supermarket to get a month's supply of food.

I wandered the aisles like an anthropologist visiting an excavation site, not only filling our grocery cart with jarred vegetables, pasta, and milk Tetra Paks but also searching for clues to Sardinians' exceptional longevity and good health. Sardinia has an abundance of people over the age of one hundred, including one region that boasts the highest concentration of centenarians in the world. In the mountainous province of Ogliastra, there is one centenarian for every two hundred people, a per capita rate that is fifty times that of the United States. Sardinia is the only place where there are nearly as many male centenarians as females, a surprising finding in an age group where there are four times as many women as men.

Amidst the uniquely Sardinian foods, we found a smoked mullet caviar called *buttariga;* pecorino, a hard cheese made from sheep's milk; and *pane carasau,* a thin flatbread that is a cross between a tortilla and a cracker and was once the shepherd's mainstay. But there was nothing that shouted "Eat me and you'll live to a hundred." As in most European grocery stores, the olive oil aisle overflowed, and there were plenty of fresh fruits, vegetables, and fish. The most memorable item I found was in the deli—a cannon-sized mortadella sausage. A single slice could have fed a family of four.

Researchers have descended on Sardinia, wondering what accounts for the population's longevity. They have drawn some conclusions, but they are still searching for more answers. Most concur that the secret to the Sardinians' long life is probably a mixture of genetics and lifestyle, such as staying fit, eating well, having low stress, and socializing. They follow the Mediterranean diet, which UNESCO lists as an "intangible cultural heritage of humanity" and defines as "consisting mainly of olive oil, cereals, fresh or dried fruit and vegetables, a moderate amount of fish, dairy and meat, and many condiments and spices, all accompanied by wine or infusions." Olive oil is a key component of their diet, drizzled on vegetables, fish, salads, and bread. Meat is generally eaten only once or twice a week, and wine is drunk daily. Sheep's cheese and goat's ricotta are also well loved.

It's impossible to know how much olive oil contributes to longevity, but the two oldest women in the world thought it was important. Jeanne Calment, the French woman who lived to age 122, credited a diet high in olive oil, along with occasional treats of chocolate and port, and rubbed olive oil into her skin to keep it youthful. Mariam Amash, an Arab Israeli who died in 2012, when she was believed to be 124 (her age has not been officially verified by the supercentenarian trackers at the Gerontology Research Group), drank an entire glass of olive oil every day. Throwing back eight ounces of olive oil daily is probably not the best choice for most people, but a growing body of evidence supports the belief that consuming olive oil every day will keep you healthy.

The idea that olive oil is healthful stretches back to ancient Greece and even earlier, when it was used to treat everything from minor cuts to debilitating diseases such as leprosy. In the 1930s, scientific publications reported on olive oil's antibacterial properties and its effectiveness in treating rickets, and two decades later, the benefits of the vitamin E in olive oil were discovered. Throughout the 1950s, researchers began to understand that oleic acid, the main fat in olive oil, and squalene, a sterol precursor, affected cholesterol and fatty acid levels. And throughout the 1970s, publications extolled the role of olive oil's monosaturated fats in reducing cardiovascular disease. Today, a search for olive oil in PubMed, the U.S. National Library of Medicine database, produces more than 6,500 articles, and another 500 are added each year. There are studies showing that olive oil lowers the risk of osteoporosis, heart disease, breast cancer, skin cancer, arteriosclerosis, stroke, dementia, depression, type 2 diabetes, metabolic syndrome, blood clotting, and rheumatoid arthritis. It reduces blood pressure, lowers cholesterol, boosts the immune system, and acts as an anti-inflammatory.

Olive oil's role in reducing the incidence of cardiovascular disease is perhaps its most researched health benefit. Dozens of studies show that olive oil consumption reduces the risk of heart attacks and strokes in a broad range of populations, from those who are at risk for cardiovascular disease to those who are young and healthy, both men and woman, as well as people of varying ethnicities. In 2012, the results of a thirteen-year study of more than forty thousand Spaniards was published, showing not only that olive oil reduced heart disease but also that it reduced overall mortality. The participants who were in the top quarter of olive oil consumption had a 44 percent reduction in diseases involving the heart or blood vessels and a 26 percent decrease in overall mortality. That benefit was directly linked to the amount of olive oil consumed, and for every extra two teaspoons of olive oil used a day, the risk of mortality dropped by 7 percent.

Another study, published in 2011 in France, found that olive oil decreased the risk of stroke by 41 percent. The study followed 7,500 seniors for five years and found that people who regularly used olive oil both for cooking and as a dressing were 41 percent less likely to have a stroke than those who used olive oil more sparingly or not at all. Those who didn't use olive oil at all had the highest incidence of strokes, and those with moderate usage had a rate between the two other groups. Both the 2011 and the 2012 studies factored the influence of other variables—such as diet, exercise, smoking, high blood pressure, and diabetes—into those results to take into consideration the differences that may exist between those who use olive oil and those who prefer other oils.

Olive oil's role in keeping the cardiovascular system healthy is linked to its ability to reduce atherosclerosis and lower blood pressure. Atherosclerosis occurs when cholesterol and other fatty materials accumulate on artery walls, effectively hardening the arteries, and is the leading cause of heart attacks, strokes, and peripheral vascular disease. Numerous observational studies show that olive oil consumption is linked to reduced risk of atherosclerosis, and in 2011, a randomized trial concurred with those findings. The Spanish study divided into three groups 187 people who were at high risk for cardiovascular disease but still asymptomatic. One group followed a Mediterranean diet high in olive oil (up to a liter a week), and the control group followed a low-fat diet. There was no change in exercise, and neither diet was calorie restricted. After a year, the change in the thickness of the inner lining of the carotid artery, known as the intima media, was measured by ultrasound. The olive oil diet reduced arterial thickness in people who had the highest levels starting out, whereas the low-fat diet didn't.

Exactly how olive oil can reverse advanced preclinical atherosclerosis isn't known, but studies indicate that olive oil lowers levels of low-density lipoproteins, known as LDL, or bad cholesterol, and raises levels of high-density proteins, frequently called HDL, or good cholesterol. Measuring levels of HDL and LDL is used to assess risk, and more recently, physicians have also begun measuring apolipoproteins, the proteins that bind fat and cholesterol to form LDL and HDL, as a more accurate predictor. In 2011, the results from the first large clinical trial measuring the impact of olive oil on apolipoproteins showed that in just three months a diet high in olive oil significantly reduced apolipoproteins associated with bad cholesterol while increasing those associated with good cholesterol. Nearly a thousand people at high risk for cardiovascular disease were divided into three groups. One group followed a low-fat diet, the second group followed a Mediterranean diet that was supplemented with nuts, and the third group followed a Mediterranean diet supplemented with olive oil. After three months, both Mediterranean diets showed a reduction in total cholesterol, including lower levels of LDL and higher levels of HDL, whereas the total cholesterol in the control group remained unchanged. Furthermore, those following a Mediterranean diet supplemented with additional olive oil showed a substantially greater reduction in levels of apolipoprotein B (the major protein of LDL) and an increase in apolipoprotein A-1 (the major protein of HDL) compared with those on the Mediterranean diet supplemented with nuts, suggesting that olive oil offers more health benefits than nuts.

Olive oil also decreases blood pressure and combats hypertension, both risks linked to cardiovascular disease. A Greek observational study of more than twenty thousand people showed an inverse relationship between olive oil consumption and both systolic and diastolic blood pressure, and another study demonstrated that patients with moderate hypertension could reduce their blood pressure-lowering drugs by 48 percent when they used four tablespoons of olive oil a day instead of the equivalent in saturated fats.

Improving blood lipid levels also reduces the risk of type 2 diabetes and metabolic syndrome. In a four-year study that assigned 418 participants to one of three diets—low in fat, high in olive oil, or high in nuts—it was found that the diets containing olive oil or nuts resulted in a 52 percent reduction in the incidence of diabetes—even though none of the diets were calorie restricted and the findings were independent of body weight or physical activity.

Mediterranean diets have long been associated with a decreased incidence of cancer, and the incidence of cancer in these countries is lower than in Scandinavian countries, the U.K., and the USA. A 2011 analysis of nineteen observational studies involving 36,000 participants found that olive oil reduces the risk of all types of cancer. Other studies show that high olive oil consumption is linked with a decrease in breast, prostate, oral cavity, and colon cancer, as well as improved prognosis for laryngeal cancer. A 2010 study in mice showed that olive oil helped prevent breast cancer, whereas corn oil stimulated it. Olive oil led to a decrease in the activity of two key proteins implicated in breast cancer and helped kill cancer cells by stimulating their death through a natural process called apoptosis.

The good news keeps coming, and we now know that olive oil is good not only for the body but also for the mind. There are fewer cases of Alzheimer's disease and dementia in Mediterranean regions where olive oil is used abundantly, and studies suggest that olive oil can help protect the brain. In 2012, researchers at Harvard Medical School reported that olive oil protects against the decline in cognitive function and memory that people experience as they age. The researchers tracked six thousand women over the age of sixty-five for four years and found that those who followed diets high in monosaturated oils, like those found in olive oil, instead of saturated fats maintained better global cognitive function and verbal memory.

Even more exciting are recent discoveries that olive oil may reverse neurological damage and could treat Alzheimer's disease, a debilitating form of dementia that affects 30 million people and has no cure. The research is still in the early stages, but it is promising. In 2011, scientists at the Saint Louis University School of Medicine showed that olive oil high in polyphenols, which are natural antioxidants, reversed symptoms of Alzheimer's in a mouse model. The mice fed extra virgin olive oil supplemented with polyphenols showed the greatest improvements in learning, thinking, and memory, followed by those fed only extra virgin olive oil. The two other groups, which consumed butter and coconut oil, did poorly; those eating butter showed no improvement, and those consuming coconut oil showed a slight improvement, but only in learning. This work suggests that olive oil's polyphenols confer important neuroprotectant properties, and one of these antioxidants has been identified as a candidate for clinical trials.

Olive oil's health benefits come from its major components (the oils) and the minor components that make up the remaining 2 percent of the oil. Olive oil is mostly made up of monounsaturated oleic acid (omega-9) but also contains polyunsaturated fatty acids, linoleic acid (omega-6), and linolenic acid (omega-3), as well as low levels of the saturated fatty acids, palmitic acid and stearic acid. The fatty acid composition of olive oil varies depending on cultivar and growing conditions. Oleic acid always makes up the bulk of the oil, with levels ranging from 55 to 83 percent. The polyunsaturated fats make up between 4 and 22.5 percent of the oil, and saturated fats make up the remaining 8 to 25 percent.

Olive oil is one of the best sources of oleic acid, which has been shown to curb cardiovascular disease, including atherosclerosis, stroke, and heart attacks. For example, a 2011 study that looked at the levels of oleic acid in 1,245 seniors found that the third with the highest oleic acid levels were 73 percent less likely to have a stroke than the third with the lowest levels.

Oleic acid decreases levels of low-density lipids (bad cholesterol) while increasing levels of high-density lipids (good cholesterol) and modulates cell membranes, lipids, and pathways linked to vasodilation and constriction, controlling high blood pressure.

Olive oil also helps achieve an optimal balance of essential omega-3 and omega-6 fats. Most Western diets include far too much omega-6 fat, and most Westerners have on average sixteen times as much omega-6 than omega-3 in their bodies. This is far from the ideal ratio of 4 to 1, and the imbalance has been linked to cardiovascular, inflammatory, and autoimmune diseases, as well as cancer. Correcting the balance has been shown to decrease mortality from cardiovascular disease by 70 percent, reduce cancer cell proliferation in colorectal cancer, decrease the risk of breast cancer, suppress rheumatoid arthritis inflammation, and help with asthma. Olive oil has a nearly 1 to 1 ratio of omega-3 and omega-6 fats, which corrects this imbalance by displacing omega-6 fats without reducing omega-3 levels.

Until recently, most of the focus on olive oil's health benefits has centered on its fatty acid profile, but we now know that the minor components that make up a mere 2 percent of the oil play a disproportionate role. Olive oil has more than 230 minor components, including polyphenols (antioxidants), sterols, carotenoids, chlorophyll, squalene, and volatile compounds.

The group that gets the most attention is the polyphenols, which are natural antioxidants and give olive oil its bitterness. The level of antioxidants depends on the cultivar of olive used, as well as the production process and age of the oil. The polyphenol concentration can range from two milligrams per kilogram or even less to five hundred milligrams per kilogram. Fresh extra virgin oil made from high-antioxidant cultivars such as Koroneiki or Coratina olives plucked while they're still green and grown without irrigation has the highest levels. Even though olive cultivars can have a range of polyphenol levels, how the olives are grown and when they are picked also make a big difference. As an olive ripens, its antioxidant levels increase, but when the olive turns black, the levels begin to diminish. Irrigating olives also decreases their antioxidant concentrations. But just because the picked olives are high in antioxidants doesn't mean the olive oil will be. Common techniques to increase olive oil yield—such as using heat, increasing malaxation time, or adding water—will also decrease the polyphenol levels. Only extra virgin and virgin olive oil have antioxidants, since the harsh chemical process of deodorizing olive oil strips the oil of its polyphenols. Olive oil must be stored in a dark, cool place to slow the inevitable polyphenol decline, and it should be used within a year.

More than thirty different polyphenols can be found in olive oil, including oleocanthal, which is both an anti-inflammatory and antioxidant, and functions like ibuprofen to reduce pain and inflammation. Oleocanthal is also what irritates your throat after ingesting some olive oils, and it's this feature that led to its discovery. When Dr. Gary Beauchamp, director of the Monell Chemical Senses Center in Philadelphia, taste-tested extra virgin olive oil in Sicily, he noticed that the bite he felt in his throat was similar to that caused by drinking a solution of ibuprofen. Intrigued, he set about finding the cause and found oleocanthal, a structurally dissimilar compound that nonetheless mimicked ibuprofen in more ways than one. In his 2005 publication in the journal *Nature*, he reported that three tablespoons of olive oil has the same anti-inflammatory properties as a low dose of aspirin or ibuprofen, and though not suitable for pain relief, it might confer the same health benefits of a low-dose anti-inflammatory, such as aspirin or ibuprofen, without the potential negative side effects such as ulcers.

Oleocanthal has since been shown to lower the risk of heart disease, stroke, certain cancers, and dementia, and new research suggests it may offer a treatment for Alzheimer's. This polyphenol targets the highly destructive proteins known as ADDLs found in Alzheimer's disease and diminishes their toxicity. Unhindered ADDL molecules bind to nerve cell synapses, disrupting the cell and eventually leading to its death and, it is believed, many of the symptoms of Alzheimer's disease. In vitro studies have found that oleocanthal increases the size of ADDL, reducing the ability of the altered molecules to bind to synapses in the hippocampus—the part of the brain first affected by Alzheimer's and associated with learning and memory—and protecting the brain from structural damage. Oleocanthal also makes the toxic protein more vulnerable to antibodies, which could increase the efficacy of immunotherapies in which antibodies are used to target and destroy ADDLs.

Olive oil also contains hydroxytyrosol, believed to be the most powerful natural antioxidant after gallic acid, with ten times the ability to absorb free radicals as green tea. Hydroxytyrosol and its precursor, oleuropein, are found in high concentrations in olive oil and contribute to olive oil's bitterness. This polyphenol has been implicated in a reduced risk of cardiovascular disease, as well as some forms of cancer. Like oleic acid, it also helps lower LDL, increase HDL, and reduce total cholesterol. Additionally, it has antithrombotic and anti-inflammatory properties and may be responsible for the decreased rate of cancer linked to olive oil. In vitro studies show that hydroxytyrosol also has powerful antiproliferative properties, scavenging free radicals, protecting DNA from reactive oxygen species, destroying tumor cells through apoptosis, altering tumor cell cycle progression, and limiting proliferation of tumors. Further cancer protection comes from the vitamin E in olive oil, which defends cells against free radicals, and carotenoids, which help reduce sun damage and ward off skin cancer.

Sardinia's hot spot of centenarians is Ogliastra, a mountainous province halfway down the eastern coast. Most of Sardinia's 1.7 million people live in the north and south, clustered in and around the cities of Olbia and Cagliari, whereas the rugged mountainous regions in the center are sparsely populated. All of Sardinia is underpopulated relative to mainland Italy, but it's rare to find a place that retains its traditional character and introverted perspective as much as Ogliastra.

OUTSIDE Marina di Olbia on Sardinia's northern tip, the wind screamed for two days, and our boat bounced and heeled like a child's Weeble toy, pushed and prodded from side to side but kept upright by its shape. When the wind weakened and the weather bulletin, taped to the marina office door, showed that calmer winds were on the way, we hoisted our sails and continued south. It was still breezy and we moved quickly, slicing through the water like a racing boat. We whipped past an endless wall of sheer rock faces and granite pillars, with few safe shelters. Capricious winds thundered over cliffs, periodically abating, only to return with renewed force. I adjusted our lines and pulled down the foresail to temper our speed, deftly moving across the deck in a way I couldn't have imagined two months earlier. Back in the cockpit, I could hear Leif's happy murmurs as Colin read a book to him.

It was my birthday, and after my sailing shift, Colin handed me a gift-wrapped box. He sang "Happy Birthday" while Leif tugged at the wrapping paper until the purple stovetop espresso maker inside was revealed. I smiled and kissed Colin. It was a thoughtful gift, not just because I love coffee, but because I prefer espressos and he'd rather drink cowboy coffee, a potent brew of grounds and water, and he was giving that up for me. After a lunch of tuna salad topped with buffalo mozzarella and Italian olive oil, and a birthday apple tart, we drank espressos.

By 10 PM we had sailed 160 kilometers and were halfway down Sardinia's coast. The small marina at the foot of Santa Maria Navarrese appeared like an oasis, the sole refuge after a marathon of cliffs. It was closed for the night, however, so we tied up at any empty berth and collapsed, exhausted after more than twelve hours of sailing.

The morning revealed a panorama of sandy cliffs, maquis-decked mountains, and stormy skies. A few sailboats sat on an otherwise empty pier. A family of four Germans with ruddy cheeks, blond hair, and high-end hiking gear advised us about where to explore. It was too late in the season to sail, they intoned, and their boat was moored here for the winter, but it was perfect weather for hiking. Another gale was forecast, and the complete absence of sailboats on the water further suggested our sailing days were coming to a close.

Hiking directions in hand, we marched up the hill and into town. Santa Maria Navarrese is named after an eleventh-century church, which we found alongside an equally old olive tree, and has a charming timelessness to it. There is a well-loved playground overlooking cobalt waters and plenty of benches where people can linger, but the streets were barren. The smattering of restaurants, most closed until spring, hinted at the town's summertime popularity with visitors who come to enjoy the rugged coastline and wilderness, and perhaps to catch a glimpse of the Mediterranean monk seals that used to live in nearby caves and beaches but are now approaching extinction.

The town borders Gennargentu National Park, and we were soon hiking along a thin goat trail, plunging through forests of maquis, cork oak, red-berried yew trees, and wild olives. The ocean was a stone's throw away, and windswept olive trees perched at the cliff's edge. Waves pummeled steep walls of granite and limestone on one side of us, and hulking mountains squeezed our other side. The landscape was wild and stunning, a mountain in the sea that reminded me of the Kalalau Trail in northern Kauai. Distant chimes tinkled, announcing a flock of white goats that clung to a faraway hill, their bells ringing as they foraged. Shepherds still roam these lands, as does the Sardinian wildcat, a striped gray cat no larger than most house cats. Not that long ago, vendettas were still a common way to enforce justice, and fugitives escaped into this wilderness.

This area has always been wild. The Roman philosopher Cicero called it the "land of barbarians," and for the most part, the Romans failed to control Sardinia. The nearby region, which was too rugged and lawless for the Romans to penetrate, was called Barbagia, derived from the Latin word *"barbària,"* meaning "barbarian." Not much changed over the next two thousand years. In 1849, the travel writer John William Warre Tyndale wrote of murderous bandits who inhabited these hills, stealing sheep, horses, and salt: "These outcasts are malviventi in the worse sense of the word—living by robbery, and sometimes accompanied with murder, and this makes the travelling in Barbagia a matter of great risk to a stranger, as well as to the natives."[2] In 2007, an eighty-two-year-old poet was shot six times at close range when he went out to get his morning newspaper. The locals blamed the shooting on a vendetta that stretched back more than fifty years, suggesting that it was payback for his role in a robbery and attempted murder. Typical of revenge killings, the poet's murder took place during the holidays, a few days after Christmas, when the family was celebrating. Even though the murder took place in broad daylight, witnesses did not come forward, and the killer remains free.

It seems ironic that lawlessness and longevity are intertwined, but it is here where the highest concentrations of centenarians reside. In the mountainous provinces of Ogliastra and Nuoro, there are nearly one hundred centenarians, and the nearby village of Villagrande Strisaili has the highest concentration in all of Sardinia. The world's oldest living siblings live here. In 2012, Guinness World Records identified a family of nine brothers and sisters who have a combined age of 818 years; the oldest is 105 and the youngest 78. Most of them live in the isolated village of Perdasdefogu, a short drive south and so inaccessible that until recently residents had to rely almost entirely on their own farming for food.

Some of the most rigorous scientific studies on centenarians have taken place in Sardinia. Finding out the true age of people born in the 1800s or early 1900s is rarely easy. Dates of birth, death, and marriage are often available from registry offices or church records, which are then cross-referenced against dates of parents, siblings, and children. The AKEA Project is a multidecade study that began examining centenarian Sardinians in the 1990s. It was undertaken by a consortium of researchers in Belgium, Italy, and France that has published numerous studies examining the diet, lifestyle, and genetics of this population of Sardinians. There is no magic fountain of youth or 1-2-3 guide to follow; rather, the Sardinians' longevity seems to be a result of a complex mingling of diet, lifestyle, environment, and genetics.

Sardinia's genetic isolation, because of its geography and lack of immigration, until recently led to the postulation that genetics played a key role. When researchers examined the Y chromosome of male centenarians, however, of which Sardinia has a disproportionate number compared with other centenarian hot spots, they found no difference in the frequency of selected genetic markers (haplotypes) from that found elsewhere in the

Mediterranean. This led them to conclude that the high level of longevity in men is either because of genes shared with females or is strongly influenced by the environment. Studies of other populations have shown that certain genes that play a role in the immune system are linked to longevity, but again, the Sardinian centenarians did not have a greater number of these genetic markers. Despite the challenges of identifying the genes that allow certain people to live longer, there is no doubt that genetics play a role, and human twin studies suggest that 20 to 30 percent of longevity is dictated by genetics and the remainder by environmental factors.

Determining what those environmental factors are can be equally complex, but studies of various populations around the globe have found consistent themes. According to the New England Centenarian Study, the largest study of centenarians in the world with more than 1,600 participants, centenarians are rarely obese and men are almost always lean. Caloric restriction was found to be a major contributing factor to the preponderance of centenarians among the Okinawan Japanese, who eat 20 percent less than the Japanese national average, and has been found to extend the health of all sorts of laboratory animals, from mice to monkeys. The study also found that centenarians rarely smoke and have a tendency to stay active. They handle stress better than most. These characteristics apply to Sardinia's centenarian population, and the researchers concluded that their longevity is a result of a mix of their diet, hard work ethic and tendency to stay active, low-stress lifestyle, and strong sense of community.

Bouncing along the trail and watching cloud shadows play over the Gennargentu masif while Leif chortled in his front carrier, I felt as though some of those habits might rub off on me. Hiking along the rugged trail felt great and was a welcome contrast to sitting in a sailboat or car. I could understand how a lifetime spent running through these hills, tending goats and picking olives, might be beneficial.

The sun hid behind clouds, and the patter of rain transformed into a deluge. A thick canopy of cork oaks sheltered us, and when the rain thinned, we joined a road that led to the sea and Pedra Longa, a 128-meter spike of granite and limestone. The beach was a tumble of boulders and iron-red sand. It was secluded, except for a traditional restaurant that was surprisingly crowded and festive. Children in velvet dresses and white shirts swirled across the floor like typhoons, while parents, grandparents, and great-grandparents lost themselves in each other's stories. A long table sagged with colorful canapés, anchovies on crisp-bread, cream-filled cookies, olives, and slivers of meat, while two waiters poured wine and coffee from behind a wooden bar. The room hummed with happiness, and several revelers looked as though they could have been centenarians.

"There are four, maybe even five generations here," I said to Colin as we entered the room. "Imagine growing up with that much family around."

Had we spoken Sardinian or Italian, we could have joined the festivities as a handful of the merrymakers mimed. But I suspected we had already glimpsed their secrets to a long and healthy life. As we left, a wrinkled woman in a dark headscarf smiled and stroked Leif's head. "*Akentannos,*" she said, the traditional Sardinian greeting, which means "May you live to be one hundred."

The marina harbormaster had warned that the "*golfe du Lion* blows all week," but by the following morning, the wind had calmed to force 4 and all that was left from yesterday's blow was a large swell. We left early to take advantage of the good weather before another storm rolled in. The coastline remained empty, mountainous, and exposed, except for the occasional marina with an overbuilt breakwater, and we spent one night at one of these.

"We should sell the boat in Cagliari," Colin said as we inched past Capo Ferrato, a mountainous jumble of granite and greenery that juts out of crescent beaches.

"What about Malta?" I said hesitantly, wanting to deny the torturous headwinds that beleaguered us and the volatile weather we'd just had.

"The sailing is getting too unpredictable," Colin said. "We could get hammered by a storm or have no winds and end up motoring the whole way."

I wanted to argue, but it was a logical decision. The sailing had been challenging for these last few days, and the weather would continue to degrade. It didn't make sense to sail another five hundred kilometers and undertake two overnight crossings.

"It could be hard to sell *Isis* in Sardinia," I said. "At least Malta is English speaking."

Our decision was made, and we spent our final night in Villasimius. The marina was new, as was the plaza of designer boutiques and gelato emporiums, but the real attraction was across the road, a huge and nearly deserted beach of fine, pale sand. Leif and I stripped down to our swimsuits and savored the late afternoon sunlight, while Colin trekked to a Genoese watchtower sitting on a nearby promontory. Even though it was October, the water was warm, and when Colin returned, we took turns swimming. I did laps between the cool deep water and the tepid shallows, swimming the front crawl until my arms tired, and then I lay back down on the beach towel. As the sun waned, we rambled back to our boat, following a boardwalk to a sandy road lined with modest houses ablaze in flowers. A gray-haired woman draped in black waved at Leif as we passed. *"Ciao, bella,"* she said. Good-bye, beautiful.

"Ciao, bella," I replied, as much to her as to the beach we were leaving.

Cagliari was disappointing. It was the end of our sailing journey, and the city was nothing like what I had expected. Postcards showed a tangle of pastel houses climbing up a mountainside, Renaissance and Art Nouveau architecture, and a Roman amphitheater, but when we arrived at Marina del Sole, none of that was visible. We were on the eastern outskirts of town, a fifteen-minute walk through litter-strewn forests and ragged streets to reach the downtown, and there was little besides an industrial boatyard nearby. The marina water was thick with algae; mussels carpeted boat lines, the boardwalk, and even boat hulls; and the bathroom was little more than a shack on the boardwalk. We had come here on the recommendation of an English sailor who had said, "It's a great place, and the water's always hot." By the time I had had my first shower and the water ran cold, I was starting to regret our decision.

I was also grumpy because selling the boat seemed unlikely. We typed up an ad, printed it in an Internet café, and postered the marina, a nearby sports club, and a handful of café-restaurants, and then spent an evening in another Internet café plastering online yachting magazines and Italian Craigslist-style websites. We tried to find a yacht broker to sell our boat, but all the yacht brokerages were in the north, and we weren't about to retrace our steps.

By the time it was karaoke night at the marina, I understood why it was so popular. Our neighbors, Tony and Tracey, a bubbly couple from England who were spending the winter readying their boat for a multiyear offshore sail, invited us to go with them, but we had too much to do. Instead we organized the boat, boxing up all the things we planned to ship home and putting the rest into piles to give away or take with us. The music pounded as the dozen or so English sailors living at the marina belted out "Hotel California" and other classics. For a Brit, this was like a home away from home, and even for us it was pretty homey.

Sardinia's post office is wildly less accommodating than its mariners, and shipping two boxes consumed the better part of a day. It took three tries before we managed to get our first carton shipped. The first time we were rejected because of improper wrapping, then because the package was overweight, and finally because we did not have a return address on land. Each time we corrected our error, waited in line for an hour, and left feeling dejected. Finally, after we had tracked down a stationery store, repacked our box, and fabricated an address, we left. Making arrangements for the rest of our travel was markedly easier, and we booked our flights to Greece for the following Monday. That would give us nearly a week to sell the boat, and if we hadn't done it by then, we'd have to figure something out.

Besides being a hot spot for centenarians, Sardinia was fascinating for its Phoenician ruins and early Nuragic civilizations. We rented a car and set off for Nora, Sardinia's oldest town, which is thirty kilometers south of Cagliari, just past the quiet village of Pula, on a Y-shaped peninsula. Phoenician inscriptions date the town to the eighth century BC, and before that it had been inhabited by Nuragic people, who lived on the island throughout the second millennium BC. Like many Phoenician settlements, this one had been chosen for its maritime advantages. The peninsula offered two sheltered harbors, one for when the winds blew from the east and another for when they came from the west.

Half of the peninsula is a military zone, and we waited for a tour guide to take us through the locked gate. Our guide, a twentysomething underwater archaeologist who documented submerged artifacts, led us and two young couples from Berlin through the ancient site. Sardinia is slowly sinking, she explained, and much of Nora is underwater, like Phoenician settlements all along the coast. Had we sailed here, we would have floated atop Phoenician artifacts and peered into the water to see an ancient Roman mosaic. The Romans conquered Sardinia in 238 BC, and although many of their buildings and roads remain, they destroyed and built over many Phoenician structures. There are still remnants of stone foundations that were once Phoenician temples and homes, but the impressive mosaics, stone roads, baths, storage cellars, and market squares are all Roman.

A handful of olive trees grew throughout the site, including two of considerable size. We didn't want to risk being denied permission, so we hung back and took samples from two large trees. The tree near the Roman marketplace was large and obviously grafted with at least two types of olives, small black ones and others that were nearly twice as large. The other tree was not much taller than a Christmas tree and had small black olives and thick corkscrew limbs. I wondered who had planted these trees. Phoenicians weren't known for grafting olive trees, but Romans were. Even though the trees didn't look large enough to be two millennia old, the meager conditions of the soil could have stunted their growth, or perhaps a generation or two separated them from the original trees. But if newcomers wanted to grow olive trees, they couldn't have asked for a more inviting climate. Hot, dry, and rocky, this was an olive tree's oasis, and Sardinia was thick with olives—wild, feral, and domesticated.

We continued to Tharros, a Phoenician site halfway up the western side of Sardinia, on a cape jutting out from the Gulf of Oristano, and searched for more old olive trees. Paths wound through the outdoor museum and past stone foundations and Roman columns, and pottery remnants and shingles littered the surrounding grassy hills. The remains of an ancient Roman wall studded the white-sand beach, and the ancient city continued underwater. Had we brought our swimsuits, we could have floated over 2,500-year-old artifacts or sunbathed lying against a Roman foundation.

Before the Phoenicians arrived some three thousand years ago, the Nuragic civilization thrived and continued to coexist with the Phoenicians until 200 AD. Wild olive trees grew on Sardinia during their reign, and we wondered if the Phoenicians used them, and if so, what for. To find out, we set off to Su Nuraxi, a prominent Nuragic settlement and UNESCO world heritage site an hour north of Cagliari, near Sardinia's center and amidst rolling farmland.

The 3,500-year-old fortress sits atop a plateau, and from the distance it looks like a giant stone igloo surrounded by leftover blocks, the beige stone contrasting sharply with the lush green fields surrounding it. It is impossible not to be struck by how complex the village is and how well it has been preserved. There are basalt towers with staircases spiraling upward, tunneled-out rooms, and a labyrinth of village foundations encircling the fortress. Our guide explained that when the Nuraghe were invaded, they covered their villages in dirt to protect them, and the island was dotted with an estimated seven thousand *nuraghes*, most of them still unexcavated and appearing as odd bulges atop hills.

Our guide didn't know whether the Nuraghe ate olives, but she confirmed that they used olive wood for building. Leading us into one of the towers, she pointed upward. "There were once wooden floors here—olive wood," she said. She explained that by carbon dating the olive wood, the *nuraghe* had been dated to 1478 BC. I could imagine that hard olive wood would make good floorboards, and I wondered again if they used the olive tree for more than wood.

When we returned to our boat, our neighbor Tony told us that a friend of his had come to see it. Pascal, a sailing instructor who worked at the offshore oil refinery, returned that evening, and the following day we agreed on a price. With only days to go before our departure, we had sold the boat for nearly as much as we paid for it. It was reason to celebrate, and over glasses of a strong red local wine made from Cannonau grapes, we toasted the sale and the British sailor who recommended this marina.

Sardinia was a place of contradictions. For millennia, the island's isolation had fostered unique and peculiar traits, and that's still true today. The remains of ancient mysterious civilizations with beehive fortresses built of basalt and olive wood coexist with flashy resorts for the uber-rich, bandit hideouts in the mountains, villages where centenarian birthday parties are commonplace, and impenetrable forests containing some of the world's last truly wild olive trees. We'd come here searching for answers to questions about how to live longer and healthier lives and where the first olive trees grew, as well as what we would do with our own journey, how we'd continue, and where we'd go. We didn't have all the answers, but we were getting closer to them.

10

THE OLIVE SOLUTION

"If truth be told, his olive oil was no better than his competitors', he could not use the common strangleholds of legitimate businessmen. He had to rely on the force of his own personality and his reputation as a 'man of respect.'"

THE GODFATHER[1]

GREECE WAS SEIZED by austerity measures and protests when we arrived. The airline strike that had silenced the skies ended two days before our flight, but city workers were still on strike and mounds of garbage festered on Athens's streets, burying parked cars and blocking driveways.

The taxi delivered us to the apartment where Colin's stepfather once lived, in a working-class suburb with gyro restaurants, barbershops, and bakeries. We rang the doorbell of the two-story townhouse and were greeted by footsteps thundering down the marble staircase.

"Looks like you're getting fat," Colin said, patting his half brother's lean stomach.

"And I bet you still have that farting problem," George said.

His daughters, Raine and Alexandra, hovered shyly nearby, and I coaxed a hug from each of them. Although they lived in London, we saw them at least once a year, and their brief vacation here gave us a chance to introduce Leif to them. The girls fawned over their new cousin as though he was the little brother they always wanted, which he looked like he could be. All three were blond, and although the girls weren't quite as flaxen as Leif, they contrasted starkly with their father's dark hair and unmistakably Greek features.

We settled onto antique furniture in the living room, a high-ceilinged, white-walled room with a mosaic tile floor and few decorations besides a bookshelf filled with volumes by Nabokov and Pushkin. George left to get lunch from the gyro shop down the road and returned with his cousin Dimitri—a spry sixty-nine-year-old chain-smoking engineer who was more interested in talking about Greece's economic crisis than his family olive farm.

"There is no hope," Dimitri said, stubbing out his cigarette in a glass ashtray. "It started two hundred years ago, when the English lent the newly formed state of Greece money. Then the U.S. took over and now the EU. They lent us money so we could buy their products."

We listened quietly. Until now, we'd only heard about Greece's woes on the news. Since Greece's debt had plummeted to junk bond status, the EU had pumped in 110 million euros in bailout loans to stave off bankruptcy. But it wasn't enough, and the EU had just agreed to inject another 120 million euros. In exchange, they demanded fiscal restraint and austerity measures that infuriated many Greeks, who voiced their disdain in headline-grabbing protests and strikes. Watching the news, I had felt limited sympathy for those who paralyzed their country because they had overspent and now had to curb their freewheeling ways, but then, I was an outsider looking in. Dimitri, who had been out of work for three years, provided another perspective; he blamed the Greeks' misfortunes on political mismanagement and foreign interest.

"First came Volkswagen, then Adidas, then Bosch. We used to make fabrics. Now we just buy from the Germans," he said.

"What about olives and olive oil?" I asked.

Greeks use more olive oil than anyone else in the world, and Greece is the third-largest olive oil producer, pressing two-thirds as much oil as Italy. They also grow excellent table olives, including the popular Kalamata olives, a staple in Greek salads around the world. But Dimitri argued that EU limitations on agriculture had stolen their thunder in that arena, too.

"The tomatoes are from Spain, the beer from Holland, the pork from Denmark—and the bill goes to Germany," George said. He laughed as he pointed to the gyro remnants on his plate and his Amstel beer.

We all laughed, except Dimitri, who looked increasingly downcast. His situation weighed on me, but it seemed ironic that there was so much negativity toward the Germans when they were footing much of the bill for averting Greece's fiscal ruin. Reining in spending was not an easy solution, but what was the alternative?

"Returning to the drachma wouldn't be so bad," Dimitri said, lighting another cigarette. "It would be hard for a few years, but then things would get better."

I wasn't so sure bankruptcy was the solution, and George, who works in the financial industry, believed the repercussions would be far-ranging.

"The whole world is watching Greece," George said. "The market dropped when Greece refused the austerity measures, and if it pulls out of the euro, it could be the end of the currency."

"I hope the strike hasn't closed the Acropolis," I said. I had suddenly realized that the olive tree that had drawn us to Athens might no longer be accessible.

We left the apartment and walked through Athens's litter-strewn streets searching for a taxi to take us to the Acropolis. Along the way, we passed overflowing dumpsters and mini-landfill sites. The nation's disillusionment was palpable. It was hard to believe that a country that had once been so powerful and influential had fallen so hard.

The Acropolis was the antithesis of Athens's current woes, a symbol of past power and global influence. Built on a limestone hill flanked by olive trees, the collection of 2,500-year-old temples dedicated to the deities of ancient Greece was a stunning sight. Strikes had shut this UNESCO world heritage site, but it had reopened, and I felt a quiver of excitement as we entered.

"Athena and Poseidon dueled to become the stewards of this city," I explained as we walked up the stone path. "The gods decided that the title would go to whoever offered the best gift. Poseidon, god of the sea, struck the earth with his trident, and water gushed out. Athena grew an olive tree."

"Is the olive tree here?" Raine asked in a lilting English accent.

"That's what we're here to find out, but first we have to find the right temple."

Past the Parthenon and other elegant temples, we found the Acropolis's youngest temple, the Erechtheion. Built in 420 BC to replace another temple, it is an elegant marble structure that was the Acropolis's holiest site in the fifth century BC. The first king of Athens, Cecrops, was buried here, in a tomb under the Porch of the Caryatids, a stunning section where six female figures replace the traditional columns used elsewhere. More important, this was Athena's temple, dedicated to her and swathed in olive symbolism. Inside, there once was an olive-wood statue of Athena, cloaked in a freshly woven peplos, the distinctive sleeveless ankle-length dress worn by women of that era, which was replaced every year. It is also here where the famous showdown between Poseidon and Athena occurred.

"I think an olive tree still grows here," I said as we circled the building. "And there are supposed to be other signs of Athena and Poseidon's battle."

Inside the temple, we found those mythological marks. A hole in the floor had once been a cistern, and deep marks in the rock had supposedly been made by Poseidon's trident. The temple architects had left a hole in the ceiling to show the path of the trident. Legend has it that when Poseidon struck the earth with his trident, horses galloped out and salt water sprang forth.

But Poseidon's gift of water was no match for Athena's gift, which we found on the other side of the temple. The nine-meter olive tree stood in the shadow of the temple, as much a part of it as the earth beneath it. It wasn't a particularly old tree, probably no more than a hundred years old. Persians had destroyed the original tree in 480 BC, when they ransacked the city, but according to lore, it sprouted again the next day. At the time, the olive tree represented Athena's gift of food, wood, and oil and the importance of the olive tree to Greece, and today none of that has changed.

ONCE WE LEFT Athens, Greece was transformed. The highway south began gently, winding along the Saronic Gulf and crossing the Corinth Canal, which slices through an isthmus to save Athens-bound ships the long detour around the Peloponnesian peninsula.

The Peloponnese, named after the Greek god Pelops, is as large as Israel and shaped like an octopus, with four ragged tentacles, one of which was our destination: the Mani Peninsula.

Mostly mountainous, the region is dotted with towns and farmland and blanketed in olive trees, and there is little that suggests its important role throughout history and even today. The Mycenaeans lived here in the Bronze Age, before the ancient Greeks built their empire and catapulted the cities into fame and infamy. Olympia, host of the first Olympic Games, lay an hour west, and we'd soon pass through Sparta, home of the fearsome Spartan army bejeweled in horsehair Mohawk helmets and circular shields.

After the Greeks came the Romans, Slavs, Turks, Crusaders, and Venetians, and it would be nearly two millennia before Greece returned to the Greeks. In the early nineteenth century, Peloponnesians ignited the twelve-year Greek Revolution against the Ottoman Empire and helped bring independence to Greece. The peninsula still exerts political influence and is the birthplace of many of Greece's politicians and business titans. Yet it also struggles with poverty and isolation. Its youth have abandoned their village homes for big-city opportunities, and now only 10 percent of Greece's population lives in the Peloponnese.

The city of Kalamata marks the entranceway to the Mani Peninsula and is, unsurprisingly, surrounded by olive trees bearing its name, as well as Koroneiki, Mavroya, and Mastoidis varieties. A few trees were already being harvested, with nets spread underneath and farmers perched on ladders, and in a couple weeks, the harvest would be in full swing, a frenzy that would last until the end of January. Unlike the high-density olive orchards of Spain or California, where olive harvesting is mechanized, here all the olives are picked by hand. Each tree was different—some tall and sprawling, others narrow and more contained—and this made mechanical picking impossible. Mechanical harvesters are like big tractors that drive over an olive tree. Inside, rotating plastic blades whack at the olive tree like a brush in a car wash, dislodging and collecting the olives. But the rough-and-tumble process of mechanical harvesting bruises the olives, adulterating the taste of the oil and tarnishing table olives, leading many growers to prefer hand-harvesting despite the added time and cost.

The owners of this olive farm have no choice. Kalamata olives cannot be picked by machine, not only because of the tree's size and shape, but also because quality table olives must be picked by hand. Even when picking olives by hand, the harvesters need to be careful. In *Producing Table Olives*, Stan Kallis explains that olives should be collected in padded bags to prevent damage and stored in the shade until they are processed. It is also crucial to know which olives to pick, and some trees may need to be picked multiple times to ensure that the olives are picked at the proper stage of ripeness. Olives need to be picked with a milking action, and using anything besides your hand will increase the likelihood of damage. This excludes the range of handheld tools for olive picking, from rakes that comb olives out of the branches to powered hand harvesters with whirling blades, since none are as gentle as a hand. Pretty much any tool will cause the olive to hit a branch or hard surface as it is removed and then again when it falls to the ground. Scars and brown spots will mar the bruised fruit, and blisters or gas pockets may form. The level of damage depends on the cultivar as well as the time of picking; black olives are more delicate than green ones. Kalamata olives are particularly prone to damage, because they are picked when they've darkened to a deep purple, the level of ripeness that is marred by an ungentle touch.

When this family finished picking their olives, they would probably be brined for table olives. Although Kalamatas can also be made into oil, most become table olives, and that is how the world thinks of this cultivar. They are one of the few olives for which the demand is almost always greater than the supply. In 2012, the price for edible olives plummeted 20 to 30 percent because of the bumper crop, but Kalamata olives weather this price fluctuation better and consistently sell for more than other cultivars. Their status comes in part from their protected designation of origin (PDO) label. Just as champagne can only come from the Champagne region in France, for olives to be called Kalamata they must come from Kalamata trees grown in this region and be a product of the microclimate, environmental conditions, and human factors specific to this area.

These laws protect the quality and origin of not only olives but also a broad range of foods—including beer, balsamic vinegar, cheese, wines, vegetables, and meats—that are considered a form of intellectual property. There are more than eight hundred geographic indications for European foods and alcohols, and within Greece alone, sixteen regions have a PDO label for their olive oil. Securing geographic protection for a product not only provides the consumer with quality assurance but also secures higher prices for the producer. When Italian Toscano olive oil received a geographic indication in 1998, it earned a 20 percent premium, and a 2009 study of Italian extra virgin olive oils showed that oils with a PDO label sold for 42 percent more than those without. Differentiation through quality and geographic origin may be the strongest ally olive growers have in securing fair prices for their crop, but that protection stops at Europe's borders.

Outside the European Union, these laws are pretty much unenforceable. Several countries, including Canada and the United States, have bilateral agreements with the EU that offer some protection, but they apply only to wine and spirits. The Kalamata olives you buy outside Europe were probably not even grown in Greece, let alone Kalamata. It is just the same with other Greek products, such as feta cheese, which, according to

EU legislation, can only be produced in Greece. Nevertheless, 72 percent of all feta cheese is made outside Greece.

We left Kalamata on a narrow road pushed against the Ionian Sea by the Taygetos mountains, jagged peaks cloaked in olive trees and cypress. It was a beautiful but savage landscape, as resolute as its inhabitants, who are descended from Spartan warriors and were once known for their fierce warring and blood feuds, vicious vendettas that went on for generations and destroyed families. All of Mani is rugged and remote, dominated by mountains and rock, and the name Mani means "dry" or "treeless." For most of history, this peninsula was accessible only by sea, and even when modern technology infiltrated the area, it was delayed here and electricity didn't reach all villages until the 1990s.

The coastline is dotted with ample sandy beaches bookended by rocky promontories, and the road unites villages of fortified homes and narrow stone towers with jail-cell windows that protected Maniots from vendettas. It's a land frozen in time, without the hardships of the past, and Colin and I dreamed of living here. Devoid of the gaudy tourism that plagues places only fractionally as becoming, we felt as though we'd stumbled on our Shangri-La. Other travelers have felt that same pull, and when we passed through Kardamili, a village featured in Homer's *Iliad,* I recalled that two of Britain's greatest travel writers lived here. Patrick Leigh Fermor, who was once known as Britain's greatest living travel writer and wrote many books, including *Mani: Travels in the Southern Peloponnese,* lived in an olive grove until he died earlier this year at the age of ninety-two. Bruce Chatwin also lived here at one time and had his ashes scattered at a Byzantine chapel overlooking the village.

At Stoupa, a village a third of the way down the peninsula, we turned into the mountains, twisting through three hamlets before reaching a modern plant, painted white with yellow doors and window trim, roofed in solar panels, and overlooking a sea of olive trees that ended when the land disappeared into the ocean. We'd heard about Mani-Bläuel from a friend who was a food writer and had traveled here with her husband several years ago. She had fallen in love with the place and the people and thought I would, too. Mani-Bläuel started the organic olive oil movement in Greece, producing the country's first organic olive oil and persuading hundreds of farmers to renounce pesticides. This initiative helped locals retain their traditional lifestyles by paying higher olive oil prices, allowing them to continue farming instead of searching for opportunities elsewhere.

"Welcome, welcome," Silvia Lazzari said as we stepped inside, flashing an infectious smile that made us feel like we were old friends. She was stylish but casual in a light blue cardigan, her straight brown hair held back by an elastic band.

"Would you like to see the plant, or would you like to have lunch first?" Silvia asked after we'd finished our introductions.

Although I was hungry after our long drive, I was more eager to learn about their olive oil. Silvia led us through the plant and into a room dominated by large stainless steel tanks filled with olive oil. Nearby, a bottling facility whirled with automated conveyers, monitored by women in hairnets, and in another sterile room, the women jarred olives, organic black Kalamatas and green Conservolias. Every year, the plant produced a staggering 750,000 liters of olive oil, about a tenth as much oil as all of France. Some five hundred farmers who lived throughout Mani grew the olives, which were picked by hand, pressed in nearby mills, and then sent here to be bottled and shipped off to stores around the world.

The oil came from the olives of Koroneiki trees, hardened trees that grow in little more than rocks and produce small, rounded olives that cling to the trees. Originating in Mani, Koroneiki olives are now a darling of Californian and Australian olive groves, preferred for their exceptional oil and compact growth, which is required for high-density farming. But nowhere else in the world will you find Koroneiki olive oil that tastes like this. The *Flos Olei* guide to olive oil describes it as an oil with "excellent organoleptic qualities" and says "the best are the productions of southern Peloponnisos."

Given the high praise, we were eager to try Mani-Bläuel's oil. To guide us through the process, Silvia introduced us to Nikko, the plant's chemist and olive oil taster. Nikko's dark, intelligent eyes were framed by horn-rimmed glasses, and he spoke in a quiet and deliberate manner as he carefully explained the complex tests and terminology of olive oil chemistry. After we'd toured his laboratory, a sterile room filled with workbenches, microscopes, scales, computer, bottles, and beakers, and he'd detailed some of the dozens of tests the plant performs—"We do more tests on our oils than any other company I know"—it was time for the tasting.

"I have two oils for you," Nikko said with a playful smile. "One oil is excellent; the other is only average. See if you can tell me the difference."

"We're getting better at this." I laughed. We had learned that the olive oil challenge is irresistible to professional tasters, and we were getting used to pitting our inexperienced palates against their vast knowledge.

Nikko set out four identical glasses and filled two of them with an inch of oil from one bottle and two of them with an inch of oil from the other bottle. As in the Pepsi Challenge, the contents of the glasses looked exactly the same. Colin and I followed our well-rehearsed protocol: swirl the glass, inhale deeply, slurp loudly, and swallow.

"This one is much better," Colin said between coughs. "It's got bite, too." I had to agree. They were both pleasant, with typical Koroneiki flavors, mellow and delicate with a slight flavor of grass and herbs and a pleasant bitterness, but with vastly different intensities; one was more like a live symphony, whereas the other was a tinny recording.

"What makes these oils so different?" I asked.

"They're both from Koroneiki trees that are about forty years old," Nikko said, passing us a bottle of intensely golden oil, "but this one is from a grove farther south, where the land is even rockier and drier."

Nikko brought the exceptional olive oil to lunch, which Silvia had prepared and set out in the company lounge, a cozy room with a long wooden table, stove, fridge, and bookshelves. There were sautéed wild greens, picked in the fields from among the olive trees; green and black tapenades; four kinds of salad; fresh bread; olives; and feta cheese. Every dish had olive oil in it, and all the ingredients came from nearby. It was a meal fit for even the fussiest health-conscious locavore.

"The salad is from Fritz's garden," Silvia said, gesturing to a bowl of leafy greens shimmering with olive oil. The other salads were wild greens—dandelion, chicory, nettles—collected from nearby fields and sautéed in olive oil; potatoes and onions and greens also liberally dressed in olive oil; and tomatoes and feta cheese doused with herbs and olive oil.

Fritz is a tall, thin man with shaggy, graying hair and a dark mustache. He looked as though a light breeze might blow him over, but his intense gaze hinted at the resoluteness of olive trees that survive in rugged mountains. He hunched over to shake our hands and folded himself into a chair at the kitchen table.

"I came here in 1978 with Austrian friends. We were the only young people in the village, and so we were accepted with even more warmth," Fritz said, nibbling on a bird's portion of wild greens. "People were very kind to us."

They lived on the beach in tents for seven months and then bought a dilapidated house, which they rebuilt, creating a roof and floor and replastering it. That winter, they ran out of money and found work picking olives. They'd wake up and start picking at 7 AM, but it was an unusually cold winter and the olives were frozen. Even though they were picking Kalamata olives destined for the table, they were too damaged and had to be pressed into oil instead. In the evenings, they'd go to the mill and watch the olives being pressed.

"The oil came out, and I thought, wow, what's that? It didn't resemble what I considered oil," Fritz said. "It was very fruity, with a strong aroma, a nice scent, and the texture..." He rubbed his fingers together as though to recreate the feeling. "The vis..."

"Viscosity," I said.

"It is a beautiful oil," Colin agreed, pouring a little more on his tomato salad.

Olive trees have long grown in the Mani Peninsula, but their popularity skyrocketed in the 1960s, when the plummeting price of flour prompted farmers to replant their wheat fields with olives. You can still see the threshing circles—large stone enclosures where the grain was separated from the wheat—throughout the countryside, but they're now surrounded by olive trees. Until the 1980s, olives were grown naturally, without chemical fertilizers, herbicides, and pesticides, but when Fritz moved here, that was changing. A hearty marketing campaign by big chemical companies and village visits by agronomists encouraged farmers to embrace nonorganic methods, just as 1950s households had welcomed TV dinners. These methods were touted as scientific and modern, and to compete with that, Fritz had to repackage natural farming.

"We marketed it as a mixture of traditional methods and new scientific methods," Fritz said. "This was really true. The traps for the olive fly had just been invented. And also organic fertilizers were just starting, because organic growing was just starting."

Organic growing was taking hold in other countries, but in Greece, it was still unheard of. Fritz pioneered not only organic olive farming in Greece but organic agriculture. When the company started in the early 1980s, the only other organic producer was a grape plantation making raisins farther north in the Peloponnese. Fritz also touted the benefits of organic growing for the land and people.

"What exactly does organic farming mean for olive trees?" I asked.

"Organic farming means organic fertilizers, organic ways of fighting insects, and organic ways of taking care of the herbs and cleaning the fields," Fritz said, counting the principles on his fingers. "That means no pesticides, herbicides, or chemical fertilizers go into the soil or groundwater. In many cases, the fertilizers were not dug in—they were just thrown on—so the rain would take it away and it would go to the sea."

I nodded, imagining how hard it would be to dig anything into the rocky soil that Mani olive trees thrived in.

"Everything from the microbes to the birds to the farmer is affected by chemicals," Fritz said, "especially the aerial spraying."

It seemed strange that farmers would move away from natural methods to techniques that cost more and had dangerous side effects, but there were strong incentives and big marketing campaigns behind this shift. The big chemical companies sent agronomy experts into the villages to convince farmers of conventional methods, and the European Union offered subsidies for chemical fertilizers. Even the government agronomists were averse to organic farming.

"It was very hard to go against this. People didn't know who to trust," Fritz explained. "And many people trusted the big companies more."

Fritz held village meetings to talk about organic farming, but few people came, and when they did, they'd say, "Why should we listen to you?" After a year of trying, one village converted to organic farming. "I was able to convince them because they were antiestablishment and didn't want to pay for the aerial spraying," Fritz explained.

Since then, he's convinced more than five hundred families to do the same, and now 10 percent of the olives grown on the Mani Peninsula are organic. This is significantly higher than in the rest of Greece, where only 1 percent of olive orchards are organic.

The next day, Fritz took us to the mountainous village where the sea change had started. It was deep in the Taygetos mountains, a tiny hamlet of stone houses, backyard gardens, and free-roaming goats surrounded by olive trees. It was a beautiful but dying town. In the 1960s, the town's population was three hundred; now it was only thirty, and most of those people were over the age of sixty. As in the picturesque hill towns of Italy, young generations had abandoned their homes and a traditional lifestyle for modern conveniences and big-city opportunities.

"Maybe now that Greece is in a recession, they will come back home," Fritz mused as we approached the rustic restaurant.

Trading Athens's grimy streets for this utopia seemed an obvious choice, but then, life here wasn't easy either. Fritz had spent a year trying to live a traditional lifestyle, growing his own food, milking goats every day, making cheese every third day, and pressing olive oil. It had been a hard year and had deepened his respect for the traditional Maniot lifestyle, but in the end he concluded, "It's not for me." Younger people didn't want to live like that, and it would take new opportunities in tourism and other employment sectors to draw them back.

Elias, a gray-haired man of ample girth, embraced Fritz when we entered the large room with a handful of wooden tables and a hearth fueled by olive wood. They chatted warmly in Greek, and it was obvious that Fritz was a part of their family, welcomed into this tightly knit community despite his striking un-Greek appearance. Against a wall near the woodstove, two gray-haired women, their faces mottled with liver spots, and an elderly man sipped water and laughed. Elias's grandmother was 103 but looked two decades younger, and they spent the next two hours fussing over Leif as though he were the last baby on earth. I suspected nothing would have made them happier than if we had left Leif behind.

Elias brought us hearty tomato and bean soup, ladled from a cauldron that bubbled over an olive wood-fired stove; sautéed wild greens; goat cheese; thick slabs of bread; and a bottle of olive oil.

"Is this your own olive oil?" I asked.

"I have two thousand trees," he said. "It takes me four months, but I pick the olives myself. I'm not as strong as I used to be, but I can still pick half the grove."

"Do you get someone else to pick the other half?" Colin asked.

"No, no," Elias said, shocked by the suggestion. "It would make me sad to let others touch my trees."

I applauded his passion, even though it made no financial sense. It was common to hire Albanians to pick olives here, and they were paid either twenty-five euros for a day's work or half the profits from the olives. Elias could have saved himself four months of work without any financial loss.

"Those who think Greeks are lazy should see Elias," Fritz said when Elias had returned to the kitchen. "He works in his olive fields all day and in the restaurant at night. He has two sons, but they cannot help him; they cannot even pick olives." Fritz looked over at two hefty men sitting at an adjacent table; they were in their thirties and had vacant gazes and made erratic movements, indicating some sort of impairment.

"Elias was born in the house I live in," Fritz continued. "When I bought it from his mother, it wasn't one house but two small houses next to each other."

I nodded, recalling his modest home with a cozy living room and kitchen and upstairs loft.

"She said it was impossible. Everyone from the village came to tell me it couldn't be done; the house would collapse if I made one big roof," Fritz said. "I knew it was possible, but because no one had ever done that, they couldn't imagine it."

"That mindset must have given you some challenges with the olive farmers," Colin said.

"It was hard." Fritz sighed. "Sometimes I wanted to give up, but slowly things changed, and it all started here. If these people didn't believe in me I couldn't have done it."

"So after you renoed your house, did people have more faith in you?" I asked.

"Elias's mother was so angry she tried to kill me. She hit me with a board full of nails and chased me across a field, which is not easy for someone that's eighty and nearly blind from cataracts." Fritz laughed. "It wasn't even over the roof. It was because I put a window in."

Local historian and Maniot Voula Kyriakea describes her compatriots' "ingrained suspicions" and their "difficulty in adopting anything new" and the challenges that posed for Mani-Bläuel in her book *Mani*.[2] She credits the Bläuels for their consistency, professionalism, and determination, concluding that "the journey was difficult, but their belief in the oil and their persistence was great, and they succeeded."[3] Like many locals, she is proud that the oil from their trees has won international awards, that it is sold in far-reaching places, and that it was here in Mani where Greece's first organic olive oil was made.

It seemed like a business model that could help Greece with its current woes. Instead of selling bulk olive oil to foreign buyers who buy it at low prices, mark up the price, and sell it under a private label, Greeks could embrace their heritage and produce world-class olive oil and olives that are coveted around the world. This is a view shared by the consultancy firm McKinsey & Company, who in 2012 issued a seventy-page report titled *Greece 10 Years Ahead: Defining Greece's New Growth Model and Strategy.*

In it the firm notes that Greece exports 60 percent of its olive oil in bulk to Italy, giving up a 50 percent premium it could earn by packaging and selling the oil itself—not to mention the additional jobs that would be created. Greece is the third-largest olive oil producer and in 2012 produced 270 million kilograms of olive oil. Bulk olive oil sells for 2.1 euros per kilogram, whereas finished olive oil fetches 3.1 euros per kilogram. If Greece stopped selling its oil to Italy in bulk and instead packaged it and sold it as Greek olive oil, it could earn an additional $162 million.

Italy and Spain are much better at tapping into lucrative export markets. McKinsey looked at the fifteen top exporting geographies, which included the U.S., Canada, a number of European countries, and nations in the Far East, and found that Greece exports a trivial amount of olive oil compared with Spain and Italy. In fact, only 4 percent of the olive oil these countries import from the three biggest olive oil-producing nations is Greek; the remaining 96 percent is produced by Italy or Spain. That's not to say that the oil wasn't made from Greek olives—much of Italy's olive oil is—but Greece did not receive the economic benefits of selling it as a finished product. McKinsey concluded, "Greece does not capture its 'fair share' in olive oil exports and forgoes significant opportunities."[4]

To change this, the report recommends that Greece build more olive oil processing plants and harness its reputation for high-quality food by certifying "original Greek" foods, packaging and branding its products instead of selling wholesale, and hitting key markets with a strong Greek marketing campaign. Basically, the report was saying that Greece needed more people like Fritz.

Fritz had worked hard to create this business over the last three decades, but now it was time to hand over the reins, and his son Felix had been managing things since Fritz had broken his pelvis in a skiing accident two years earlier. Still, retirement wasn't on the horizon. Besides being on the company advisory board, Fritz was absorbed by Sonnenlink, the feng shui retreat he and his wife had created, and the music concerts, yoga retreats, and olive tours they offered.

We had been staying at Sonnenlink, and I was sad to leave. Perched on the hillside, we overlooked olive groves peppered with terra-cotta-roofed houses and the Mediterranean, its torturous shoreline and endless promontories jutting out like finger docks at a marina until adjacent mountains blotted them out. We woke up watching the sunrise through a wall of glass patio doors and windows and sipped our morning coffee on the wooden deck while Leif hurled pinecones and rocks into the shrubs. Marble mounted on the wall radiated heat when temperatures dipped, and solar panels warmed our shower water. I don't know if it was the view or the feng shui, but I felt more relaxed and at peace than I had in years.

There was something magical about walking along stone paths winding under olive trees and past delicate flowers and lounging in a stone amphitheater surrounding a stage with a baby grand piano that comes alive during the summertime concert series. In the main house, which housed the yoga studio and conference room, we perused books about the local history and chatted with the other couple staying there, yoga instructors from Germany. Fritz had again captured the essence of the Mani

Peninsula and created a way for outsiders to partake in it. This time it was not through food but through tourism and a combination of both in the tours that gave people the chance to pick olives, press them, and taste the fresh oil. There was so much hope and possibility here, and it was such a stark contrast to the disenchantment of Athens.

Olives could engender prosperity, despite the historically low prices for olive oil and the glut of fraudulent oils. But this would require a shift in thinking, a move away from producing anonymous oil sold to bulk buyers and a focus on quality and identity. Abandoning a way of life that was millennia old wasn't the answer, but embracing and inviting others to share in it was. Tilling the soil and living in a stone hilltop hamlet may seem tedious to a Greek teenager aching for Athens excitement, but to many, it seems to be a magical way of life, a return to simpler times. Agritourism is a growing industry, and Greece has more than its share of alluring destinations and delicious foods. Sometimes picking olives can be more prosperous than pressing them.

11

SOMETHING OLD AND SOMETHING NEW

"The olive being pure, ought to have them that gather it chaste; and they ought to swear that they come from their own wife's, not from another's bed; for it will thus produce a great abundance of fruit for the time to come."

Geoponika, TENTH-CENTURY BYZANTINE COMPILATION[1]

BY NOVEMBER, CRETE'S olive harvest was in full swing. Its more southerly location meant the Koroneiki olives, which were so prevalent in Mani but just beginning to ripen, were fully ripe and ready to be pressed. We drove westward from the Heraklion airport along the northern coast, its rugged but populated terrain squeezed between the ocean and mountains, the plateaus thick with holiday homes and olive trees crawling up hillsides. Nets carpeted the ground beneath the olive trees like Christmas tree skirts, and pickers beat the branches with sticks or waved their electric brushes through the leaves. Nearly half of Greece's olive oil is made here, Greece's largest and most populous island, with 600,000 Cretans and 2 million visitors a year. A region half the size of New Jersey produces 5 percent of the world's olive oil.

Olive oil has always been big business here. Crete is home to Europe's first civilization, the Minoans, who, beginning 4,700 years ago, relied on olive oil to help build their prosperous empire. Minoans grew olives and produced olive oil as food, soap, a perfume base, fuel, medicine, and a lucrative export commodity, and the island is littered with archaeological discoveries, from ancient vessels called *pithoi* used to hold oil to stone presses, older than any others in Europe. Their olive legacy lives on today through the island's abundance of ancient olive trees, and some say the oldest olive tree in the world grows here. This tree, known as the Olive Tree of Vouves, is reputed to be up to four thousand years old, meaning that it was alive during Minoan times. Today, Crete embraces the modern along with the ancient, and we timed our visit to coincide with a conference for olive researchers from around the world.

On the western edge of Crete, we left the highway and turned south into olive groves punctuated by hamlets where chickens scratched in roadside dirt and laundry hung outside stone houses. Deep in the island, we reached one of Crete's most iconic olive farms. Biolea is an organic olive farm that merges modern and traditional technology, using stone grindstones to crush olives and stacks of round discs to press the oil but also working with modern materials according to the most up-to-date EU standards. I found Biolea's olive oil in a Greek specialty store in Vancouver years ago, and when I contacted the owners, they invited us to join them for the first pressing of the season.

We climbed a slight hill and parked amidst their olive trees, in a mostly empty lot that fronted their olive press and tasting room, a modern and tasteful building not unlike what you'd find in a Sonoma County vineyard. A man with floppy salt-and-pepper hair and a full moustache walked toward us.

"George Dimitriadis," he said, sticking out his hand and inviting us upstairs into his home. His wife, Christine, greeted us warmly and crooned over Leif, confiding that she was eager for grandchildren. At this, their daughter, Chloe, laughed. She's in her twenties and a recent graduate of McGill University's political science program.

"The olive season is bad this year," George said as we settled into his soft living room couch. "Often it takes three months to harvest, but it will be much quicker this year."

"How much oil will you produce?" I asked, sipping the tea Christine brought us.

"We have eleven hectares of trees, and this year it'll be half of what we pressed last year," George said.

The farm has been in George's family for five generations, and he has been running it since 1994. When he returned to Greece from Canada and discovered his family was losing money, he decided a different approach was warranted. "There were 210 olive farms in Chania. I didn't want to be number 211."

He converted the farm to organic and began experimenting with traditional pressing methods, which he believed were more healthful. Traditional olive presses retained more of the water-soluble antioxidants, he explained, and the olive oil was more healthful, part of the reason Cretans used to live to one hundred. But creating a traditional press according to EU standards proved to be more of a challenge and took years.

"People said it couldn't be done," he said. "There was no EU-approved traditional mill equipment available, so we had to make it ourselves."

George led us downstairs and opened the heavy doors to the mill. As promised, he had waited for us to start the first press of the season. He whirred the stainless steel machinery to life, and a trio of young men, interns through a farm exchange program, poured olives onto the conveyer belt, which chugged upward, washing the olives and separating out the leaves and twigs. The clean olives dropped into large stainless steel cauldrons, where they were crushed. Three large granite grindstones, each weighing 2.5 tons and attached to a central axle, rolled over the olives like a car driving through mud. The entire device was covered with a Plexiglas shield that curved outward like the cockpit on a fighter jet, a futuristic take on a process that was thousands of years old. George had built this modern version of the traditional millstone grinder from scratch, sourcing the grindstones from the Swiss Alps, hiring expert engineers, and then making adjustments to comply with EU regulations. The ground olives then went into a malaxator, which kneaded the olive paste and coaxed the oil out.

"The temperature is very important," George said, drawing my attention to a thermometer.

Malaxation warms the olives, but the temperature needs to stay under twenty-seven degrees Celsius, according to regulation. Heating the olive any more causes degradation. Many olive oils claim to be cold-pressed, but this term is archaic, a remnant of dated technology in which hot water was poured over the olives as they were being pressed to extract additional oil and producers who didn't employ this shoddy practice differentiated themselves by calling their oil "cold-pressed." Nowadays, hot water is never added to olive oil that is destined to be virgin or extra virgin, and most olive oil is extracted with centrifuges not presses. "First press" is another antiquated term that is still commonly used. It refers to oil pressed from freshly crushed olives, as opposed to oil from subsequent pressings, but today, all extra virgin and virgin olive oil is made from freshly crushed olives and once again rarely "pressed."

Once the olive paste was sufficiently mixed, an intern spread it onto large circular microfilament mats shaped like oversized records. Traditionally, these would have been made from hemp, but Biolea used modern fibers for sanitary reasons. The mats were stacked on top of each other in the press, and when the third one was in place, olive oil already began to dribble out. When the stack was waist high, the oil flowed freely, trickling from between the mats and collecting in the base below.

"Now we press the oil," George said as he turned on the hydraulic press. It rumbled to life and the base moved upward, squeezing the stack of mats against another metal plate above it. The pressure was intense and oil gushed out, a river of green that pooled beneath the press and disappeared into a holding tank. Both water and oil are squeezed from the olive paste, leaving behind the skins and stones, called pomace, which will be sold to a factory that will turn it into pomace oil. A high-speed centrifuge separated the oil from the water, and some two hours after the olives entered the press, we had olive oil.

"Our first oil of the season," George announced as the olive oil began to flow out of a spigot, frothy and golden green, like a beer dyed for Saint Patrick's Day. Chloe caught the oil in a glass jug and poured it into a collection of tiny cups, one for each of us.

It was a pregnant moment—their first taste of the year's oil and our first time tasting freshly pressed oil. I was worried that they'd want an appraisal, testing my taste buds, as so many professional olive oil tasters seem to enjoy doing. Everyone swirled, sniffed, slurped, and swallowed the oil. It was raw and green, and the silky texture coated my mouth pleasantly. I liked it, and I looked around to gauge the others' reactions, but everyone was silent, waiting for the first appraisal. Finally, Christine spoke. She was unhappy with the oil and detected an unexpected flavor, which she attributed to the machinery, which had been unused since the previous season. The next run would taste different she said, and she suggested we try the oils from their previous harvests.

In the tasting room, we sampled more olive oils and watched grindstones slowly crush olives in a millennia-old process that is more romantic and captivating than modern presses, but whether it's more healthful is less certain. Some argue that stone mills are hard to clean, potentially resulting in off flavors, and that the process exposes the oil to more oxygen, which reduces antioxidant levels. Others contend, however, that because the grindstones roll over olives, pulping their flesh without damaging the skin or stone, and the olives are pressed without adding water, more of the antioxidants and aromas are retained. Whatever impact the milling process has on the wholesomeness of the oil, there was no denying that their oils were lovely, and I soon found my favorite: a lemon oil made by crushing lemons alongside the olives, creating a delicate, refreshing flavor that seemed destined for salads and fish. Another oil, made with bitter oranges, reminded me of oils we tasted in Italy. Christine and George explained that the fruit is added during the crushing process and not afterward, a process that creates a better flavor and is less common than adding flavors to the finished oil.

Before we left, Colin asked about Crete's oldest olive trees, and George smiled like the Cheshire cat. "There are many old olive trees in Crete, but they are not all accessible. There are a few right where you want them, so they say this is the oldest tree." He explained that old olive trees attract tourists. "Experts" come and verify its size, a sign is erected, and a café is built to monetize visitors. "If you want to see Crete's oldest olive tree, you have to go to Sitia in eastern Crete."

"Go there. You'll see the way Crete used to be," Christine said. "Tourism hasn't reached it yet, so they are earning their living mainly from farming, whereas every other province depends on tourism and farms very little."

Back at our hotel, Colin made a salad dressed with Biolea's olive oil, while Leif and I played in the spacious apartment. The family-run complex was nearly empty, and our one-bedroom apartment was the cheapest hotel we'd stayed in so far. Whether that was a reflection of Greece's ailing economy or just typical off-season rates, I didn't know, but I was grateful for the space and kitchenette.

"Is that your only one?" our host asked when I took Leif to the lobby to use the Internet.

"Yes," I said, putting Leif down on the couch to play with some stray toys.

"I have four," he said, pointing to three boys riding their bikes on the patio and a baby in a stroller.

"You make parenting look so easy," I said as I picked Leif up, trying to quell his cries before he woke the baby.

"It gets easier when you have more. One is a psychopath, two is a split personality, three is a family, and four is even better," he said.

Yeah, right, I thought, and retreated to a corner to check my e-mail. But before we left, our talkative host returned. Thankfully, this time the conversation wasn't on parenting but Greece's national obsession: the economy. Like Dimitri in Athens, he felt Greece had been exploited and concluded, "If you want to rule a country, you don't start a war; you lend them money. The Germans want to build a pipeline for solar power, and the Americans want our oil."

I vaguely wondered if he meant olive oil, but soon I realized he was talking about petroleum, the oil boom of today not of ancient Greece.

CRETE'S RELATIONSHIP to the olive tree was a mix of old and new. Olives have been harvested here since Minoan times, and in some traditional corners of the island it seemed like not much had changed in millennia. But olive cultivation and olive oil production have modernized, and Crete was on the cutting edge of this research. It was also the host for this year's Olivebioteq conference. The four-day event focused on biotechnology in olive growing and, like our expedition, was an amalgamation of modern technology and ancient practices. Biotechnology in agriculture does not mean genetically modified foods, as people often assume. It is a tool that olive researchers use for everything from classifying olive trees to creating tests that can detect adulterated oil. New olive cultivars are created mostly by clonal selection and to a lesser extent by crossbreeding. For us, the conference was an opportunity to meet nearly two hundred olive researchers from dozens of countries and to reconnect with Dr. Luciana Baldoni, from the University of Perugia, to discuss the progress of our project analyzing ancient olive trees.

The lobby of the waterfront resort bustled with academics, and tables were laden with olives and olive oil. This was the third day of the conference, and Luciana had already given two talks on her laboratory's research, both related to using genetics to identify and track olive cultivars. Today, she had some free time, and I was looking forward to telling her about the ancient trees we'd found and the areas we planned to search.

"Luciana," I called, when I spotted her hunched over her laptop computer.

"Welcome," she said, wrapping us in hugs. "I'm so glad you could make it." She hoisted Leif into the air and settled him against her waist.

"I have some olive samples for you," I said, offering a plastic bag stuffed with ziplock bags, each containing olive branches from different ancient and wild trees. She extricated Leif from her necklace and handed him to Colin.

"This is wonderful," she said, opening the bag as though it was a Christmas present. "You've marked the locations? And did you take samples from the rootstock? You know, we need that to know if the trees were grafted."

"Yes, yes," I assured her.

"We sampled an ancient olive tree in Vouves yesterday," she continued in her delicate Italian accent. "And tomorrow we will search for other old olive trees."

"I heard the Vouves tree is supposed to be the oldest tree in the world," I said.

"I don't know about that." She laughed. "But it is very large, and the trunk is intact."

Leif squirmed and moaned, reaching for the marble stairs we'd just descended. "I'll take him outside," Colin said. "Just meet me upstairs when you're ready." Leif crawled up the stairs with Colin close behind, while Luciana talked olive research and introduced me to passing colleagues.

No one picking up a bottle of supermarket olive oil could suspect how thoroughly all aspects of the olive tree were researched. Every facet was examined in excruciating detail, from the risks olive trees faced, from climate change to the battle against fraudulent olive oil. It was both enlightening and overwhelming, flooded with scientific jargon that was too complex for me to understand. But what was clear was the passion these researchers felt and the multifaceted nature of olive research. My curiosity about the tree's origins was just one of thousands of questions researchers had, and there were many brilliant people pursuing the answers. Luciana introduced me to academics who studied olive trees in Syria, Israel, Jordan, and the Palestinian territories, and I made connections that would help us on the final leg of our journey. The olive tree was at least as important to the Middle East as to Europe, and, fittingly, the next Olivebioteq conference was going to be held in Aleppo, Syria, in 2014.

The olive trees in the Middle East have not been as extensively studied as those in the countries we'd been to, and Luciana was disheartened to hear we would not be able to end our journey in Syria. It had already been two weeks since we had decided that it was too dangerous, and every day, news headlines reinforced that decision with alarming reports of escalating violence. I kept hoping for good news, but there was nothing cheery to report from this Arab Spring uprising. Even though we were unhappy not to be able to return to Aleppo to see my family and the olive farm that inspired this journey, we were thankful my family was still safe, harvesting their olives as they did every year. But neighboring olive groves had been destroyed, and because their trees were close to Turkey, people hid among them as they escaped across the border. There had been gunfire in the olive groves, and in other areas, trees had been burned down.

We said good-bye to Luciana and drove through the countryside, following street signs for the "Monumental Olive Tree of Vouves." A few kilometers away, we reached the handful of houses that was Vouves. The hamlet is dominated by the ancient tree whose trunk is a tornado of knotted ropes spiraling upward and ending in a cloud of silver-green leaves and black olives. It was a singular tree, in part because it was so obviously one tree. The center of the trunk was hollow, but enough of the tree remained to see that it was one tree. I ducked inside and ran my fingers along its twisted interior, circled the perimeter, and held Leif up to touch its shiny leaves. I could see why some believed this was the oldest olive tree in the world, but no one could ever prove it—one of the many secrets the olive tree keeps.

We visited a nearby museum and restaurant before returning to Deliana for lunch. It was our third visit to this restaurant in as many days; we kept returning because it served some of the best food we'd had in Greece. Named the Gorge after the nearby rocky chasms, it was a cozy place with an olive-wood fire in the corner and chunky homemade tables with tree-stump legs. A woman cooked, and her son waited tables. Bottles of olive oil from their Koroneiki trees sat on every table, and a trio of old men with faces as craggy as the mountains surrounding us sat in the corner drinking coffee and watching the Greek economy unravel on TV.

"*Yahsu*," the son said, greeting us in Greek. He placed toasted bread and bowls of cured green Koroneiki olives on the table and glanced up at the televised politicians. "It's bad; they've messed everything up."

I asked him what could be done and picked up an olive to nibble. These were also Koroneiki olives, which are usually pressed into oil, and despite being smaller than most table olives, they had a nice robust flavor.

"We have to return to the drachma," he said, his twentysomething face serious beyond its years. "If we stay in the euro, we have to pay thirty to forty years. With the drachma, in five years we have growth."

"What about your olive oil?" I asked. "How are the prices this year?"

"You know, in Italy and Spain they don't have very good olive oil, so they mix it with ours," he said. "But we don't make any money on our trees. We have three thousand trees and pick fifty tons of olives every year. You know what we make for that? One point three euros a liter."

It was a pittance, not enough to cover costs, let alone pay minimum wages to all those involved. Each liter of olive oil was made from approximately seven kilograms of olives, so a kilogram of olives was worth nineteen cents. What other fruit could you sell for a mere quarter a kilogram? If a tree produced twenty kilograms of olives a year, it would earn the farmer less than five euros a year.

This was barely enough to cover the cost of picking the olives. A seasoned picker could pluck as much as 250 kilograms of olives per day, which would fetch fifty euros. But that was only if the conditions were ideal. When Chloe from Biolea spent a full day picking olives, she collected fewer than 50 kilograms, worth a mere ten euros. From that money, all other costs associated with olive growing had to be deducted, including pruning, pest control, fertilization, weed management, irrigation, transportation of olives, and equipment maintenance.

The mill that pressed the olives into oil then sold it to a bulk buyer for slightly more, around 1.8 euros a liter. Organic olives might fetch a slight premium, but not always. The previous year, there was no price difference, and everyone was paid poorly. When an average olive oil sells for 1.99 euros a liter in a Spanish supermarket and a premium one sells for 3.25 euros, it is hard to imagine how traditional farmers like this could continue to survive.

Our host brought us sautéed greens, mostly dandelion leaves, swimming in olive oil and drizzled with lemon, followed by meatballs with green beans in a light cream sauce and roasted lamb with potatoes in a tomato puree. The mother, a cheery woman with deep creases in her face who spoke no English, brought out a soft-boiled egg and mimed that we should dip bread into the yolk for Leif. When the son brought us quince compote with thick Greek yogurt for dessert, we asked about the olive tree of Vouves.

"That's not the oldest tree. The mayor is from Vouves." He chuckled. "If you want to see an older tree, go to the village down the road."

He returned with directions and two shot glasses filled with raki—Crete's national spirit—a clear liquid that smelled as though it could peel paint. Made every autumn with fermented and distilled leftovers from winemaking, it was a vile creation that I quickly downed, trying not to look too pained.

AS WE HEADED east into the part of Crete Christine from Biolea had said was more authentic, I wondered what we'd find. Despite the sprawling developments and proliferation of motels catering to the annual influx of tourists, much of what we had experienced so far felt authentic. Maybe the olive trees were a little tarted up for tourists, but the mom-and-pop places serving their own olive oil and backyard vegetables reflected an ethos from yesteryear. But more important than the changes the island had undergone in the last two decades was the colossal olive tree rumored to grow here. Like those searching for the magical Tree of Souls in the movie *Avatar,* we needed to find it; yet we were uncertain if our vague directions would lead us there.

When we arrived in Heraklion, Crete's largest city, we checked into a hotel named after the 3,500-year-old Minoan fresco *Prince of the Lilies.* The original fresco was in a palace at Knossos, the Minoans' most important city and one of the places that documented early use of olive oil. The next morning, we went there to see the fresco.

Knossos is not far from Heraklion, on a hill next to the Kairatos River. It is Europe's oldest city, built in 1900 BC, and during the fifteenth and seventeenth centuries BC, when the Minoan civilization peaked, it housed an estimated 100,000 people. The excavated palace and surrounding complex was the Minoans' political and cultural center, an expansive area with apartments, hundreds of rooms, a courtyard, storerooms, workshops, bathhouses, and a throne room, and much of that has been preserved and reconstructed. Earthquakes destroyed the palace twice, but when the Mycenaeans conquered Crete in 1400 BC, it was one of the few palaces they left standing.

It is a maze of foundations, frescoes, and reconstructed rooms. Three brick-red columns mark an entrance to the palace; a bull charges in the fresco behind the entrance. Remnants of the columns lie elsewhere in the complex and are noticeably different from other ancient Greek pillars—wider at the top than at the base and made from cypress trunks, painted red and turned upside down, instead of stone. In the throne room, there are gypsum benches and a high-backed alabaster chair, the oldest throne in Europe, bookended by frescoes of two mythical griffins, which have an avian head on a lion's body.

The scale and opulence of the palace are overwhelming, especially for a structure that is 3,500 years old. But there is something about the brilliant colors and ambitious reconstruction that seems too new, and on a placard we read that the British archaeologist Arthur Evans, who had done much of the restoration, came under criticism for his heavy-handed approach. Nonetheless, his work has shed light on many of the mysteries of this ancient civilization, including its production and use of olive oil.

"That must be where they stored the olive oil," Colin said, pointing to a row of clay vases against a stone wall. The waist-high *pithoi* are flat bottomed and range in color from eggshell to ocher and are decorated with circles, angular lines, and waves. Dr. Evans found four hundred *pithoi* in the palace, which held olive oil as well as grain, fish, and wine. The archaeologist hypothesized that olive oil production and exportation was such a mainstay of the Minoan economy that when the invading Mycenaean Greeks destroyed the olive oil presses, the Minoans fled Crete.

Thousands of clay tablets found here also attest to the importance of olive oil. The Minoans wrote in Linear A and the Mycenaeans in Linear B, ideogram-based scripts with at least ten representations for olives and olive oil between the two languages. Little is understood from the Minoan record keeping, as Linear A is largely indecipherable, but from the Mycenaeans we know how much oil was stored in the palace, the number of olive trees they owned, where the oil went, and what it was used for.

We also know that the Mycenaeans grew olive trees, harvested wild olives, and made oil from both cultivated and wild varieties. Oil from the wild olives was more abundant and used for industrial uses—perfumes, tanning, and textiles—whereas domesticated olives were pressed into cooking oil. Olives were also eaten, and from the size of stones—larger than wild olives and smaller than domesticated cultivars—found in Knossos, experts have hypothesized that the olive tree was early in its domestication.

The palace had an "Olive Press Room," and we came upon a stone bowl the size of a child's bathtub, with a quarter-sized hole as a spigot near the bottom, and I wondered if it had been used for olive oil. Prehistoric oil production consisted of little more than a mortar and pestle—the olives were crushed, perhaps slightly heated, and the oil floated to the top—but during Minoan times, primitive oil presses were being developed, just as they were in Syria and Palestine. The Minoans crushed olives with a mortar and pestle and then transferred the paste to a press, which consisted of a large stone basin with a stone on a wooden lever suspended above it. The weight came down and squeezed the oil out of the olives, and it flowed from the bowl into a small *pithoi*. The olive oil was then separated from the water and vegetative matter by decanting or by using a spouted clay tub called a *lekanai*.

We traveled to the nearby Minoan city of Vathypetro to see an even older olive press. It sat outside, next to a crumbling wall, and was surprisingly simple—merely an elongated boulder that had been chiseled out to have a slight depression and a spigot at one end. The rock leaned at a slight angle, and you could imagine the oil from the crushed olives flowing down the slope and collecting in the rock bowl carved beneath the spigot.

THE FOLLOWING DAY, we went east, into the Crete of the past, before tourism had replaced farming. This is where the island's oldest olive tree was rumored to live. We weren't sure where to look, so we asked in Sitia, the region's largest town, a pretty port with beachside cafés and mostly locals. The owner of the restaurant where we had lunch concurred that there were many old olive trees and we just needed to drive south to see them. But none of the trees along the roadside compared to the ancient specimens we'd already seen, and another family we asked pointed inland and said, "Vroda."

"That's the place I read about," Colin said, and he pulled out the map to search for it.

We turned onto thin roads caked in dust and carved through the mountains. Goats with heavy bells clanged on the hillside and flowed across the road like a leisurely school group jaywalking. The roads were clearly made for hooves and not economy rental cars, and our tires spun as we corkscrewed upward. We worried that we'd rip out our oil pan and void our insurance, which didn't cover off-roading, but soon, retracing our route seemed more dangerous than continuing. At a hillside of terraced olive trees, we finally reached a brown sign marking archaeological sites, and I was relieved to see an ancient olive tree on the list.

The olive tree of Kavusi is old and beautiful, perfectly symmetrical like the tree of Vouves but even bigger. The center has hollowed with time, and it is filled with stones, a precaution to give it extra strength. It has a voluminous canopy and semi-ripe olives, but its trunk is the showstopper, twisted and tortured, like roots that have grown upward. We measured it, took samples and photos, and read the information on the placard.

Dated using tree ring analysis, the tree is believed to be 3,250 years old, 250 years older than the tree of Vouves and probably the oldest olive tree on Crete, if not in the world. We knew from meeting other researchers that estimating olive tree age is part science and part art, with a good dose of luck thrown in. In this case, the diameter of the trunk was measured to be 4.90 meters at a height of 0.8 meters, and the olive tree was assumed to grow 0.75 millimeters per year. Dividing the radius (2,450 millimeters) by the growth per year (0.75) gave a rough estimate of age (3,267 years old).

This method isn't that accurate, but then, little about measuring the age of an olive tree is. More importantly, the surrounding story supports the notion that this was a Minoan olive tree. The Mycenaeans wrote on their tablets about grafting olive trees, and like the Vouves tree and other trees on Crete from this era, this tree is grafted onto a wild olive tree. The grafted cultivar, Mastoidis, is still popular today, and many of the large, unruly trees on Crete are Mastoidis, or Muratolia, as the locals call them.

On a hilltop a few kilometers away lie the remains of a Minoan settlement where archaeologists found olive-pressing equipment and *pithoi* in which the olive oil was stored. We wandered alone among stones overgrown with grass, imagining the walls and rectangular foundations as the storerooms, courtyards, houses, shrine, potter's kiln, and graveyard that once stood here. The village has been reclaimed by nature and left unscarred by overzealous archaeologists. Yellow buttercups grew amidst crumbled buildings, olive shrubs proliferated, and we were surrounded by gray conical mountains that dropped into the sea and hills terraced with olive trees. An ancient plaster church, with white walls and a deep-red roof, sat in an adjacent valley, but there was nothing else to hint at human habitation. We were alone with antiquity, pondering Crete's astounding olive history, trees that are more than three millennia old and olive presses from four thousand years ago. But the story of the olive is even older, and our final destination was to the very beginnings of olive cultivation.

12

THE BIRTHPLACE OF THE OLIVE

"Olive trees represent everything that roots us, anchors us, identifies us and locates us in this world—whether it be belonging to a family, a community, a tribe, a nation, a religion, or, most of all, a place called home . . . we fight so intensely at times over our olive trees because, at their best, they provide the feelings of self-esteem and belonging that are as essential for human survival as food in the belly."

THOMAS L. FRIEDMAN, *The Lexus and the Olive Tree*[1]

WHEN WE ARRIVED at the airport on the outskirts of Tel Aviv, it was late and we were tired. It had taken three flights and all day to travel from Crete, and poor Leif had a cold that made him howl during landings. We almost missed our flight when the Athens customs agents interrogated us for being in the European Union for more than three months, the limit for tourists without a visa. Our taxi charged us more than the set flat fee, and our hotel was a dingy, overpriced coffin with a stringy-haired troll of an owner.

Yet it was a relief to finally be in our room, though the short, curly hairs of dubious origin in the carpet and used bandage in the corner made it less than appealing. The bathroom had no toilet paper or soap, and when I trudged back downstairs to get a blanket for our barren bed, the scowling owner plucked one off the floor of the laundry room. Sleep was also elusive, as Leif tossed and turned all night with a stuffed-up nose. Finally, the sun rose, we walked to the waterfront, and Leif settled into his most peaceful sleep in twenty-four hours.

The beach was wide and sandy, with an endless boardwalk and gentle waters dotted with buoys marking swimming areas. We saw an occasional swimmer, despite the cool chill of an early-November morning. A muscled man hung from a chin-up bar in an outdoor gym, and two recumbent bikes powered by amputees zipped past. With its palm trees, modern apartments, grassy parks, and exercise enthusiasts, it felt more like California than the Middle East.

As we explored Tel Aviv and cemented our travel plans for Israel, we started to appreciate just how odd the mix of values, religions, and opinions that coexisted here was. On the main street leading downtown, you find everything from sex-toy shops to falafel diners. The air-conditioned mall has global franchises such as the Body Shop next to clothing stores featuring fatigue-wearing models with machine guns. Armed guards are everywhere, and before you enter many buildings, you must pass through security. Orthodox Jews cloaked in black with black hats and long beards walk next to scantily clad women with handguns poking out of their belts. Twenty-year-olds in dreadlocks stroll alongside men in suits carrying high-end leather briefcases.

With nearly a half million people, Tel Aviv is Israel's second-largest city and its most liberal, often rated as a top destination for lesbians and gays. It is halfway down Israel, a central location from which to plan our itinerary. Our goal was to visit Israel's most historic olive trees and the storied trees of Gethsemane garden at the base of the Mount of Olives, as well as ancient Phoenician sites where olives were first pressed. Equally important, we wanted to visit the West Bank and meet the Palestinian people to find out what olive trees mean to them and how the occupation has affected their livelihood. It was an ambitious agenda, and after three days in Tel Aviv, we booked a car and headed into the Negev desert.

More than half of Israel is covered by desert, a pie-shaped wedge in the south that bleeds into the Sinai desert and borders Egypt and Jordan. It is rocky and mostly barren, home to a mere 8 percent of the country's population, a disproportionate number of whom are Bedouins. The Bedouin encampments are shabby towns of tents and trailers, without electricity, pavement, or running water. Their camels are tied up outside, and on the road we passed signs warning drivers to watch out for wild camels. We passed a prison, a firing range, and a few small towns, but most of the Negev is barren and dusty. How can they grow olive trees here? I wondered. And what is so special about the cultivar they've created?

At Mitzpe Ramon, a town near the center of the desert and on the lip of the Ramon Crater, we searched for the ecolodge where we had reserved a hut. The ecolodge was guarded by a high wall of rock, rebar, and adobe studded with bottles and tires. It was crumbling and looked bizarre, like a prop for an apocalyptic movie set. Our adobe hut had two rooms, and we spread the blankets we'd been given over the mattress and unpacked in the other room. The walls, floor, and ceiling were all made of thick mud, and we slowly became covered in dust, but there was a silence and peacefulness to the place that made up for the dirt. The sky was cloudless, the moon full, and the crater empty and endless.

The next day, we explored the crater, which is not really a crater but a *makhtesh*, a forty-kilometer-long depression formed by receding waters and rivers wearing away at soft rock, and it is unique to Israel. It was a swirl of contours and rocks, now roamed by ibexes, impressively horned ungulates, and was once part of the spice-trade route. More than two thousand years ago, Nabataeans crisscrossed the Arabian Desert from the Persian Gulf to Gaza, cashing in on their expert knowledge of the desert to transport spices, perfumes, oils, and silk from the Far East to the Mediterranean for ships bound for Egypt and Rome.

What gave these nomadic Arabians their advantage is also what we were searching for—a trickle of water that forms oases and gives some plants the ability to survive this unforgiving environment. A researcher at Israel's Ben Gurion University told us there were wild olive trees in the desert, but so far we hadn't seen any. Near the crumbling remains of a Nabataean settlement, we found a patch of greenery that was fed by a spring. There were acacia trees and prickly shrubs with leaves that sparkled with salt crystals but no olive trees.

It wasn't until we met Benny from Halutza Olive Oil at the entrance of the company's olive grove that we saw our first desert olive trees. Benny had short, graying hair, thick eyebrows, and a confident, easygoing manner. We piled into his truck, and when Leif started to moan, Benny pulled him onto his lap, immediately putting an end to his complaints. "I have three boys," he explained with a smile. We bounced over fields of rock and hard-packed sand to a hilltop in the center of the olive grove. The panoramic desert view, endless sand colored by blocks of verdant olive trees, seems schizophrenic and drives home the seeming impossibility of what has been accomplished.

"We have 7,000 *dunum* of olive trees. About 150,000 trees," Benny said as he turned off the engine.

We got out of the car and walked through a patch of the seven-hundred-hectare farm. Many of the olive trees had already been picked, but others were heavy with olives, glistening green and black under the midday sun.

"This was once a vineyard, about a thousand years ago," Benny said, squinting against the bright sunshine. "There was terracing everywhere, but the sand has covered it."

He explained that olive trees had been growing here for fifty years, but most of the trees are younger and have been producing oil for the last fifteen years.

"How do you get enough water?" I asked, for there were no irrigation hoses.

"We use drip irrigation and bury the hoses. They last longer that way."

"Do you use recycled water?" I asked. The owners of our eco-lodge used recycled wastewater from the prison to irrigate their vineyard, and the gas station café we'd lunched at had a sign in the bathroom explaining that the wastewater was recycled to water their garden.

"No, no. The government will never give us a license for that amount," Benny said, kicking the parched earth. "We've drilled seven wells that are eight hundred to a thousand meters deep. It's not easy or cheap. The water is brackish water, and every five years, we have to replace the hoses because the salt plugs them up."

"I didn't know olive trees could grow in salty water," Colin said.

"Not too salty, about 4.5 ppm, and some varieties are more salt tolerant than others." Benny rhymed off their cultivars: Picual, Manzanillo, Souri, Ferantoio, Coratina, and Barnea.

The Barnea cultivar was particularly interesting because it was created to be salt tolerant, developed by Israeli scientist and former International Olive Oil Council president Dr. Shimon Lavee, and is now popular throughout Israel and in other desert climes, such as Australia. Later, Benny would show us the dry research agricultural center next door, where researchers grew passion fruit, marula, jojoba, and even cotton, all bred to grow in drought conditions.

"I'm sorry I cannot show you the mill," Benny said as we returned to the car. "It is closed today for Shabbat."

"Of course," I sputtered, embarrassed by our oversight. I'd forgotten that today was Saturday and most of Israel was shut down for the Sabbath. Before I could apologize for our faux pas, he continued, "Instead, we can go to the kibbutz and watch them pick olives."

The kibbutz wasn't the utopian collective I expected but an industrial warehouse where workers made valves and raised chickens. Eight hundred people worked on this kibbutz, one of five kibbutzim in the Negev desert. Throughout Israel, there are more than two hundred kibbutzim, and together they are an economic powerhouse, producing 4 percent of the nation's agricultural products and $8 billion in industrial goods.

We parked on a hard-packed dirt road and strode along a grid of tall, unruly olive trees. Benny picked an olive and clucked, "The trees aren't cared for. They're not pruned, and look at these olives." He showed me a half-green orb, pockmarked by olive flies. "They're not our trees but belong to the kibbutz, and these olives will go to the north to be pressed."

Nets were spread along the ground and empty crates were stacked by the road, but no one was picking. We had come at lunchtime, and a half dozen olive pickers sat in a grassy patch at the edge of the grove, containers of yogurt and hummus resting on the ground, and a blackened kettle steamed over a small fire of olive prunings. A deeply lined man wearing a checkered keffiyeh shook our hands, and others nodded a greeting. He gave us plastic cups filled with sweet black tea and mint leaves and chatted in Arabic.

They were Palestinians from Hebron and had been here for two weeks, and in another month and a half, when the olive harvest ended, they would return. It was good money for them, badly needed money. Many of Israel's olive pickers were from the West Bank, Benny explained, but it wasn't always easy to get work permits for them. The banter between Benny and the Palestinians was jovial and friendly, and I wondered about the divide between Israelis and Palestinians; maybe it wasn't as fractious as the news reported. As we walked back to the car, I steered the conversation toward politics, and Benny said, "If the governments let us make peace, we would have made peace a long time ago."

THERE ARE TWO Palestinian territories, the West Bank and Gaza. Gaza is a narrow strip along the Mediterranean that butts up against Egypt and is tightly controlled and inaccessible to foreigners. The West Bank begins in East Jerusalem and encompasses an area the size of Delaware. When I called these regions Palestine, an Israeli scientist corrected me. "What is Palestine?" he said, his jovial tone suddenly icy. "You must mean the Palestinian Territories." Naming conventions are just one of the many heartaches of this complicated dispute.

We took a small bus from Jerusalem to Ramallah, since we were not allowed to cross the border in our rental car. It's a quick trip between the two cities, fewer than ten kilometers, but the checkpoint can make the cities seem a continent away. Sometimes things go awry, and the week before, a rabbi had been shot and killed at a border crossing. For tourists, the ordeal is generally uneventful, and when we pulled up to the heavily armed and fortified gates, we passed through without stopping.

Buses and cars waited on the Palestinian side, bustling with arrivals and departures, and we called Mohammad, an olive researcher we'd been introduced to through acquaintances, to let him know we had arrived. A few minutes later, a dusty Hyundai Santa Fe pulled up, and a dark-haired man limped out. He greeted us without a smile, his weary face looking much older than his forty years. Mohammad slipped back into the driver's seat, lifting his injured leg with his hands, and Colin joined him in the front.

Soon we learned that Mohammad is from a village south of here, near Hebron, and has four children, aged four to twelve. He has a degree in chemical engineering and is finishing his MSc in Palestinian olive oil quality, which he talks about with frustration. "I can't import the chemicals I need to analyze the olive samples. Instead, we have an agreement with a university in Jordan to do the analysis, but I've been waiting on the samples for months."

His research demonstrated that Palestinian olive oil has higher levels of select sterols than most European oils as a result of the climate, olive cultivar, and geography, which includes richer soil with less limestone than many other Mediterranean regions. It's what gives Palestinian oils their distinctive taste, but high sterol levels can also be an indication of adulterated oil, so the International Olive Oil Council set limits of 0.5 percent. But high-quality extra virgin Palestinian olive oil often has levels higher than that.

"I am trying to change the regulations," Mohammad said, "but I cannot present our results, because Palestine is not recognized as a nation. Instead, I have given it to researchers in Jordan, and I hope they will present it."

In addition to his graduate degree research, he examines ancient olive trees, works with the Palestinian NGO Association for Integrated Rural Development, known by its acronym, AIRD, and is involved in olive cooperatives. It seemed like an exhausting schedule, and when I commented, he said, "I have to work day and night to feed my family."

Ramallah is surrounded by caramel-colored hills ringed with olive trees like ripples cast from a skipping stone. There are 10 million olive trees in the West Bank, covering nearly half of the arable land, and they're a lynchpin to the region's economy. Palestinians earn up to $100 million a year from olive trees. The region's most impoverished families depend on olive trees for survival, and for two-thirds of the people living in rural areas, it is the primary source of income.

Most of the olive oil is pressed through cooperatives, and at a modest house in the village of Kufr Ein, we met Daoud Barghouthi, a retired teacher with a mustache, short gray hair, and a gold tooth. He is the head of an organic oil cooperative, where he oversees olive oil production from five villages, and as with all olive farmers, it didn't take long for our conversation to turn to the challenges of the olive oil industry.

"Our central problem is the Israeli occupation," Daoud said, pausing to sip the tea his wife had brought us. "This year, we have a huge problem sending olive oil to Gaza. Gaza would consume seven thousand tons of oil, but we can't send them any."

Daoud explained that they haven't been able to send olive oil into Gaza since 2008, when the Gaza War rocked the area, killing more than a thousand Palestinians. He detailed the lengthy application process to send goods into Gaza, which required numerous approvals and in the end was refused "99 percent of the time." People also cannot enter Gaza, Daoud explained, recounting the struggles the farmers' union faced when they traveled to Gaza via Jordan and Egypt, unable to pass through Israel, and waited eight days at the border before being denied permission to enter.

"Why didn't they use the tunnels?" Mohammad asked. "It's the only way."

"The tunnels are also dangerous; a lot of people have died," Daoud said. "It's a big jail. Economically, it's a bad situation. The people in Gaza are dependent on humanitarian aid and the generosity of Israelis to allow aid and fuel in."

"Before the occupation, they lived from olive oil," Mohammad said, his face as bleak as his voice. "Now the population has increased two to three times, but they have the same amount of land and much of that has been destroyed."

Today, 1.7 million people live in Gaza, nearly five times as many as recorded in the 1967 census, when Israel occupied Gaza following the Six-Day War. Yet they have only 360 square kilometers of land, less than the city of Denver, and much of that has been devastated by Israeli incursions, war, and the construction of the barrier. Oxfam reported that between 2001 and 2008, 112,000 olive trees were uprooted, and the war that followed destroyed 60 percent of the arable land, according to the World Health Organization. How can a population with half a million people living in refugee camps and one of the highest population growth rates in the world survive on devastated land cut off from the rest of the world?

"I can't see an end," Daoud said as we finished our tea. "We are in a black tunnel without a light."

Walking through Daoud's olive groves lightened our moods. We trod across a grassy field, stepping over a low stone fence and entering a grove of a dozen ancient trees. Like Crete's aged trees, they had twisted trunks with fairy-tale charm and a plume of frosted leaves.

"My great-grandfather picked these trees," Daoud said, touching an aged tree. "And his grandfather, and his grandfather, and so on."

Some of the trees were numbered with blue paint on the trunk, indicating the ones Mohammad studied. Their age was estimated to be in the thousands of years, and Daoud reminded us that the tree came back from the roots, so that although the trunk could be a thousand years old, a tree could have stood there for multiple millennia and the roots might be much older. Each time the trunk died or was felled, new shoots would erupt from its base.

"So the tree could be much older than the trunk we see?" Colin inquired.

Daoud nodded. "Now what do the Israelis do? They steal these trees. They pull them out by bulldozer and move them inside Israel, plant them there, saying this is history." He looked both outraged and disbelieving, shaking his head as though it were a bad dream. "They are stealing history."

I didn't know what to say, so I asked about his earliest memories of the olive harvest. It was of his great-grandparents. "They would pick olives all day," he said. "And when they got hungry, they would eat the fallen olives."

I'd never heard of people eating uncured olives. "These olives must taste better than any I've tried," I said, recalling their bitter and unpalatable taste.

"Try one," Daoud said, picking an inky olive off the ground and biting into it.

I bit into it—just a little nibble, expecting to spit it out. Instead, I chewed it. The flesh was soft, like a peach that had finally ripened, and the flavor was deep, earthy, and ripe, like thick tapenade. It wouldn't make the pages of *Gourmet* magazine, but it was palatable and surpassed many of the more unusual delicacies found around the world. Fallen olives would have made an easy, nutritious, and plentiful snack, and it wasn't difficult to imagine people acquiring a taste for them.

"Well, that answers our question," Colin said, chewing on an olive. "People must have eaten olives before olive oil."

"There's one more test we can do," I said, recalling the advice a Greek historian had given us. "If Leif likes it, we know early people would have, too."

I searched for an unblemished dark olive and held it before Leif's mouth. He eyed it and poked it, turned away, and then took it. Chomping down on the olive, he left the pit and remaining olive half in my hand. He chewed, swallowed, and came back for seconds. If Leif could eat uncured olives, early people struggling for nourishment could have, too.

We said good-bye to Daoud and continued on to the olive mill, winding through a sea of olive trees and hilltop towns of white buildings with red roofs. Some towns were more substantial than others, and one looked like a new suburb plonked into an olive grove. When I commented on it, Mohammad told me it was an Israeli settlement.

"Can't drive from one village to the next without seeing settlements," he said. "This is occupation; they want to take our land."

The settlements are illegal under international law, but there are more than 300,000 Israelis living in settlements in the West Bank, and much of that land comes from farmers. Olive trees are lost not only in the construction but in violent attacks by settlers. An EU report estimates that ten thousand olive trees were destroyed by settlers in 2011. It noted that the violence is especially targeted toward farmers with the aim of destroying their livelihood and includes en masse burning and felling of olive trees. In 2011, there were 411 attacks against Palestinians by settlers, a threefold increase in the last three years.

I was beginning to understand more and more why Mohammad seemed so tired, as problems continued to pour out. Irrigation would greatly improve olive yields, but Palestinian water usage is highly regulated. Palestinians have water only two or three days a week, and there is no water for agriculture. Currently, 80 percent of the West Bank's water is used by Israelis; a more balanced approach could add $100 million to Palestinian agriculture.

Shipping and transporting oil is also fraught with challenges. All products leaving the West Bank have to go through security, but the machine can take only a partially loaded pallet. Half the Palestinians' space is lost, and their shipping costs double. The delivery truck drives to the border, a forklift unloads the pallets, a security clerk inspects them, and because the Palestinian driver can't continue into Israel, the pallets are transferred to an Israeli truck and brought to the port. Each step costs money. The farmers need to pay two truck drivers, the security clerk, the forklift operator on the Palestinian side, and then another on the Israeli side. If the ship doesn't leave immediately, they have to pay storage fees, and once the ship sails, they are still not home free.

"Sometimes the forklift hits the glass and shatters the bottles, but we don't know that until the importer calls us and tells us his shipment is destroyed," Mohammad said, sounding more tired than ever.

Like many Palestinians, Mohammad has never lived in an unoccupied West Bank. He lives a life that is made harder than it should be, where every action feels like swimming up current. He sounded weary and hopeless, as though all his energy had been used up, and so when I asked about his children, I expected him to say he wanted them to search for opportunities elsewhere. But he didn't.

"This is their home," he said in the most cheerful voice I'd yet heard. "I hope they stay here and make it a better country."

BACK IN Jerusalem, we wandered through the market in the Old City, walking in the footsteps of Jesus, pausing at the Western

Wall to watch Jews worship at their most sacred site, and admiring the golden Dome of the Rock and neighboring mosque, Sunni Muslims' third-holiest site. A ten-minute walk away lies the Mount of Olives, a hill covered in graves and olive trees, where scripture says the Resurrection will begin when the Messiah arrives. Tens of thousands of taupe tombs engraved with Hebrew sit atop the sand, tightly packed together like boxes in a warehouse. There are an estimated 150,000 graves here, some more than three thousand years old. A road carves up the hill, sandwiched between the cemetery and a park, and at the top, there is an Arab village where uniformed children play in a schoolyard and a handful of shops sell food.

After trudging up the road, we returned to the base and entered the iron gates of Gethsemane garden; *Gethsemane* originates from a Hebrew term meaning "oil press." Eight mighty olive trees sit in the garden next to the basilica. It is another holy site, and many believe that Jesus sat under these olive trees on his final night before he was arrested, that these trees are, as it is often said, silent witnesses to Jesus's prayer and suffering. In 2000, Luciana and her team tested the trees and found that they were all the same cultivar, and they had all been grafted onto wild olive trees. The cultivar was Nabali, a type of olive that has been growing in the Middle East for a very long time and is often called the Roman olive. Nabali olives are high in oil and plump and have a good texture, making them ideal for oil production and as table olives. They are still popular and are commonly grown in Palestine, Israel, Syria, and Jordan.

This cultivar was probably in existence during Jesus's time, but the challenges of carbon dating olive trees make it difficult to ascertain whether these specific trees were. In 2012, Italian researchers completed carbon dating of three of the eight trees and found them to be between 920 and 814 years old. Other trees could not be tested, because the center of their trunks—the oldest part—had decayed with age; they could be older than the three that were tested. The researchers stressed that this did not mean that the olive trees were not standing during Jesus's time. Of the trees they tested, they found that the roots were older, suggesting that the trees might have been regrafted when the original trees became unproductive or dried out. Crusaders may have rearranged the olive trees during the reconstruction of the nearby Basilica of the Agony in the twelfth century. Either way, they are beautiful, stately trees, and their religious importance is eternal. "For every Christian, the olive trees of the Garden of Gethsemane serve as a 'living' reference to the Passion of Christ," stated Father Pierbattista Pizzaballa, who worked with the researchers and is the Custos of the Holy Land, a high position in the Franciscan order that owns and cares for holy sites throughout the Middle East.

Three hours west of Christianity's most revered olive trees is the world's oldest olive press. A few kilometers south of the city of Haifa sits the submerged, seven-thousand-year-old village of Kfar Samir. The Carmel coast is littered with ancient settlements and evidence of olive oil use, but the olive press here predates by five hundred years any other ever found. On the seafloor, half-buried in mud, Dr. Ehud Galili, a marine archaeologist with the Israel Antiquities Authority, found a treasure trove of olive artifacts, from crushed olive stones to pulp concentrate, potsherds to hold the oil, concave stone mortars and grinding tools to crush the olives, woven reed baskets, and wooden bowls. Large pits of crushed olives and pulped pomace were also found, interpreted to be the waste from olive oil pressing. Carbon dating demonstrated that the oldest crushed olive pits were 6,500 years old. Pollen analysis showed that many olive trees were growing at that time, and the size of the olive pits suggests that they were wild olive trees. Here lies the proof that in 4500 BC, people picked wild olives and made oil.

We walked along the Mediterranean seashore, staring out into its blue waters and imagining the civilizations that lived here millennia ago. A few kilometers farther south is Atlit, another seven-thousand-year-old village, and here we searched for signs of the sunken Phoenician harbor, ashlar blocks lining the seabed to create one of the first known breakwaters. But now a military base sits at the tip of the promontory, and a surly fisherman eyed us suspiciously and yelled at Colin when he pointed his camera toward the base.

Although the Phoenician harbor wasn't visible, the Phoenicians' ancient road was. Crusaders had built a post on it, crumbling stone walls that obliterated and obscured any signs of their predecessors' settlements, but the Phoenicians left an enduring mark. They created the first widely used phonetic script, a precursor to our current alphabet, and in the high cliffs that paralleled the ancient road, two enormous letters were carved into the stone. A circle and a capital T, laid on its side with an extra line. The letters ayin and taw probably stood for the ancient name of the settlement, and their presence today is a reminder of all that the Phoenicians gave us.

We clambered over the scrubby terrain and burst out at the bluff near the script. A crumbling rock sat opposite it, like a ledge meant for viewers, and all three of us huddled on it, staring at the large letters. Even Leif, who was still too young to know his ABCs, seemed entranced. Our alphabet began on these rocks, and olive oil first flowed on nearby stones. The olive tree was domesticated somewhere not too far away, and along this coast, Phoenicians built an empire on trade, shipping olive oil to distant lands and spreading the olive tree throughout the Mediterranean. It felt like we were at the origin of everything. We had traveled thousands of kilometers retracing the migration of the olive, discovering its importance to cultures throughout the

Mediterranean and throughout time, and we had now reached a place where all the elements of our journey converged.

WE BEGAN this journey searching for answers, unsure of what we'd find and at times doubtful that we'd be able to retrace any of the Phoenicians' maritime routes. We also questioned the wisdom of traveling with an infant. But slowly, confidence replaced uncertainty, and we found the rhythm of our travels. A quarter of Leif's life had been spent on our olive odyssey, and he seemed to revel in the new experiences, his constant colic replaced by an unquenchable curiosity about his surroundings. Colin and I now had a better understanding of how to balance family with work and travel, and we had become better parents as a result. We had faced setbacks and had learned to accept what we couldn't change, including the growing unrest in Syria that had prevented us from going there. But in the end, our journey and the destinations en route had offered many answers. In many ways, our olive odyssey reflected its Homeric roots, and perhaps just as the Greek goddess Athena had been Odysseus's protector during his ten-year journey, the goddess of olive trees had looked after us, too.

EPILOGUE

"And peace proclaims olives of endless age."

SHAKESPEARE[1]

WE RETURNED HOME with notebooks brimming and hard drives full of video and photographs. There were countless hours of interviews to sift through and a couple bags of olive samples to send back to Luciana. The experts we'd spoken with and the archaeological evidence we'd seen strongly supported the idea that the Phoenicians had played an important role in popularizing the olive tree throughout Europe, but our collection of samples from ancient olive trees promised the most conclusive evidence.

Luciana and her team carefully cataloged all the samples and examined their genetic structure, studying eleven molecular markers in two types of DNA (nuclear and plastid) for each tree. The results were then compared with a database of thousands of olive samples, and statistical analysis determined genetic relationships. Could genetics unlock some of the mystery behind the ancient trees we'd searched for throughout the Mediterranean?

I was ecstatic when Luciana sent me an e-mail with the results from their initial set of tests. The results were grouped in a circular diagram called a dendrogram, a word derived from the Greek *"dendron,"* "tree," and *"gramma,"* "drawing," both linguistically and functionally suited to our olive trees. In it, I could see our samples interspersed with other known cultivars. Most of the trees we found in Israel and Palestine were grouped together with other known Middle Eastern cultivars, whereas those from Spain, France, Italy, and Greece were in separate clusters. But there were exceptions, and some ancient trees in Spain and Greece were closer to Middle Eastern trees than their local wild counterparts. This analysis came from the nuclear DNA, Luciana explained, and the real evidence that Phoenicians spread the olive tree throughout the Mediterranean came from the plastid DNA.

All the ancient trees we sampled in Palestine and Israel had a common plastid marker (chlorotype) that is found only in Middle Eastern olive trees and is thought to have originated in this region. This chlorotype is also the most common marker in cultivated olives and suggests that cultivated trees originated from olive trees in the Middle East. Interestingly, some of the ancient trees we sampled in Spain and Crete also had these markers, proof that these trees or their predecessors originally came from the Middle East. The Cretan olive trees were estimated to be up to 3,200 years old, whereas the Spanish trees might have been relics from Roman times, supporting the early influence of Middle Eastern olive trees in the western Mediterranean. Even if the trees were younger, the long life span of the olive tree meant there might be only one or two generations separating the trees we sampled from the original domesticated olive trees that grew there. Olive stones or saplings must have been carried westward to give rise to these trees, and the age of the trees indicates that this happened a very long time ago, during the era when Phoenicians amassed fortunes trading olive oil and other wares throughout the Mediterranean.

The olive trees they brought or grew from stones would have interbred with local olive cultivars, creating new variants throughout their colonies and ports. Although we can never say with certainty what life was like thousands of years ago, we know from shipwrecked amphorae, clay lamps, and blown glass perfume bottles that olive oil was widely traded and highly cherished, and the living archaeological record of ancient olive trees tells us the story that would otherwise be lost.

I was thrilled that we were able to contribute to the understanding of the olive tree's origins in some small way. But this journey was about more than that, and we had come away with a profound understanding of the olive tree's importance throughout time. Olive oil treated diseases in the Bronze Age, and today, clinical trials have demonstrated its efficacy for prominent diseases plaguing Western countries, from cancer to cardiovascular disease. Olive trees were eulogized in ancient Greek mythology and are still revered in modern-day religions, used in ceremony and symbolism. The olive tree is a symbol of peace and a victim of war; UN peacekeepers wear olive-branch logos, and conflicts defile olive groves with fire and axes. Olive oil has been a magnet for corruption since at least Roman times, when only vigilant monitoring could prevent fraud, and the controversy continues today, with exposés revealing that nearly half of supermarket extra virgin olive oil is not what the label promises.

The olive has been a silent witness to mankind's great achievements and follies, sculpting humanity in a way that no other tree has. It grows for thousands of years, its silver leaves shimmering in the distance, beguiling us with a beauty that our greatest artists struggle to capture, while its wizened trunk hints at an inner strength. It is a tree that has been with us since the dawn of civilization, and it will continue to exert its influence for millennia to come.

ACKNOWLEDGEMENTS

ALTHOUGH AT TIMES writing a book feels like a solitary pursuit, it isn't, and I could not have done this without the generous and unwavering support of many people and organizations.

On the writing side, a big thank you goes to my editor, Nancy Flight at Greystone Books, who provided invaluable guidance that made this book even better than I imagined; my copy editor, Shirarose Wilensky; and my publicist, Zoe Grams. I am also extremely grateful for financial support from the Canada Council for the Arts, the British Columbia Arts Council, the Access Copyright Foundation, and *National Geographic*'s Expeditions Council.

My family's olive farm in Syria provided the inspiration for this book and journey, and I'll never forget my aunt's delicious meal at which the idea first hatched. Since then, many people have helped with the research and journey. It's thanks to their wisdom that this book could be written, and even though I've had wonderful teachers, any mistakes are entirely mine.

These wonderful people include Dr. Luciana Baldoni from Perugia's Institute of Plant Genetics and her laboratory for analyzing the DNA from our olive samples; Dr. Ignasi Batlle and Dr. Agusti Romero from Spain's Institute for Food Research and Technology for introducing us to our first ancient olive trees; French chef Philippe Gion for preparing a divine Provençal meal; Marie-Pierre Desaize for opening our eyes to how artists view the olive tree; Christine Ceylan for her tour of Château Virant; and George Spentzos for a home in Athens. Fritz Bläuel and everyone at Mani-Bläuel made me fall in love with the Mani Peninsula, and George Dimitriadis allowed us to witness Biolea's first pressing of the year. In Israel and the West Bank, Dr. Zohar Kerem, Halutza Olive Oil, Dr. Eitan Ayalon, the Association for Integrated Rural Development, Mohammad, and Daoud Barghouthi were of invaluable assistance. And to the many others who helped but are not listed here, thank you.

But perhaps the biggest thank you goes to my husband, Colin. He is always my biggest cheerleader, providing unlimited encouragement and helping me however he can. This journey would not have been possible without his sailing talents and curiosity to explore. And this book would not have been the same without the countless hours he spent poring over my manuscript, reminding me of key moments in our journey and critiquing my prose. And last but not least, Leif, our beautiful son who wasn't yet born when the idea for this project germinated and who spent a quarter of his infant life on a sailboat, making our journey richer and more fulfilling as a result.

NOTES

CHAPTER 1: *A Modern Boat for an Ancient Voyage*

1 Lawrence Durrell, *Prospero's Cell: A Guide to the Landscape and Manners of the Island of Corcyra* (London: Faber and Faber, 1945), 111.

2 Theophrastus, *Enquiry into Plants and Minor Works on Odours and Weather Signs*, trans. Sir Arthur Hort (London: William Heinemann, 1916), 447.

3 Ibid.

4 Ibid., 459.

5 George Duhamel, quoted in Joules L. Quiles, *Olive Oil and Health* (Oxfordshire: CAB International, 2006), 1.

6 Rick Gore, "Who Were the Phoenicians?" *National Geographic*, October 2004, accessed October 11, 2013, ngm.nationalgeographic.com/print/features/world/asia/lebanon/phoenicians-text.

CHAPTER 2: *Ancient Olive Groves*

1 Pliny, quoted in Waverley Root, *Food* (New York: Konecky & Konecky, 1996), 296.

CHAPTER 3: *Searching for Wild Olives*

1 Homer, *The Odyssey*, trans. Robert Fangles (New York: Penguin Books, 1996), book five, line 527–28, accessed October 15, 2013, iris.haverford.edu/myth13/files/2013/01/Homer Odyssey59.pdf.

2 Theophrastus, *Enquiry into Plants and Minor Works on Odours and Weather Signs*, trans. Sir Arthur Hort (London: William Heinemann, 1916), 459.
3 Ibid.
4 Ibid.

CHAPTER 4: *An Ancient Food for Modern Foodies*

1 "Johnny Carson," Quote Corner, accessed October 15, 2013, quote-corner.com/Johnny-Carson-quotes.html.
2 "Frédéric Mistral," Wikipedia, accessed October 15, 2013, en.wikipedia.org/wiki/Fr%C3%A9d%C3%A9ric_Mistral.
3 Jean-Charles Brun, quoted in Flandrin et al., *Food: A Culinary History from Antiquity to the Present* (New York: Columbia University Press, 1999), 512, accessed October 15, 2013, books.google.ca/books?id=FnwnXzTRA44C&pg=PA512&lpg=PA512&dq=Jean-Charles+Brun+olive+oil&source=bl&ots=YdRwOQtSwU&sig=ELWooNQeldSxrhL3d6T_ByQxQvM&hl=en&sa=X&ei=voFdUqOjNrCgyAH9soD4CQ&ved=0CCwQ6AEwAA#v=onepage&q=Jean-Charles%20Brun%20olive%20oil&f=false.
4 Juvenal, "Satire 5: How Clients are Entertained," in *Juvenal and Persius*, trans. G.G. Ramsay (London: William Heinemann, 1918), accessed October 15, 2013, www.tertullian.org/fathers/juvenal_satires_05.htm.
5 Ibid.
6 Ibid.
7 "Book I. The Careful Experienced Cook" in *Apicius, Cookery and Dining in Imperial Rome: A Bibliography, Critical Review and Translation of the Ancient Book Known as "Apicius de re Coquinaria,"* trans. Joseph Dommers Vehling (Chicago: Walter M. Hill, 1936), accessed October 15, 2013, penelope.uchicago.edu/Thayer/E/Roman/Texts/Apicius/1*.html.
8 *Geoponika: Agricultural Pursuits, volume 1*, trans. Thomas Owen (London: W. Spilsbury, 1805), 292, accessed October 15, 2013, www.ancientlibrary.com/geoponica/0314.html.
9 Ibid.
10 Anaxandrides, quoted in Gene A. Spiller, *The Mediterranean Diets in Health and Disease* (New York: Van Nostrand Reinhold, 1991), 48.

11 Martin Luther, *Works of Martin Luther: With Introductions and Notes, Volume 2* (Philadelphia: A.J. Hoolman Company, 1916), 196, accessed October 15, 2013, books.google.ca/books?id=L4RRFI1r5r8C.

12 Marcus Cato, *De Agricultura*, line 119, trans. W.D. Hooper and H.B. Ash (Cambridge: Loeb Classical Library, 1934), accessed October 15, 2013, penelope.uchicago.edu/Thayer/E/Roman/Texts/Cato/De_Agricultura/G*.html.

13 L. Junius Moderatus Columella, *L. Junius Moderatus Columella of Husbandry: In Twelve Books: and His Book, Concerning Trees*, trans. A. Millar (London: A. Millar, 1745), 558, accessed October 15, 2013, books.google.ca/books?id=qcNbAAAAMAAJ.

14 Ibid.

15 Ibid.

16 Vincent Van Gogh, letter to Theo Van Gogh, written c. 25–28 April 1889 in Arles, translated by Mrs. Johanna Van Gogh-Bonger, edited by Robert Harrison, number 587, webexhibits.org/vangogh/letter/19/587.htm.

17 Archestratus, quoted in Oxford Symposium, *Look and Feel: Studies in Texture, Appearance and Incidental Characteristics of Food: Proceedings of the Oxford Symposium on Food and Cookery* (Devon, U.K.: Prospect Books, 1994), 242.

18 Archestratus, quoted in Kathryn Koromilas, "Feasting with Archestratus," *Odyssey*, Nov/Dec 2007, www.kathrynkoromilas.com/files/pdf/Feasting_With_Archestratus.pdf.

19 *The Deipnosophistae of Athenaeus*, volume 1, trans. Charles Burton Gulick (Boston: Harvard University Press, 1927), 107, accessed October 19, 2013, penelope.uchicago.edu/Thayer/E/Roman/Texts/Athenaeus/1C*.html.

20 Ibid.

21 Ibid.

22 Ibid.

23 Ibid.

24 Ibid.

25 *Apicius: Cookery and Dining in Imperial Rome*, trans. Joseph Dommers Vehling (Project Gutenberg, August 19, 2009), 62, www.gutenberg.org/files/29728/29728-h/29728-h.htm.

26 Ibid., 148.

27 L. Junius Moderatus Columella, *L. Junius Moderatus Columella of Husbandry: In Twelve Books: and His Book, Concerning Trees*, trans. A. Millar (London: A. Millar, 1745), 556, books.google.ca/books?id=qcNbAAAAMAAJ.

28 Ibid., 559.

29 *Apicius: Cookery and Dining in Imperial Rome*, trans. Joseph Dommers Vehling (Project Gutenberg, August 19, 2009), 55, www.gutenberg.org/files/29728/29728-h/29728-h.htm.

CHAPTER 5: *Coveting Virginity*

1 "Marseille Soap Information," Frenchy Bee: Everyday French Living, www.thefrenchybee.com/marseille_soap_information.php.

2 "Olive," Botanical.com, www.botanical.com/botanical/mgmh/o/olive-06.html.

3 Julie Butler, "New Twist on Traditional Olive Press," *Olive Oil Times* (September 25, 2012), www.oliveoiltimes.com/olive-oil-making-and-milling/oleapure/29130.

CHAPTER 6: *Illumination and Inspiration on the French Riviera*

1 Bible, New International Version, Psalm 128, www.biblegateway.com/passage/?search=Psalm+128&version=NIV.

2 Bible, New International Version, Deuteronomy 24, www.biblegateway.com/passage/?search=Deuteronomy+24&version=NIV.

3 The Life of Adam and Eve, biblical.ie/Apocrypha/Life_of_Adam_and_Eve.asp.

4 Bible, New International Version, Exodus 27:20, www.biblestudytools.com/exodus/27-20-compare.html.

5 Bible, New American Standard Bible, 2 Kings 9:3, biblehub.com/2_kings/9-3.htm.

6 Hebrew Bible, Exodus 27, www.mechon-mamre.org/p/pt/pt0227.htm#21.

7 Quoted in Yitzhak Buxbaum, *A Person is Like a Tree: A Sourcebook for Tu BeShvat* (North Bergen, NJ: Rowman & Littlefield, 2000), 97.

8 Ibid., 97.

9 Ibid., 99.

10 Hazrat Abu Huraira (R.A.) narrated Rasullullah (Sallallaho Alayhi

Wasallam) as cited in I. Farooqi, *Ahadith Mein Mazkoor Nabatat, Adwiya Aur Ghizain* (Lahore: Ilm-o-Irfan Publishers, 1998), 151-52, 168.

11 *English Translation of the Holy Quran: With Explanatory Notes*, 95:1, trans. Maulana Muhammad Ali (Wembley, U.K.: Ahmadiyya Anjuman Lahore, 2010), 783.

12 *The Koran Interpreted: A Translation*, 24:35, trans. A.J. Arberry (New York: Touchstone, 1955), 50-51.

13 Bible, English Standard Version, Exodus 30:23-25, www.biblestudytools.com.

14 Guy de Maupassant, *The Complete Works of Guy de Maupassant Vol XIII* (New York: Wildside Press LLC, 2010), 14.

15 Ibid.

16 Aldous Huxley, *Collected Essays* (New York: Harper & Row, 1971), 15.

17 Lawrence Durrell, *Prospero's Cell: A Guide to the Landscape and Manners of the Island of Corfu* (London: Faber and Faber, 1945), 105.

18 Baron George Gordon Byron, *The Works of Lord Byron Complete in One Volume* (London: Francfort O.M., 1837), 552.

19 Lord Byron, *Don Juan* (London: George Routledge and Sons, 1906), 130.

20 William Shakespeare, *Antony and Cleopatra* (London: J. Bell British Library Strand, 1786), 104.

21 William Shakespeare, *The Dramatic Works of William Shakespeare* (London: C. and C. Whittingham, 1826), 114.

22 William Shakespeare, *Henry VI* (New York: Modern Library, 2012), 312.

23 William Shakespeare, *The Sonnets and Other Poems* (New York: Modern Library, 2009), 282.

24 Derek Fell, *Renoir's Garden* (London: Frances Lincoln Limited, 1995), 8.

25 Ibid., 40.

26 Ibid., 16.

27 Renoir, quoted in Kathryn Bradley-Hole, *Villa Gardens of the Mediterranean: From the Archives of Country Life* (London: Aurum Press, 2006), 70.

28 Aldous Huxley, *Collected Essays* (New York: Harper & Row, 1971), 15.

29 Ibid., 16.

30 John Lichfield, "The Meek Shall Inherit the Negresco," *The Independent* (July 22, 2009).

CHAPTER 7: *Ancient Civilizations, Ancient Oil*

1 Marcus Aurelius, *The Meditations of Marcus Aurelius*, trans. George Long (New York: Digireads.com Publishing, 2005), 22.

2 Seneca, quoted in George Smallfield, *The Monthly Repository of Theology and General Literature, Volume 18* (London: Sherwood, Jones & Co., 1823), 730, books.google.ca/books?id=w38UAAAAYAAJ.

3 Ferdinand Gregorovius, *Wanderings in Corsica, Its History and Its Heroes*, trans. A. Muir (Edinburgh: Thomas Constable & Co, 1855), 463.

4 Ibid., 196.

5 Ibid.

6 Marcus Porcius Cato, *On Agriculture* (Cambridge: Harvard University Press, 1954), 75.

7 Ibid.

8 Ibid., 77.

9 Pausanias, *Pausanias Description of Greece IV* (London: W. Heinemann, 1935), 463.

CHAPTER 8: *The Science of Olives*

1 Aldous Huxley, *Collected Essays* (New York: Harper & Row, 1971), 11.

2 Bible, New International Version, Romans 11:17 (Colorado Springs: Biblica, 1984).

3 Tom Mueller, quoted in Ron Doering, "Losing Virginity: The Adulteration of Olive Oil," *Canadian Manufacturing* (April 2012), www.canadianmanufacturing.com/food/news/losing-virginity-the-adulteration-of-olive-oil-59894.

CHAPTER 9: *How to Live Like a Centenarian*

1 Letter to George Wythe, September 16, 1787, in *The Works of Thomas Jefferson*, Federal Edition, vol. 5 (New York and London: G.P. Putnam's Sons, 1904-5).

2 John Tyndale, *The Island of Sardinia: Including Pictures of the Manners and Customs of the Sardinians* (London: Richard Bentley, 1849), 232.

CHAPTER 10: *The Olive Solution*

1 Mario Puzo, *The Godfather* (New York: New American Library, 1969), chapter 13.

2 Voula Kyriakea, *Mani: A Magic Trek to the Villages of Outer Mani with a Taste of the Inner Mani* (Athens: Manh, 2011), 182.

3 Ibid.

4 "Greece 10 Years Ahead: Defining Greece's New Growth Model and Strategy," McKinsey & Company (March 2012), 49.

CHAPTER 11: *Something Old and Something New*

1 *Geoponika: Agricultural Pursuits, volume 1*, trans. Thomas Owen (London: W. Spilsbury, 1805), 292, accessed October 15, 2013, www.ancientlibrary.com/geoponica/0314.html.

CHAPTER 12: *The Birthplace of the Olive*

1 Thomas L. Friedman, *The Lexus and the Olive Tree: Understanding Globalization* (New York: Farrar, Straus and Giroux, 1999), 31.

EPILOGUE

1 William Shakespeare, Sonnet 107, in Stephen Bretzius, *Shakespeare in Theory: The Postmodern Academy and the Early Modern Theater* (Ann Arbor: University of Michigan Press, 1997), 45.

REFERENCES

INTRODUCTION

- Statistics for Syria's olive production from:
  www.syriangate.com/syria-news-10/2/Syria-2-million-olive-trees-enter-production-boosting-oil-export.htm.

CHAPTER 1: *A Modern Boat for an Ancient Voyage*

- Statistics for Spain's olive oil and table olive market from:
  Olive Oil Times, www.oliveoiltimes.com/olive-oil-business/spanish-olive-oil-harvest-sets-record/26303.
  International Olive Council, www.internationaloliveoil.org/estaticos/view/132-world-table-olive-figures.
- Details about Spain's olive production facilities and companies from:
  "Economic Analysis of Olive Sector," European Commission, Directorate-General for Agriculture and Rural Development (July 2012), http://ec.europa.eu/agriculture/olive-oil/economic-analysis_en.pdf.
  Olive Oil Times, www.oliveoiltimes.com/olive-oil-business/acesur-gonzalo-guillen/20861.
  Hojiblanca company website, www.hojiblanca.com/cooperative/?lang=en.
  International Olive Oil Council, www.internationaloliveoil.org/estaticos/view/307-the-olive-oil-value-chain-in-spain.

- Botanical and evolutionary history information comes from:

P. S. Green, "A Revision of Olea L. (Oleaceae)," *Royal Botanic Gardens* 57, 1 (2002), 91–140.

Julian Cuevas et al., "The Role of Staminate Flowers in the Breeding System of Olea europaea (Oleaceae): An Andromonoecious, Wind Pollinated Taxon," *Annals of Botany* 93, 5 (2004), 547–53.

Melinda A. Zeder, *Documenting Domestication: New Genetic and Archaeological Paradigms* (Berkeley: University of California Press, 2006).

Joules L. Quiles, *Olive Oil and Health* (Oxfordshire: CAB International, 2006).

- Archaeological olive history comes from:

Yolana Carrión et al., "Olea Europaea L. in the North Mediterranean Basin during the Pleniglacial and the Early-Middle Holocene," *Quaternary Science Reviews* 29, 7–8 (April 2010), 952–68, digital.csic.es/bitstream/10261/32465/3/YCarri%C3%B3n02.pdf.

Jean-Frederic Terral et al., "Beginnings of Olive Cultivation in Eastern Spain in Relation to Holocene Bioclimatic Changes," *Quaternary Research* 46 (1996), 176–85, www.umr5059.univ-montp2.fr/doc_terral/2_QR96.pdf.

Jean-Frédéric Terral, "Exploitation and Management of the Olive Tree During Prehistoric Times in Mediterranean France and Spain," *Journal of Archaeological Science* 27 (2000), 127–33, www.umr5059.univ-montp2.fr/doc_terral/8_JAS2000.pdf.

Carlos E. Cordova, *Millennial Landscape Change in Jordan: Geoarchaeology and Cultural Ecology* (Tucson: University of Arizona Press, 2007), 76, books.google.ca/books?id=1eWaveyEIlcC.

- Ancient Greek olive history comes from:

Theophrastus, *Enquiry into Plants and Minor Works on Odours and Weather Signs*, trans. Sir Arthur Hort (London: William Heinemann, 1916), 459, archive.org/stream/enquiryintoplant02theouoft/enquiryintoplant02theouoft_djvu.txt.

- Mediterranean geology details from:

Open University, *The Ocean Basins: Their Structure and Evolution* (Oxford: Butterworth-Heinemann, 1989), 142, books.google.ca/books?id=9rSp1q7A21YC.

▸ Phoenician ship history from:

Lionel Casson, *The Ancient Mariners: Seafarers and Sea Fighters of the Mediterranean in Ancient Times* (Princeton: Princeton University Press, 1991), 6, books.google.ca/books?id=4Ls6MczXvBEC.

Rick Gore, "Who Were the Phoenicians?" *National Geographic* (October 2004), accessed October 11, 2013, ngm.nationalgeographic.com/print/features/world/asia/lebanon/phoenicians-text.

"Phoenician Mining," accessed October 20, 2013, phoenicia.org/minning.html.

CHAPTER 2: *Ancient Olive Groves*

▸ All chapter details about olives during Roman times from:

Jarrett A. Lobell, "Trash Talk," *Archaeology* (March/April 2009), www.archaeospain.com/images/Testaccio.pdf.

▸ Facts about the illicit olive tree trade from:

William Snyder, "A New Market for Old Olive Trees," *Wall Street Journal* (April 2008), online.wsj.com/news/articles/SB120846638155724155.

▸ Olive-growing details from:

Juan Francisco Hermoso et al., "Mediterranean Clonal Selections Evaluated for Modern Hedgerow Olive Oil Production in Spain," *California Agriculture* 65, 1 (2011), ucce.ucdavis.edu/files/repositoryfiles/ca6501p34-82943.pdf.

CHAPTER 3: *Searching for Wild Olives*

▸ Chapter information about dating trees from:

Paolo Cherubini et al., "Olive Tree-Ring Problematic Dating: A Comparative Analysis on Santorini (Greece)," *Plos* (January 2013), www.plosone.org/article/info:doi%2F10.1371%2Fjournal.pone.0054730;jsessionid=21C9DC2B0213EB8C76354AAD41B64DE9.

Joules L. Quiles, *Olive Oil and Health* (Oxfordshire: CAB International, 2006).

R. Lumaret and N. Ouazzani, "Plant Genetics: Ancient Wild Olives in Mediterranean Forests," *Nature* 413, 6857 (October 2001), 700.

▸ Olive biodiversity and wild olives details from:

"Celebrating the International Year of Biodiversity with Success Stories from the Field," United Nations Environment Programme, accessed

October 20, 2013, www.unep.org/dgef/CelebratingtheInternationalYearofBiodiversi/tabid/4996/Default.aspx.

"Crop Wild Relatives: IUCN Red List Status," European Commission, accessed October 20, 2013, ec.europa.eu/environment/nature/conservation/species/redlist/plants/wild_relatives_status.htm.

Lumaret et al., "Allozyme Variation of Oleaster Populations (Wild Olive Tree) (Olea Europaea L.) in the Mediterranean Basin," *Heredity* 92 (2004), 343–51.

Baldoni et al., "Genetic Structure of Wild and Cultivated Olives in the Central Mediterranean Basin," *Annals of Botany* 98, 5 (2006), 935–42.

CHAPTER 4: *An Ancient Food for Modern Foodies*

▸ Middle Ages and earlier use of olive oil from:

Maguelonne Toussaint-Samat, *A History of Food* (Paris: Blackwell Publishers, 1987), 189.

Joules L. Quiles, *Olive Oil and Health* (Oxfordshire: CAB International, 2006), 27.

Geoponika: Agricultural Pursuits, volume 1, trans. Thomas Owen (London: W. Spilsbury, 1805), 292, accessed October 15, 2013, www.ancientlibrary.com/geoponica/0314.html.

John Wilkins and Shaun Hill, *Archestratus: The Life of Luxury Introduction* (2004), http://latis.exeter.ac.uk/classics/undergraduate/food3/archestratus.htm.

Apicius: Cookery and Dining in Imperial Rome, trans. Joseph Dommers Vehling (Project Gutenberg, August 19, 2009), www.gutenberg.org/files/29728/29728-h/29728-h.htm.

Barbara Damrosch, "Salsify, a Root Vegetable that Does Double Duty," *Washington Post* (January 4, 2012), www.washingtonpost.com/lifestyle/home-garden/salsify-a-root-vegetable-that-does-double-duty/2011/12/20/gIQAxL6GaP_story.html.

Columella, *Husbandry in Twelve Books and His Book Concerning Trees* (London: A. Millar, 1745), play.google.com/books/reader?id=qcNbAAAAMAAJ&printsec=frontcover&output=reader&authuser=0&hl=en&pg=GBS.PR1.

▸ Statistics for olive oil and butter consumption from:

Julie Butler, "Global Olive Oil Consumption Forecast to Climb, Led by

U.S., China, Brazil," *Olive Oil Times* (December 14, 2011), www.oliveoiltimes.com/olive-oil-business/europe/world-olive-oil-consumption/22944.

United States Department of Agriculture Foreign Agricultural Service, Production, Supply and Distribution (PSD) online database, www.fas.usda.gov/psdonline/psdHome.aspx.

World Olive Oil Figures, International Olive Council, www.internationaloliveoil.org/estaticos/view/131-world-olive-oil-figures.

World Table Olive Figures, International Olive Council, www.internationaloliveoil.org/estaticos/view/132-world-table-olive-figures.

Country Profiles, International Olive Council, www.internationaloliveoil.org/estaticos/view/136-country-profiles.

▸ Details about early use of butter and invention of margarine from:

Leanne Kitchen, *The Dairy* (London: Murdoch Books, 2008), 29.

Katharine Sarah Macquoid, *Through Normandy* (London: W. Isbister & Co., 1874), 28, books.google.ca/books?id=z5kBAAAAQAAJ.

CHAPTER 5: *Coveting Virginity*

▸ Details about olive varieties from:

Joules L. Quiles, *Olive Oil and Health* (Oxfordshire: CAB International, 2006), 2.

"Oil Quantity and Quality are Highly Dependent on the Olive Variety," Amazing Olive Oil, accessed October 20, 2013, www.amazingoliveoil.com/olive-varieties.html.

International Olive Council, *France* (International Olive Council, 2012).

▸ Production and attributes of olive oil soap from:

Alessandra Giuliani, *Developing Markets for Agrobiodiversity: Securing Livelihoods in Dryland Areas* (U.K.: EarthScan, 2007), books.google.ca/books?hl=en&lr=&id=rCTqOA2XebcC.

Soap Story, accessed October 20, 2013, www.historische-aleppo-seife.de/engl_story.html.

Marcie Doyle, "What Are the Benefits of Olive Oil Soap?" www.ehow.com/facts_5043106_benefits-olive-oil-soap.html.

Cricket Webber, "The Amazing Benefits of Olive Oil Soap," www.dailyglow.com/the-amazing-benefits-of-olive-oil-soap.html.

"Marseille Soap Information," French Bee: Everyday French Living, www.thefrenchybee.com/marseille_soap_information.php.

- Information about olive processing to produce oil from:

Anna McElhatton, *Novel Technologies in Food Science: Their Impact on Products, Consumer Trends and the Environment* (New York: Springer, 2011), 67, books.google.ca/books?id=Xa4KxpujNLUC.

Maurizio Servili et al., "Technological Aspects of Olive Oil Production," *Olive Germplasm—The Olive Cultivation, Table Olive and Olive Oil Industry in Italy*, ed. Innocenzo Muzzalupo (InTech, 2012), www.intechopen.com/books/olive-germplasm-the-olive-cultivation-table-olive-and-olive-oil-industry-in-italy/technological-aspects-of-olive-oil-production.

European Union Network for the Implementation and Enforcement of Environmental Law, "Impel Olive Oil Project" (Impel, 2003), www.installationsclassees.developpement-durable.gouv.fr/IMG/pdf/olive_oil_project.pdf.

Costas Vasilopoulos, "New Phase for Greek Olive Mills," *Olive Oil Times* (July 2012), www.oliveoiltimes.com/olive-oil-making-and-milling/new-phase-olive-oil-mills-greece/27303.

CHAPTER 6: *Illumination and Inspiration on the French Riviera*

- Ancient Greek use of olives in literature sourced from:

The Deipnosophistae of Athenaeus and interpretations of this ancient Greek book. See: latis.exeter.ac.uk/classics/undergraduate/food3/archestratus.htm.

- Religious material from:

Nerses Manoogian, *From the Pastor's Desk: Pastoral Talks to His Flock* (Bloomington: AuthorHouse, 2008), 69–71, http://books.google.ca/books?id=V9u4BnMyPgkC.

"Bible Plants," Old Dominion University, ww2.odu.edu/~lmusselm/plant/bible/olive.php.

"Roman Catacombs," New Advent, www.newadvent.org/cathen/03417b.htm.

"Olive," Botanical.com, www.botanical.com/botanical/mgmh/o/olive-06.html.

"Mystery of the Olive Tree," Triumph Prophetic, www.triumphpro.com/olive-tree-mystery.htm.

"Olive Oil, the Very Heart of the Greek Orthodoxy—Make Your Own Aromatic Oil," Orthodox Christian Channel, philotimo-leventia.blogspot.ca/2012/04/olive-oil-very-heart-of-greek-orthodoxy.html.

"History of Ancient Olive and Olive Oil to Present Day," Eden Aromata, edenaromata.com/About/AllAboutOliveOil/HistoryofOliveOlive Oil.aspx.

- Literary references to the olive from:

Alexander Kilgour, *Anecdotes of Lord Byron: From Authentic Sources; with Remarks Illustrative of His Connection with the Literary Characters of the Present* (London: Knight and Lacey, 1825), 110.

George Eric Mackay, *Lord Byron at the Armenian Convent* (Venice: Office of the "Poliglotta," 1876), 81.

William Shakespeare, *Tragedies of Shakespeare in Plain and Simple English* (BookCaps Study Guides, 2012).

- Renoir material sourced from:

Jean Renoir, "My Memories of Renoir," *Life Magazine* 32, 20 (May 1952), 90–99, books.google.ca/books?id=G1YEAAAAMBAJ.

Derek Fell, *Renoir's Garden* (London: Frances Lincoln Limited, 1995).

CHAPTER 7: *Ancient Civilizations, Ancient Oil*

- Olive history in Corsica from:

Ferdinand Gregorovius, *Wanderings in Corsica, Its History and Its Heroes*, trans. A. Muir (Edinburgh: Thomas Constable & Co, 1855), 61–63.

Melinda A. Zeder, ed., *Documenting Domestication: New Genetic and Archaeological Paradigms* (Berkeley: University of California Press, 2006), 149-150, books.google.ca/books?id=EaVTxjrbIFQC.

- Roman shipyard details from:

Nick Squires, "Largest Ever Roman Shipyard Found in Mediterranean," *Telegraph* (September 2011), www.telegraph.co.uk/news/world-news/europe/italy/8779281/Largest-ever-Roman-shipyard-found-in-Mediterranean.html.

- Information about Mount Testaccio and Roman olive oil from:

Jarrett Lobell, "Trash Talk," *Archaeology*, March/April 2009, www.archaeospain.com/images/Testaccio.pdf.

Anthony R. Birley, *Septimius Severus: The African Emperor* (London: Eyre & Spottiswoode, 1971), 6, books.google.ca/books?id=pcyPrVltTEkC.

CHAPTER 8: *The Science of Olives*

▸ Olive genetics details from:

Guillaume Besnard, "Genomic Profiling of Plastid DNA Variation in the Mediterranean Olive Tree," BMC *Plant Biology* 11, 80 (2011), www.biomedcentral.com/1471-2229/11/80/.

▸ Olive fraud and testing details from:

Julie Butler, "Two Plead Guilty in Olive Oil Fraud Scheme, Sentenced to Two Years in Jail," *Olive Oil Times* (December 2011), www.oliveoiltimes.com/olive-oil-basics/jail-term-for-olive-oil-fraudsters/23081.

"Sovena USA First Ever Lab to be Certified by International Olive Council in United States," www.prnewswire.com/news-releases/sovena-usa-first-ever-lab-to-be-certified-by-international-olive-council-in-united-states-135028643.html.

"Can the FDA Have an Impact on Olive Oil Fraud?" *Olive Oil Source*, www.oliveoilsource.com/article/can-fda-have-impact-olive-oil-fraud.

Ron Doering, "Losing Virginity: The Adulteration of Olive Oil," *Canadian Manufacturing* (April 2012), www.canadianmanufacturing.com/food/news/losing-virginity-the-adulteration-of-olive-oil-59894.

CHAPTER 9: *How to Live Like a Centenarian*

▸ Details about longevity from:

Graziella Caselli et al., "Survival Differences among the Oldest Old in Sardinia: Who, What, Where, and Why?" *Demographic Research* 14, 13 (March 2006), 267–94.

"World's Oldest Person Dead," *McCook Daily Gazette* (August 1997), news.google.com/newspapers?id=VqEgAAAAIBAJ&sjid=7GgFAAAAIBAJ&pg=6026%2C3313956.

"Israeli Arab Says She's World's Oldest Person," NBC News (January 2008), www.nbcnews.com/id/23194445/#.USVtv6U9AfE.

▸ Olive oil and its health benefits from:

Tom Baker, "Olive Oil Joins the Fight Against Osteoporosis," *Olive Oil Times* (February 2007), www.oliveoiltimes.com/olive-oil-health-news/olive-oil-and-osteoporosis/12257.

G. Ruckland et al., "Olive Oil Intake and Mortality within the Spanish Population," *American Journal of Clinical Nutrition* 96, 1 (July 2012), 142–49.

Manuel Murie-Fernandez et al., "Carotid Intima-Media Thickness Changes with Mediterranean Diet: A Randomized Trial," *Atherosclerosis* 219, 1 (June 2011), 158–62.

Rosa Sola et al., "Effect of a Traditional Mediterranean Diet on Apolipoproteins B, A-I, and Their Ratio: A Randomized, Controlled Trial," *Atherosclerosis* 218, 1 (February 2013), 174–80.

T. Psaltopoulou et al., "Olive Oil, the Mediterranean Diet, and Arterial Blood Pressure: The Greek European Prospective Investigation into Cancer and Nutrition (EPIC) study," *American Journal of Clinical Nutrition* 80, 4 (October 2004), 1012-18.

Elena Paravantes, "Olive Oil Diet Reduces Risk of Type 2 Diabetes," *Olive Oil Times* (May 2011), www.oliveoiltimes.com/olive-oil-health-news/olive-oil-diet-reduces-diabetes-risk/15948.

L. Filik et al., "Olive-Oil Consumption and Cancer Risk," *European Journal of Clinical Nutrition* 57 (2003), 191.

Elena Paravantes, "Eating Olive Oil Can Help Prevent Cancer," *Olive Oil Times* (December 2012), www.oliveoiltimes.com/olive-oil-health-news/top-5-health-benefits-of-olive-oil/31463/3.

Roberto Fabiani et al., "Inhibition of Cell Cycle Progression by Hydroxytyrosol Is Associated with Upregulation of Cyclin-Dependent Protein Kinase Inhibitors p21WAF1/Cip1 and p27Kip1 and with Induction of Differentiation in HL60 Cells," *Journal of Nutrition* 138, 1 (January 2008), 42–48.

R. Sirianni et al., "Oleuropein and Hydroxytyrosol Inhibit MCF-7 Breast Cancer Cell Proliferation Interfering with ERJK1/2 Activation," *Molecular Nutrition & Food Research* 54, 6 (June 2010), 833–40.

M. Solanas et al., "Dietary Olive Oil and Corn Oil Differentially Affect Experimental Breast Cancer through Distinct Modulation of the p21Ras Signaling and the Proliferation-Apoptosis Balance," *Carcinogenesis* 31, 5 (October 2009), 871–79.

"Olive Oil Clarifies Thinking," Saint Louis University, www.slu.edu/rel-news-farr-research-1110.

S. Teres et al., "Oleic Acid Content is Responsible for the Reduction in Blood Pressure Induced by Olive Oil," *Proceedings of the National Academy of Sciences* 105, 37 (2008), 13811-16.

P. Haban et al., "Dietary Supplementation with Olive Oil Leads to Improved Lipoprotein Spectrum and Lower n-6 PUFAs in Elderly Subjects," *Medical Science Monitor* 10,4 (April 2004), 149–54.

A.P. Simopoulos, "The Importance of the Omega-6/Omega-3 Fatty Acid Ratio in Cardiovascular Disease and Other Chronic Diseases," *Experimental Biology and Medicine* 233 (June 2008), 674–88.

▸ Polyphenols:

Dean Moyer, "Health Benefits of Polyphenols in Olive Oil," *Olive Oil Source*, www.oliveoilsource.com/article/health-benefits-polyphenols-olive-oil.

"Polyphenols and Antioxidants in Olive Oil," Agbiolab, www.agbiolab.com/files/agbiolab_Polyphenols.pdf.

"Natural Compound in Extra-Virgin Olive Oil—Oleocanthal—May Help Prevent, Treat Alzheimer's," *Science Daily* (September 2009), www.sciencedaily.com/releases/2009/09/090929133123.htm.

K.L. Tuck et al., "Major Phenolic Compounds in Olive Oil: Metabolism and Health Effects," *Journal of Nutritional Biochemistry* 13, 11 (November 2002), 636–44.

"Extra-Virgin Olive Oil Mimics Painkiller," *Nature Publishing Group* (August 2005), www.nature.com/drugdisc/news/articles/050829-11.html.

Christian Brazil Bautista, "Olive Oil Found to Help Prevent Skin Cancer," *Olive Oil Times* (December 2010), www.oliveoiltimes.com/olive-oil-health-news/olive-oil-prevent-skin-cancer/10302.

▸ Sardinian longevity and other centenarian populations:

Michel Poulain et al., "A Population Where Men Live as Long as Women: Villagrande Strissaili (Sardinia)," Gender Inequality, In Death as in Life?, XXVI IUSSP International Population Conference (September 2009), iussp2009.princeton.edu/papers/93003.

Nick Squires, "Centenarian Sister Helps Sardinian Siblings Set World Record," *Christian Science Monitor* (August 2012), www.csmonitor.com/World/Global-News/2012/0822/Centenarian-sister-helps-Sardinian-siblings-set-world-record.

D. Lio et al., "Association between the HLA-DR Alleles and Longevity: A Study in Sardinian Population," *Experimental Gerontology* 38, 3 (March 2003), 313–17.

G.M. Pes et al., "Association between Longevity and Cytokine Gene Polymorphisms: A Study in Sardinian Centenarians," *Aging Clinical and Experimental Research* 16, 3 (June 2004), 244–48.

Leonie K. Heilbronn et al., "Calorie Restriction and Aging: Review of the Literature and Implications for Studies in Humans," *American Journal of Clinical Nutrition* 78, 3 (September 2003), 361–69.

CHAPTER 10: *The Olive Solution*

▸ Information about geographic protection for olive oil and table olives from:

Costas Vasilopoulos, "Table Olives: Kalamata PDO a Mixed Blessing," *Olive Oil Times* (November 2012), www.oliveoiltimes.com/olive-oil-making-and-milling/kalamata-pdo-a-mixed-blessing/30901.

"Canada EU Discuss Geographic Indications," Canadian Association of Importers and Exporters (March 2010), www.iecanada.com/ienow/2010/mar_10/inside_1.html.

Costas Vasilopoulos, "Two More Greek Regions Apply for Olive Oil PDOs," *Olive Oil Times* (October 2012), www.oliveoiltimes.com/olive-oil-basics/chalkidiki-messinia-pdo/29380.

C. Bramley et al., "The Economics of Geographical Indications: Towards a Conceptual Framework for Geographical Indication Research in Developing Countries," World Intellectual Property Organization, accessed October 20, 2013, www.wipo.int/export/sites/www/ip-development/en/economics/pdf/wo_1012_e_ch_4.pdf.

L. Roselli et al., "Olive Oils Protected by the EU Geographical Indications: Creation and Distribution of the Value-Adding within Supply Chains" (paper presented at 113th EAAE Seminar "A Resilient European Food Industry and Food Chain in a Challenging World," Chania, Crete, Greece, September 2009).

"Greece 10 Years Ahead: Defining Greece's New Growth Model and Strategy," McKinsey & Company (March 2012).

CHAPTER 11: *Something Old and Something New*

▸ Traditional olive press views from:

"Commitment to Quality and Traditions," www.sierradecadiz.com/pajarete/ingles2008.htm.

▸ Details about Minoan and Mycenaean history from:

James Baike, *The Sea-Kings of Crete* (Fairford, U.K.: Echo Library, 2007).

Melena Jiménez and José Luis, "Olive Oil and Other Sorts of Oil in the Mycenaean Tablets" (Universidad de Salamanca, 1983), gredos.usal.es/jspui/bitstream/10366/73447/1/Olive_Oil_and_Other_Sorts_of_Oil_in_the_.pdf.

APPENDIX A

TIPS ON HOSTING AN OLIVE OIL TASTING PARTY

THE BEST WAY to hone your olive oil tasting prowess is through practice, so besides being adventurous in your supermarket olive oil aisle and visiting olive oil specialty shops, try throwing an olive oil tasting party. You can either host an event just for tasting olive oil, or tack it onto a dinner party by asking everyone to bring a bottle of olive oil.

The best time to try olive oil is when you're hungry but not too hungry, and ideally in the morning. This is when your perception of tastes and smells peaks and is why olive tasting panels often meet between 10 AM and noon. Professional tasters are forbidden coffee and cigarettes for thirty minutes before the tasting and must fast for the preceding hour. This might be a little excessive for a friendly gathering. However, if your olive tasting is tied to a dinner event, it would be best to do the tasting before dinner and definitely prior to an after-dinner coffee.

These tips and guidelines on tasting olive oil are from a number of excellent sources including certified olive oil tasters, an international olive oil competition judge, and the International Olive Council guidelines for olive oil tasting.

WHAT YOU NEED

Tasting Glasses

Ideally, each person will get a separate glass for each oil. As this can mean dozens of glasses, it may be easiest to use disposable cups. Professional tasting panels use opaque glasses that resemble stemless wine glasses, as wide as they are high and narrowing slightly at the opening. The opaqueness of the glass prevents the tasters from focusing on the color of the oil, which is irrelevant to the taste. The shape of the glass enhances the ability to smell the oil, the wideness provides lots of space to swirl the oil, and the slight narrowing at the rim helps contain the scent.

Green Apple Slices

Between each oil tasting, you'll need to cleanse your palate by taking a bite of green apple. Rusks or plain crackers are a suitable substitute.

Water

To drink between tastings.

Spittoon

Not everyone may want to swallow the olive oil, and a container should be provided for those who wish to spit it out.

THE TASTING

Assign each oil a number and mark the glasses appropriately. Pour a shot glass's worth of olive oil, about fourteen to sixteen milliliters, into each glass. Set out plates of sliced green apples and supply each person with a glass of water. Provide a tasting sheet or paper and pens so that people can record their observations (you can find a tasting sheet at angusadventures.com/olivetasting).

Smell the Oil

Cup the glass in one hand and place the other hand on top, covering the glass. Swirl the oil. This warms the oil, bringing it to body temperature, and releases its volatile compounds, scents that are then trapped in the glass by your palm. Lift your hand and inhale deeply and slowly. Do not smell the oil for more than thirty seconds. If you have not yet reached any conclusions, cover the glass again with your hand, and after a short break, resume your olfactory test.

Taste the Oil

Take a small sip of oil, about four milliliters, sucking it into your mouth with air to aerate the oil and further bring out its taste. Gently move the oil throughout your mouth, gliding it from the tip of your tongue to the back. The receptors on your tongue differ in each region, and this will help you notice the progression of flavors. Note the order in which the pungent and bitter flavors appear. Take small breaths through your mouth to help the oil spread throughout your mouth and allow you to detect volatile compounds at the back of your nose.

Swallow the Oil

Swallowing the oil allows you to detect tactile compounds and further access the oil's pungency, the burning sensation in your throat that accompanies high-antioxidant oils.

Record Your Observations

There are three main positive attributes you are assessing in an extra virgin olive oil: fruitiness, pungency, and bitterness. You can also look for distinct scents and flavors. It is also important to note any negative attributes that preclude an oil from being classified as extra virgin. An oil that has any negative scents or flavors cannot be called extra virgin, but instead will be virgin oil, or even worse, depending on the severity of the deficits.

Fruity, Pungent, Bitter

Rate the oil on the intensity of each of these flavors, determining whether each is intense, medium, or light.

Fruity: This is perceived through smell and depends on the variety of olives and when they were picked.

Pungent: This biting taste is noticed throughout the entire mouth and particularly in the throat. If an olive oil makes you cough, it is very pungent. Generally, oil made from green, unripe olives has a higher pungency.

Bitter: This is perceived through taste, particularly in the circumvallate papillae on the V region of the tongue. Bitterness is characteristic of green olives or olives turning color.

Note Characteristic Positive Scents

The following is a list of positive scents commonly found in olive oils:

- Almond
- Apple
- Artichoke
- Chamomile
- Citrus fruit (lemon, orange, bergamot, mandarin, and grapefruit)
- Eucalyptus
- Exotic fruit (pineapple, banana, passion fruit, mango, papaya)
- Fig leaf
- Flowers
- Grass

- Green complex (typical odor of fruit before it ripens)
- Green peppercorns
- Greenly fruity (typical of oils obtained from green or mostly green olives)
- Herbs
- Olive leaf
- Pear
- Pine
- Ripely fruity (typical of oils obtained from fully ripe olives)
- Soft fruit (blackberries, raspberries, bilberries, blackcurrants, redcurrants)
- Sweet pepper
- Tomato leaves
- Vanilla
- Walnut

Look for Negative Attributes

Remember, for an olive oil to be extra virgin it has to be free of negative attributes. The following are some negative traits to look for and their causes:

- Fusty/muddy sediment: anaerobic fermentation; often caused by sediment in tanks and vats
- Musty-humid-earthy: mud in the olive oil from improperly washed olives or yeast from olives that have been stored too long in humid conditions before pressing
- Winey/vinegary: aerobic fermentation of olives or waste left on improperly cleaned pressing mats
- Rancid: oxidation of olive oil
- Frostbitten olives (wet wood): olives damaged by frost prior to picking
- Burnt: too high heat used during processing
- Hay/wood: oil made from dried-out olives

- Rough/thick: a pasty sensation resulting from old oils
- Vegetable: oils that have been in contact with fermented vegetable water
- Brine: oil made from brined olives
- Metallic: protracted contact with metallic surfaces during processing
- Grubby: olives infested by olive fly
- Cucumber: prolonged hermetic storage in containers causing the formation of the aldehyde 2,6-Nonadienal

Taste the Next Oil

Repeat the same process with the next oil, taking a bite of green apple to cleanse your palate. It's best to taste no more than four oils at a time so that you don't overwhelm your taste receptors. Then take a fifteen-minute break and taste another four oils, with no more than three tasting sessions a day.

APPENDIX B

TOP QUESTIONS ABOUT OLIVE OIL

BEFORE BEGINNING this project, I knew nothing about olive oil, but I had a lot of questions. These are my top questions and the answers I learned along the way.

1. How Do I Choose an Olive Oil?

Picking an olive oil shouldn't be an intimidating process. If you can choose a wine to pair with your meal, selecting an olive oil will be child's play. In fact, our two-year-old is already developing a discerning olive oil palate.

Olive oil boutiques are becoming increasingly popular, and if you're lucky enough to have one of these in your city, go visit it. You will probably be able to taste test a variety of oils and learn a lot from their expertise. Next time you have a dinner party or potluck, make it an extra virgin olive oil (EVOO) tasting and get everyone to bring a bottle. (See my tips on hosting an olive oil tasting party.) If you're going on a vineyard tour in olive country, stop by some olive mills as well. Often, olives and grapes are grown side by side, and it will complement your trip nicely. The best way to develop a taste for olive oil is by trying different cultivars from various brands.

Even before tasting the oil, there are several things you can do to improve the chances that the bottle you bring home is a high-quality oil.

Make Sure It's Fresh

Olive oil that has just been pressed is the best it's ever going to be. From then on, the oil begins to degrade. Ideally, olive oil should be consumed within the first year, but an oil's longevity depends on a number of things, and some oils may keep for two years, whereas others, especially those that are improperly stored, will spoil earlier. In general, oil with high levels of polyphenols (the stuff that makes your throat burn) will last longer.

Make sure your olive oil had a best before date or, better yet, a date of harvest or bottling. If the oil doesn't have any of these figures, don't buy it; it's like buying bread without knowing when it was baked or when it will go stale. Furthermore, a date of harvest is the most accurate figure, as you know exactly when that olive oil was made. A date of bottling is a little less accurate, as companies may store the oil for months before bottling, waiting for prices to improve. Oil stored in these huge stainless steel vats augmented with inert gas will degrade less slowly than bottled oil, but it's still better fresh. A best before date is the least accurate, as often they are set at two years following harvest and you can't be sure what criteria the oil producer used.

Make Sure It's Stored Properly

Heat and light quicken the rate at which an olive oil degrades. Make sure you buy oil that is in a darkened bottle. When you bring the oil home, store it in the cupboard, preferably one that is cool. Olive oil should not be stored in the fridge, because it may solidify. You can freeze olive oil to prolong its life span.

Look at the Olive Cultivar and Where It Was Grown

Some companies buy their oil in bulk from a number of producers across many countries, while others produce their oil from a single grove. Some oils are made of a single cultivar, whereas others are blended. Olive oil is affected by both the cultivar of olive and the place the olives are grown, just as a grape variety influences the taste of a wine and the region where the grapes grow affects its terroir.

Some olive oil will provide this information, and for added assurance, Europeans have certification processes that guarantee an oil is made in a certain region. These geographic indications, either protected designation of origin (PDO) or protected geographical indication (PGI), are only bestowed on olives grown in specific regions and in a manner that complies with practices specific to that area. There are hundreds of such geographic indications; Italy alone has fifty.

The only drawback is that enforcement of these claims is pretty much impossible outside Europe. It is illegal in Europe for a Tuscan olive oil to contain oil from olives from any other region. However, as of yet there are no bilateral agreements with non-European countries to enforce these regulations, though efforts are underway to change this. Both Canada and the United States have bilateral agreements like this in place for wine, so that we are confident the champagne we buy is from the Champagne region in France, and I hope non-Europeans will soon have that same guarantee when they buy their Tuscan olive oil or Kalamata olives.

Be Prepared to Pay a Little Extra

There are no guarantees that paying more for an olive oil ensures quality. However, a rock-bottom price is unlikely to get you a top-notch oil. When you consider that an average bottle of wine costs $20 and that you can pay many times that for a special bottle, it's not unreasonable to fork over a little extra for a good olive oil. Plus, unlike wine, which is gone by the next morning, you'll be using your olive oil for months. This is not to say that all your olive oil has to be top of the line. We generally have at least two oils in the house, one unremarkable EVOO for cooking and a high-quality one for drizzling onto foods. You lose a lot of an oil's flavor when it's heated; therefore, it seems sacrilegious to waste an expensive bottle like that.

2. How Can I Be Sure My EVOO Is Extra Virgin?

With so many reports of fraudulent extra virgin olive oil, it's easy to wonder if you're being duped. For an olive oil to be called extra virgin, it needs to meet a stringent set of requirements, including having an acidity level below 0.8 percent; it has to pass a panel of chemical tests and a taste test by a qualified olive oil tasting panel. The oil has to be made exclusively using physical methods, no chemicals allowed, and in temperatures that never exceed thirty degrees Celsius.

Olive oils could fail these tests for a number of reasons, some worse than others. The most troubling is when an olive oil contains non-olive products; for example, when it is cut with a cheaper oil, such as hazelnut or vegetable. Another possibility is that it is a subpar olive oil, such as virgin or refined olive oil. And the third possibility is that when it was bottled, it was EVOO, but because of poor storage or because it's too old, it degraded and no longer meets those standards. Outright fraud is clearly worse than shoddy storage, and the difficulty of validating the contents of a bottle of olive oil have made this a lucrative crime for some.

There are some tests you can do at home, but they're notoriously inaccurate, and without a laboratory and spectrophotometer, you'd be hard-pressed to get reliable results. The best way to protect yourself is to learn what good olive oil should taste like. Despite all the fancy equipment in modern laboratories, the best tool to detect fraudulent olive oil is still a professional taste panel. The human palate can detect minuscule discretions that multimillion dollar equipment can't. If you're not yet confident in your taste buds, here are two tests you can try, but don't count on them being accurate.

The Fridge Test

This test is little more than a well-propagated myth that real EVOO will solidify in your fridge and fakes won't. This is based on the fact that monounsaturated oils will solidify in the fridge, whereas polyunsaturated oils won't. But the reality is that olive oil is made of a mixture of fatty acids, whose composition varies depending on the olive cultivar. Thus, there is no set freezing point for all EVOO, and some EVOO will freeze whereas others won't, and non-olive oils such as canola and safflower will also harden in the fridge. Furthermore, fridges can vary in temperature by several degrees, which, when compounded with temperature variability inside the fridge (the door is warmer than a shelf), adds to the uncertainty.

The Fire Test

Olive oil should burn when you put a lit wick in it, but just because it burns doesn't mean it's EVOO or even olive oil. The poorest quality olive oil is called lampante oil, because it was traditionally used to fuel lamps.

3. What Is the Most Healthful Olive Oil?

Olive oil's health benefits come from not only the type of lipids it's composed of, primarily monounsaturated oleic acid, but also its minor components: polyphenols, chlorophyll, and vitamin E. Polyphenols play a particularly important role, and clinical trials have shown that olive oil high in polyphenols is more effective at preventing cancer, heart disease, and cognitive decline. Thus, the most healthful olive oil is an extra virgin olive oil high in polyphenols.

There are a few tricks to selecting this oil. The two main polyphenols implicated in health benefits, tyrosol and hydroxytyrosol, have a peppery taste, giving olive oil its characteristic bite. Some olive cultivars are higher in polyphenols than others. These include Koroneiki, Picholine, and Coratina. EVOO has the highest levels of polyphenols, whereas virgin and refined olive oils have much lower levels. Polyphenols also degrade with time.

4. Given All the Olive Oil Fraud, Should I Even Bother?

It's easy to get caught up in the hype of being swindled, but don't let that cause you to forsake olive oil for some other oil. There is no other oil with the same health benefits and the scientific studies to back it up. No other oil has such a range of flavors, with thousands of olive cultivars made even more diverse by a range of growing conditions offering the opportunity to pair the subtleties of an oil with a specific dish, just as you would with wine.

Olive oil is the only mainstream oil made in such a simple and natural way. Seed oils are primarily extracted using hexane, and even when they are cold-pressed, they have to be refined afterward using filters and chemicals. The same is true for many cold-pressed or expeller-pressed coconut oils. Olive oil is good and good for you, and the best way to ensure you're getting the real deal is to educate yourself, which means trying lots of olive oils.

5. What Is the Difference Between Virgin, Extra Virgin, and All Those Other Olive Oils?

Only virgin and extra virgin oils are made by squeezing olives and nothing more. Extra virgin is a higher quality than virgin, requiring acidity levels below 0.8 percent and superior taste.

Virgin oil can have an acidity level up to 2 percent, and the taste only needs to be moderate.

All other olive oils, such as light or pure, have undergone a refinement, either using chemicals, charcoal filters, or other means. These are oils that were so inferior, not even making the virgin cutoff, that their negative flavors had to be stripped away, along with most of their positive flavors and polyphenols. Sometimes, a little virgin olive oil is thrown in to provide taste and dye is added for color.

After olive oil is made, the leftover skins and stones, known as pomace, are brought to factories where chemicals are used to coerce the remaining dregs out of the waste, and that product is called pomace oil. It is unlikely you have to worry about accidentally buying pomace oil, as most supermarkets don't stock it, but it is widely used in the restaurant business.

6. Is Frying with Olive Oil Bad?

A common belief is that olive oil is not well suited to frying because of a low smoke point. This is not true, and there are many things about olive oil that make it better for frying than other oils.

As with any oil, you want to ensure that you keep it from smoking, which results in chemical changes and undesirable flavors. The smoking point of olive oil is around 410 degrees Fahrenheit but depends on the quality, as higher quality olive oil has lower free acidity levels and thus a higher smoke point. Oil used for most panfrying, sautéing, and deep-frying should be between 350 to 370 degrees Fahrenheit when you add food, which is well below olive oil's smoke point.

The other misconception is that olive oil changes from a "good oil" to a "bad oil" when you fry with it. This is also untrue. Many of olive oil's health benefits come from being an unsaturated oil versus a saturated or trans oil. Heated olive oil is every bit as much of an unsaturated oil as unheated oil.

Furthermore, frying with olive oil is healthier than frying with other oils for two main reasons. First, fried foods absorb the oil they are cooked in, and the healthy benefits of olive oil are incorporated into the food. Second, olive oil creates more of a seal around foods, limiting the amount of oil that is absorbed. This means that foods cooked in olive oil are less greasy than foods cooked in other oils.

7. How Can I Substitute Olive Oil for Other Oils, or Even Butter, in My Recipes?

Olive oil can be used to replace other oil or butter in sweet and savory dishes. I've baked biscotti and chocolate cake with olive oil, used it in puddings and brownies, made béchamel sauce with it, and use it in pretty much every dish that requires oil.

If you are substituting olive oil for butter, you use three-quarters of a cup of olive oil for every cup of butter. It will give brownies and cakes a moister texture than butter, as well as a characteristic taste. For desserts, I prefer an olive oil that is mild and buttery. Because of the oil's distinctive taste, it goes best in desserts that have a robust flavor, such as chocolate or lemon cake. If you are substituting olive oil for other oils, you'd use the same amount and remember to pair the intensity of the oil with the dish. Roasted eggplant or yams would be best with a robust oil, whereas a delicate white fish such as sole or halibut would be better with a milder floral oil.

8. What Are the World's Best Olive Oils?

There are dozens of contests every year pitting olive oils against each other, where you can find out what oils the experts like best, and there are guidebooks to help you make your selections.

The biggest international contests are the New York International Olive Oil Competition, L.A. International Extra Virgin Olive Oil Competition, International Olive Council Mario

Solinas Quality Award, Zurich's International Olive Oil Award, Israel's TerraOlivo, Italy's Sol d'Oro, and many more. These competitions evaluate hundreds of oils from around the world, highlighting the best, and usually the results are freely available on their websites.

Competitions often group olive oils into categories: green and fruity, and mature and fruity. The former is made from olives that are picked when they're less ripe, more green than black, and is generally more peppery. As the olives remain on the tree and ripen further, their polyphenol levels dip and they become mellower. In North America, the oils are more frequently categorized as delicate, medium, and robust.

Several guidebooks deal exclusively with extra virgin olive oil. Perhaps the best known is *Flos Olei*, which is published in Italian and English every year, and reviews around 750 oils. They have a free app that lets you see the top ten oils, and you can pay for more detailed information. The Italian slow food movement also puts out an annual publication, but it is entirely in Italian.

APPENDIX C

OLIVE OIL AND OLIVE RECIPES

ONE OF THE best things about traveling through the Mediterranean and Middle East researching olive oil and olives was trying each country's cuisine and their masterful incorporation of these ingredients. The food was delicious and diverse, with each country using olive oil and olives widely and in innovative ways that highlight their region's unique cuisine.

Here are a few recipes for both savory and sweet dishes I enjoy, from a number of the countries we traveled through. Also, keep in mind when cooking that olive oil can often be substituted for butter and other oils, even in baking. When substituting olive oil for other oils use a one to one ratio. When substituting olive oil for butter, use three-quarters of a cup of olive oil for one cup of butter.

Greek Potato Salad with Olive and Egg

Green cracked olives are used for this dish. They have been slit or gently bruised prior to brining so that they lose their bitter taste and absorb more flavor from the brine. If you cannot find green cracked olives, you can substitute any green olives.

SALAD

- 2 lbs potatoes
- 5 eggs
- 1 yellow onion, finely chopped
- 1 cucumber, sliced
- 4 green onions, thinly sliced
- 2/3 cup green cracked olives
- 2 Tbsp capers
- 4–5 anchovy fillets, chopped
- 1 parsley sprig, chopped
- Handful of fresh basil leaves, chopped

DRESSING

- Juice of 2 oranges
- 4 Tbsp heavy cream
- 2 Tbsp mustard
- 1/2 cup extra virgin olive oil
- 4 Tbsp white vinegar
- Salt, freshly ground pepper

Salad: Rinse the potatoes and boil them in lightly salted water until soft, about half an hour. Drain, peel, and quarter the potatoes.

While the potatoes are boiling, cook the eggs. Use a pot large enough to lay the eggs in a single layer. Cover them with cool water and bring to a boil. Once the water has reached a rapid boil, remove the pot from the heat, cover, and let sit for 10 minutes. Remove the eggs and let cool before peeling and quartering.

Combine potatoes, eggs, yellow onion, cucumber, green onions, olives, capers, and anchovies.

Dressing: Using a whisk, mix the orange juice, cream, mustard, olive oil, and vinegar. Add salt and pepper to taste. Pour over salad and garnish with parsley and basil.

Mediterranean Spaghetti with Olives, Feta Cheese, and Baked Peppers

In Greece, Conservolia black olives are used in this recipe. These mid-sized olives are the most common variety grown in Greece and are eaten both in their green and black state. The olives ripen naturally on the tree, unlike canned black olives, which are sometimes artificially blackened using chemicals such as ferrous sulfate. They are also cured naturally and without sodium hydroxide, a weak lye solution that can be used to extract bitterness from olives.

- 1/2 cup extra virgin olive oil
- 1 green pepper
- 1 red pepper
- 1 yellow pepper
- 2 tomatoes, peeled and finely chopped
- 2/3 cup black olives, pitted and finely chopped
- 2 garlic cloves, minced
- 1/2 tsp oregano
- Salt, freshly ground pepper
- 1 lb spaghetti
- 1 cup feta cheese, chopped
- Handful of fresh basil leaves, whole

Preheat the oven to 450°F. Brush peppers with 4 Tbsp olive oil and bake them until their skins are blackened. Let cool, peel, and cut into strips.

In a bowl, combine tomatoes, olives, garlic, 4 Tbsp olive oil, and oregano. Add salt and pepper to taste. Refrigerate for an hour to let flavors mingle.

Add the spaghetti to a pot of boiling salted water and cook until al dente. Drain and mix with feta cheese. Add the peppers and tomato sauce. Mix and garnish with basil and more freshly ground pepper.

Kourabiedes (Greek Almond Cookies)

These Greek cookies are popular during holidays and especially at Christmas.

1/4 tsp baking soda
1/4 cup ouzo
3/4 cup extra virgin olive oil
1/4 cup sugar
1/2 tsp lemon juice
3 cups flour
1 cup blanched roasted almonds, chopped
Extra ouzo for sprinkling
Icing sugar

Preheat oven to 375°F. Dissolve baking soda in ouzo. Beat olive oil with sugar and slowly add ouzo, lemon, flour, and almonds. Roll mixture into a ball.

Line a baking sheet with wax paper. Roll small balls of dough, about the size of a walnut, between your hands and make a depression in the middle with your thumb. Place on baking tray. Bake for approximately 35 minutes—do not let them brown. While the cookies are warm, sprinkle them with ouzo and icing sugar.

Olive Oil Aioli

Aioli is a Provençal sauce that can be served with a variety of foods, including seafood, vegetables, and bread. The French also make a dish called *le grand aïoli*, which is a complete meal that consists of boiled vegetables, such as carrots, potatoes, and green beans, as well as boiled salted cod, boiled eggs, and snails—all served with aioli.

2 egg yolks, at room temperature
4–6 garlic cloves, crushed using a mortar and pestle
1/2 tsp sea salt
Freshly ground black pepper, to taste
2 tsp lemon juice
3/4 cup olive oil

In a bowl, whisk egg yolks, garlic, salt, pepper, and lemon juice. Slowly drizzle in the olive oil, careful not to add it too quickly. Continue to whisk until the mixture is thick and emulsified.

This can be made in a food processor on low speed.

Almond Biscotti

These twice-baked cookies originated in Italy and are usually served with a drink to dunk them into, such as coffee or fortified wine.

- 2 cups whole unblanched almonds
- 5 eggs
- 3 tsp orange zest (about 2 oranges)
- 2 cups sugar
- 1 cup olive oil
- 3 tsp vanilla extract
- 2 tsp almond extract
- 5 cups all-purpose flour
- 3 tsp baking powder
- 1/2 tsp salt
- 1 egg white

Preheat oven to 350°F. Place almonds on a baking sheet and toast in the oven for 10–15 minutes, or until they are browned and fragrant. Allow to cool, then coarsely chop.

In a medium bowl, whisk eggs, orange zest, sugar, olive oil, vanilla extract, and almond extract. In a large mixing bowl, combine flour, baking powder, salt, and almonds. Slowly add the wet ingredients to the dry, mixing to form a slightly sticky dough. If the dough is too sticky, add more flour. Do not overmix.

On a floured cutting board, knead the dough into a smooth ball. Divide into 6 pieces and roll each piece into a 30-inch log. Place the logs on a cookie sheet lined with parchment paper and bake for 18 minutes, turning halfway through. Transfer logs to a wire rack and allow to cool.

Using a serrated knife, cut each log into ½-inch-thick slices. Space the slices ½ inch apart and return them to the oven for 20 minutes, or until golden brown, turning halfway through. Allow the biscotti to cool and store in an airtight container for up to 6 months. They also freeze well.

Moules à la Provençale

Mussels are popular throughout France, and this Provençal recipe offers a nice change from the cream-based sauces, relying instead on ingredients that are fresh and plentiful in Provence.

6 Tbsp extra virgin olive oil
4 shallots, chopped,
3 garlic cloves, chopped
1 15-oz can plum tomatoes
3/4 cup black olives
1/2 cup dry white wine
1 rosemary sprig, chopped
2 thyme sprigs, chopped
4 lbs mussels
Handful of fresh basil leaves, torn

In a large frying pan, heat 3 Tbsp olive oil and cook shallots for 3 minutes until soft. Add garlic and cook for another 2 minutes. Add tomatoes, olives, wine, rosemary, and thyme. Cover and simmer for 20 minutes.

Scrub the mussels under cold running water and remove beards. Throw away any mussels that are damaged or won't close when you tap them.

Add the mussels to the sauce, along with the remaining olive oil. Stir gently. Cover and cook for 5 minutes, or until mussels have opened. Discard any that remain closed.

Garnish with basil and serve with crusty bread.

Chicken with Forty Cloves of Garlic

Chef Philippe Gion taught us this recipe in Provence. It produces a succulent and flavorful chicken thanks to the generous use of olive oil and garlic.

1 whole chicken
1 Tbsp *herbes de Provence* (mixture of savory, fennel, basil, and thyme)
Salt, freshly ground pepper
1 lemon
1 rosemary sprig
1 thyme sprig
1 cup olive oil
40 garlic cloves
¼ cup flour
1 Tbsp water

Preheat oven to 350°F. Season the chicken, inside and out, with *herbes de Provence*, salt, and pepper. Stuff lemon, rosemary, and thyme inside. To increase the lemon flavor, make several punctures in the lemon with a knife and microwave it for 30 seconds before stuffing in the chicken.

Place the chicken in a Dutch oven and pour olive oil over it. With the flat edge of a knife or a rolling pin, put gentle pressure on the garlic cloves so that the peel is slightly damaged. Add the garlic to the oil.

Mix the flour and water to form a thick dough. Add more flour if needed. Roll into a long cylinder about the width of a pencil and place between the edge of the pot and the lid. This will seal the pot, so that the chicken is extraordinarily tender.

Bake the chicken between 70 and 90 minutes depending on its size, until the juices run clear and it is no longer pink at the bone. A thermometer inserted into the thickest part of the thigh should read 180°F.

Remove the chicken from the pot and cover it loosely with aluminum foil, allowing it to rest for 10 minutes. While the chicken is resting, remove the peels from the roasted garlic cloves. Mash garlic and add a little olive oil from the pan to create a thick sauce to serve with the chicken.